THE WORLD DIRECTORY OF THEOLOGICAL EDUCATION BY EXTENSION

THE WORLD DIRECTORY OF THEOLOGICAL EDUCATION BY EXTENSION

Wayne C. Weld

William Carey Library

533 HERMOSA STREET • SOUTH PASADENA, CALIF. 91030 • TEL. 213-682-2047

Copyright © 1973 by Wayne C. Weld

Library of Congress Cataloging in Publication Data

Weld, Wayne.
    The world directory of theological education
by extension.

    Bibliography: p.
    1. Seminary extension--Directories. I. Title.
II. Title: Theological education by extension.
BV4164.W44   207'.8   73-8894
ISBN 0-87808-134-8

Published by the William Carey Library
305 Pasadena Avenue
South Pasadena, Calif. 91030
Telephone: 213-799-4559

Contents

PART TWO: *DIRECTORY*

Figures

Foreword

This has to be one of the most exciting reference tools around: it provides the hard data to document the stunning growth and now world scope of a movement that began only ten years ago (and had gained much momentum only five years ago).

More than that - it adds a narrative analysis of more than a hundred pages that neatly solves the mystery of why this sudden, spectacular growth. This extra packing material is a vital accompaniment simply because so many onlookers fail to grasp the most significant novelty of the movement. They may think that TEE is just another educational gimmick.

But what transforms the gimmick into a revolutionary breakthrough - what makes TEE breathtakingly more than a tardy application of longstanding extension techniques to the training of ministers - is that one most weighty fact, often unnoticed, *that it allows a far wider selection process in the development of church leadership.*

What does this mean? It means bluntly that a local church, or a church denomination, is no longer limited to uncertain leadership gifts of a stream of young candidates going into the ministry as a one-way-trip career. TEE can reach out to any man in any local congregation anywhere, at any age, any stage of life, in any occupation, and screen him, prepare him, and elevate him to whatever level any church desires for whatever leadership position his God-given gifts will take him.

But I must let Weld tell this exciting story. This book does not try to prove that one hundred schools can't be wrong. Weld is very cautious in his evaluations. What it does say is that one hundred schools are now dealing with 14,000 men in a vast new program that may in the 70's become the single most significant innovation in the world mission of the Church.

RALPH D. WINTER

ix

Acknowledgements

My first contact with theological education by extension was in a class led by Merle Crouse in Cajas, Ecuador in October of 1966. The following year, while at the Fuller School of World Mission, I was to hear much from Ralph Winter, Peter Wagner and Peter Savage. In August of 1968 I began a four year term of service in Colombia, South America in which my primary assignment was to the United Biblical Seminary. There I learned much more from Wallace Rehner and others. The best teacher, however, has been the experience of hours of interaction with students and many hours more in the preparation of materials to be used in extension studies.

All the persons mentioned above and many more, some of whom are named in the text, have contributed to my knowledge of TEE, imperfect as it still is. To each one I gladly acknowledge my indebtedness. Much of what is set forth in the following pages has been impressed upon me through correspondence and conversation with others who informally have been my tutors. Special thanks must go to Ralph Winter who has guided in the assembling of the data on the following pages and in the topics discussed in the narrative sections.

Recognition is due also to those men and women who took time from busy schedules to fill out questionnaires or to write letters. The data in this book would be much less complete without their cooperation. It is to help such people in their programs of theological education by extension and to inform others of the progress of this movement that has motivated the production of this book.

Its appearance would have been impossible, however, without the continued help and support of my wife, Mary Anne, who has done much of the "busy work" involved in data collection as well as the final typing of the manuscript. Her understanding of programmed instruction has come through the typing of hundreds of pages of it and the equally tedious task of serving as an informant in testing it. In spite of all this she has been a constant encouragement in this project as in all of our ministry together.

Abbreviations

AATS   American Association of Theological Schools
AEBICAM   Association of Evangelical Bible Institutes and Colleges of Africa and Madagascar
AETTE   Evangelical Theological Association for Training by Extension
ALET   Latin American Association of Theological Schools
ALISTE   Latin American Association of Institutions and Theological Seminaries by Extension
ASIT   South American Association of Theological Institutions
CAMEO   Committee to Assist Missionary Education Overseas
CATA   Advisory Committee on Self-teaching Texts
CLATT   Latin American Committee on Theological Texts
PABATS   Philippine Association of Bible and Theological Schools
PACTEE   Pakistan Committee on Theological Education by Extension
PAFTEE   Philippine Committee on Theological Education by Extension
PI   Programmed Instruction
TAFTEE   The Association for Theological Education by Extension
TAP   Theological Assistance Program
TEE   Theological Education by Extension
TEF   Theological Education Fund
UNICO   Union of Biblical Institutions of Colombia
WEF   World Evangelical Fellowship

Introduction

Theological Education by Extension (TEE) has been the most exciting and widely disseminated innovation in ministerial training certainly in the last ten years and probably in many decades. No longer can it be called an experiment. With varying success it has been used in many areas of the world and extension students now number in the thousands. The idea has spread from Latin America to every continent in a stunning reversal of the usual flow of influence and structures to the Third World. Even the United States has begun to copy this form of theological education.

PURPOSE OF THIS STUDY

Often TEE has been misunderstood and been identified only with a particular kind of program. More frequently its principles have been applied with amazing diversity. Furthermore, in its application TEE has forced many groups to reevaluate their very concept of the ministry and has even challenged the sacredness of congregational and denominational structures and policies. By its introduction of programmed instructional materials and techniques the extension movement has called into question the educational philosophies and methods observed in the traditional residence programs. TEE has run parallel to one of the emphases of the "church growth" school of thought as it has insisted on setting goals and measuring progress toward those goals. Perhaps this is a partial explanation for the fact that some of those entrenched in traditional forms of theological education find the extension seminary movement threatening.

A movement of such wide scope and implications certainly merits close study. The history of the movement up to 1969 has been well set out in a book entitled *Theological Education by Extension* (Winter 1969). In a real sense the present study is a sequel to that book. However, the approach taken here is

quite different. Although we begin with a short historical
survey to put TEE into perspective the main thrust of this presentation is to sum up the situation in 1973, ten years after
the extension seminary movement was launched in Guatemala. The
central part of this study, therefore, is a directory of TEE
programs around the world. They are presented in a standard
format so that institutions and regions may be compared, and
so that additional data may be readily added.

Although the various extension programs constitute an essential emphasis of this study, they do not account for the
whole movement. Many supportive agencies and associated activities have made valuable contributions to TEE. As part of
the movement they must be described and their participation
evaluated. Cooperation between institutions, particularly in
the production of materials, has been necessary. We must examine the associations formed to promote and coordinate TEE.
Institutions are also related to associations of theological
schools which do not restrict their interest to extension programs. We will attempt to define relationships between extension programs and such associations and also the policies
and programs of some representative denominations. Finally,
we must assess the value of workshops and consultations on TEE
and the publications which are devoted wholly or in part to
this subject.

Lest the items above appear exhaustive it should be mentioned that it is not within the scope of this study to discuss
the educational materials used in extension or even to list
them. This would require a catalogue subject to constant revision. We shall not attempt to explain how an extension program can be administered. The administration of an extension
center, for example, is covered in the third section of Winter's book (1969). Educational psychology and methodology are
beyond the competence of the author and will not be dealt with.

The author would have liked to have made a thorough evaluation of theological education by extension with particular reference to its contribution, if any, to the growth of the
church. Unfortunately this presented insurmountable obstacles.
In general terms the movement is too young for evaluation.
Most of the programs listed in the directory have begun since
1970. This method, and even more so the materials which it
uses, are in a developmental stage. The first experiments in
TEE may not be a valid model for what this method of leadership
training can and will do.

The final proof of such a pastoral and lay training program
is in its products. The Cali Division of the United Biblical
Seminary of Colombia has had two graduates in extension, both
of whom began their studies in residence. Such a small sample
would be inconclusive even if we had an adequate control group
with which to compare them. In Guatemala the Presbyterian
Seminary has now graduated approximately the same number of men
by extension as it did previously in residence. A higher proportion of the extension graduates are actively serving in the

churches, but who knows where they will be twenty years after graduation?

The evaluative section which has been included in this study indicates, on a rather subjective basis, that TEE contributes to higher levels of biblical knowledge in the congregation, more confident and competent leadership and a degree of capacitation for evangelism.

In few cases can concrete data on increases in membership be validly ascribed to TEE at this time. In the Presbyterian Seminary of Guatemala we find a denominational program in which it might be possible to compare the progress of the Church with that of another denomination if this were the only variable. It is not. Policies, conditions, varying degrees of receptivity, previous histories of the Churches all are factors which would have to be weighed since they can not be controlled. In the United Biblical Seminary of Colombia the analysis is further complicated by the fact that most denominations have a few students in extension studies, but no denomination trains all its leaders in this way. This makes denominational comparisons impossible even if the previously mentioned factors did not exist.

At a later date, as programs are perfected, more field data become available and situations with relatively controlled conditions are discovered, evaluation will be more feasible. As a small contribution to such future evaluation, the present study has set three projects in motion. One is this directory, the second is the permanent archive on TEE at the School of World Mission, Fuller Theological Seminary and the third is the monthly air mail newsletter, *Extension*. It is the desire of the author that these three projects which he has begun in the course of his studies will be able to continue and thus provide a basis for the further research which needs to be done in this area. The archive contains most of the unpublished materials mentioned below and in the bibliography.

METHODOLOGY

Questionnaires were sent to every institution engaged in TEE of which the author has any knowledge. In many cases a second questionnaire was sent after a period of time. A separate inquiry was sent to obtain data for years previous to 1972. At this stage response is as yet far from 100 per cent and this accounts for the omission of some extension programs. A Spanish version of the questionnaire was sent to institutions in Latin America. Samples are found in the appendix.

Letters requesting information on programs or policies toward TEE were sent to mission boards and to associations of theological schools. Key men in the movement were asked for information and efforts were made to secure constitutions, minutes and other documents from the associations of extension institutions.

With regard to publications, the archive now contains a fairly complete collection of periodicals related to the extension movement. Mimeographed materials and some articles have also been gathered. No attempt has been made to include books.

Information on the extension program of the United Biblical Seminary of Colombia was collected by the author, as he was a member of the residence faculty and also taught in the extension program for nearly three and one half years. Data on student body composition and other matters was gleaned from application forms and questionnaires. The evaluations of the program by missionaries and national leaders were given in taped interviews, in letters and were expressed in meetings which the author attended.

PART ONE

Background

The Crisis in Theological Education

It will be appropriate to present in this first chapter some
of the problems of traditional theological education, some of
the possibilities of TEE and a brief history of the development
of this movement, since theological education by extension
(TEE) must be seen in its historical, theological and structural context to be properly understood. This requires a description of the factors which have produced such a movement,
a comparison with alternative systems of theological education,
and a biblical justification for this innovative form of training the ministry.

THE PROBLEMS OF TRADITIONAL THEOLOGICAL EDUCATION

The rapid growth of the Church throughout the world and the
retreat of the western powers before divers forces including
rising nationalism, along with many other factors, have placed
almost unbearable strains on theological education around the
world. Common to most institutions, Churches and regions has
been a growing dissatisfaction with present systems for training the ministry and laity in the churches. Criticisms which
are frequently heard are that the patterns established in the
United States and Europe are not applicable to the Third World.
Or that the training imposed upon the Churches by their found-
ing missions is culturally irrelevant and is not meeting the
needs of the men who must minister to situations for which they
have not been prepared. Ministerial training is perhaps the
weakest element in many Churches. Even when ministers are
academically well trained this preparation is not capable of
contributing to the spiritual and theological life of the
churches served by these ministers (Consultation on Theology
of the Indonesian Council of Churches 1971:25). Before taking
up specific areas of inadequacy in traditional forms of theological education, let us look briefly at the development of
the patterns to which we have been accustomed.

Novelty of the Seminary

   Theological seminaries are a relatively recent innovation of
the Church. The Dutch Reformed Church founded the first seminary in the United States in 1784 (Jencks and Riesman 1968:
208). Up to that time the only form of ministerial training
was that received from the local minister, but other denominations soon followed the pattern of more formally institution-
alized theological training. Seminary training helped to re-
inforce the already established separation of clergy and laity.
The creation of two classes of Christians in the Roman Catholic
Church had led eventually to ministerial exemption from the
jurisdiction of civil courts and a multitude of abuses which
the reformers resisted. Even today in Roman Catholic countries
the priest is set apart as one who has prestige, must be submitted to, has access to the powerful, is able to deal with
problems, can give infallible advice and accomplish what is
impossible for other men (Guzman 1969:21). Protestant ministerial associations which so far only set standards for ordination and judge the errors of the members of the profession fall short of the Roman attitude which would free the
clergy entirely from responsibility to the whole church.
   One basic issue is whether the theological student should
be initiated into a body of esoteric knowledge which separates
him from and gives him authority over laymen. Biblical, theological, historical and linguistic studies have made such a
body of knowledge available. Should the study of such subjects be that which sets a man apart as a minister of the Gospel? Although a theological seminary may be considered a professional school similar in function to a medical or law
school, there seems to be a distinction in the exercise of
these professions. Only a medical doctor who has graduated
from an accredited school may practice medicine. The physician
does not share his knowledge with others because it is generally believed that a little knowledge is a dangerous thing. The
minister, on the contrary, is expected to share what he has
learned so that the members of his congregation may not only
use the knowledge imparted but even teach it to others. If
the ministry is to be distinguished from the other professions
in this way we would do well to ask whether the exercise of the
Christian ministry should depend upon a professional school
type of training.
   Even if we were to concede that a pastor needs professional
education, we should be reminded that professional schools of
any type have appeared very recently. During the last century
it was more common to read law under the tutelage of a local
lawyer, perhaps in a kind of apprenticeship, in preparation for
bar exams. It has been already pointed out that there were no
separate seminaries in the United States two centuries ago.
Only since the Second World War has the Church of England made
theological college obligatory (Barry 1966:44).
   Efforts are constantly being made to upgrade academically

theological education in the Churches of the Third World.
While this goal has merit, it must be asked if traditional
seminaries with constantly rising entrance requirements will
meet the needs of churches where educational and economic
levels are closer to those of the United States two centuries
ago than to present conditions. Jencks and Riesman point out
that in the eighteenth and nineteenth centuries applicants to
colleges in the United States were often little more than functionally literate. Few had had any secondary schooling (1968:
28). As late as 1960 about one-sixth of those who listed the
ministry as their principal occupation had had no college preparation (1968:211). In 1926 over 40 per cent of the ministers
in the seventeen largest white Protestant denominations were
graduates neither of college nor theological seminary (Niebuhr
and Williams 1956:274-275).

In the light of the conditions in most Third World Churches
is it wise to impose our recently acquired educational standards for ministers upon them? Is it reasonable to expect
churches largely gathered from the lower classes to support
full time pastors just because this is the pattern in the af-
fluent West? And at the same time that we accuse ourselves of
cultural overhang it might be appropriate to mention national-
istic pride.

> But like other more recent victims of colonialism, Ameri-
> cans during these years were eager to have the outward
> trappings of equality with the mother country, even if
> these trappings were neither relevant to the American set-
> ting nor notably productive in the mother country itself...
> But in America as in Africa today, collegiate promotors
> could and did charge such critics with selling their coun-
> try short and perpetuating subordination to Europe. Eng-
> land had a few colleges, so America had more (Jencks and
> Riesman 1968:2).

No one can deny to the Third World Churches and seminaries the
right to form first rate theologians who can formulate an indigenous expression of Christian theology for their own people.
But let us remember that the desperate need of the churches is
not merely for theologians but for pastors. Resources and
programs must not be directed primarily towards preparing a
few well trained men for seminary teaching and urban pulpits
while millions of Christians remain in relative ignorance of
biblical truths. The specific criticisms of traditional theological education which follow attempt to point out the folly
of such a policy.

Inability to Supply the Churches

A shortage of pastors is felt in many areas of the world.
In the relatively static Church in the United States some denominations are hard put to keep their pulpits filled. Pres-

tigious seminaries have experienced a drop of enrollment. The
Church of England also laments a ministerial shortage (Barry
1962:43). Secularism has taken its toll and political and social activists question the relevance of the Church and its answers to the problems which this generation must face. Consequently the traditionally conceived roles of the Christian ministry are considered by many as antiquated or even antagonis-
tic to the work of God in the world today. Roman Catholics as
well as Protestants face this problem in the United States and
in countries in which they represent the official religion. In
Colombia, one of the most strongly Roman Catholic nations of
Latin America (the nation picked for the Pope's first visit to
the New World) a 70 per cent decline in candidates for the
priesthood and for religious orders is reported (Sepulveda
1971:19). Even minimally trained national pastors are available to serve only about half the churches of the historic
Protestant denominations in Brazil (Sapsezian 1971:260).

The ministerial crisis is multiplied in the more rapidly
growing Churches. A study commission of the Church in Latin
America reported in 1967 that some 75,000 congregations and at
least that many more preaching points existed in that area of
the world. Probably 90 per cent of those responsible for ministering the Word of God to the members of those congregations
and groups had received no formal pastoral training (Winter
1967c:13). Moreover, approximately 5,000 new congregations
are being formed in Latin America each year. All the seminaries and Bible institutes graduate less than half this number
annually. When we consider that at least one third of these
students are girls, whose ministerial role is not yet well
accepted in Latin America, and another one third are either not
capable or have no thought of formal church leadership, it becomes clear that these traditional institutions are able to
supply even partially trained men for less than 20 per cent of
the new congregations formed each year and will never be able
to touch the tremendous backlog of churches, some 100,000 of
which are without trained leadership.

The desperate situation in Central and South America is repeated in Indonesia and some areas of Africa where the growth
of the Church has far outstripped the capacity of the theological training institutions. A tragic result of the lack of
trained leaders has been the formation of schismatic and syn-
cretistic movements whose understanding of Christianity has be
been seriously distorted. This numerical inadequacy of traditional theological education is enough alone to make those responsible cast about for an alternative or supplementary means
of pastoral training. However, as we shall see, there are
other deficiencies in the system.

Inordinate Expense of Pastoral Training

Some of us who have pursued out theological training in the
United States have often been reminded as we pay our $1,500

or more per year for tuition and fees that this really only represents one third of the cost of our schooling. It may be mildly surprising that the true cost of theological education is four or five thousand dollars a year in the United States. However, it is much more shocking to realize that this same figure is not uncommon in the training of national pastors in other lands. A comparable figure could be calculated for the seminary in Colombia in which the author taught. To operating expenses we must add salaries of missionary professors, perhaps $10,000 per couple (the United Presbyterians now calculate $20,000). When this dollar total is divided by the number of students at institutions with small enrollments the cost per student suddenly appears astronomical. This does not even include the cost of student scholarships which may add another $1,000 per year. Since most seminaries are located in urban centers with high living costs it is not unheard of for a student to receive a scholarship which alone is higher than the salary which he will later receive as a pastor.

The elevated cost of theological education is a fact of life in small institutions around the world. In a study of all Bible schools on mission fields Reynhout noted that the average number of faculty members was seven (4.4 missionaries), and the average ratio of faculty to students was one to six (1959: 7-8). Calculations in this case may produce a per student cost of less than $2,000. However, it should be remembered that there are generally fewer students per faculty member in the seminaries and theological colleges than in the lower level schools included in these averages. In Taiwan eleven evangelical schools training ministerial candidates have a total enrollment of 175 full time students and 87 full time teachers of whom 49 or 62 per cent are missionaries (Chao 1972:6).

In addition to salaries and other operating expenses which we have examined in terms of cost per student, other items must be included to grasp the full cost of traditional ministerial training. Scholarships and the cost of transportation to seminary, sometimes to a foreign country, raise the figure. Some seminaries have investments in land, buildings and equipment of over one million dollars. Total investment of this kind would amount to many millions of dollars.

The problem of finances, however, is not just that some missionary agencies find it increasingly difficult to amass such sums of money and that national Churches see no possibility of doing so. The resulting standard of living often has unfortunate effects on those who are supposed to benefit by it. The students whose standard of living in seminary is higher than that which he will be offered in the pastorate is obviously going to dissatisfied if he accepts a call to a church. Some theological students feel that the more (free) education they receive, the higher their pay should be upon graduation and placement. Perhaps the most serious consequence of receiving scholarships to study in residence programs is that many students establish in that way a pattern of financial depend-

ence upon the mission or the church which grants the scholarship. It is difficult to become independent on graduation. In
such a case the ministry is the only profession for which the
student has been prepared and candidates usually expect job security with minimum salary scales and other benefits.

Cultural Dislocation of its Students

The most common complaint concerning traditional theological
education stemming from those who are its recipients (or vic-
tims), is the foreignness or lack of indigeneity. The principal objection is that it is designed to perpetuate the western
pattern of the ministry. This is part of the nearly universal
complaint among students that in general colleges do not help
the students develop the capacity for critical thinking. The
institutions have become part of the socialization process,
oriented in part by those representatives of industry who visit
the campuses to recruit those graduates who will fit into their
organizations without questioning the operation or values of
the system into which they are incorporated. This is not just
the complaint of radical students who would be misfits in any
system, but also the observation of perceptive professors
(Jencks and Riesman 1968:20). In any event, whether the criticism is just or not, it has filtered down from the secular
schools to the theological seminaries.

In an age of increasing nationalism it is felt that the socialization process is oriented toward cultural patterns foreign to the students. While the professor's cultural background may not be very significant in certain subjects, it is
usually an absurdity to assign a course in homiletics or pastoral theology to a missionary. In this respect the efforts of
the Theological Education Fund and others to help nationals
train as seminary professors are well directed. For this reason many national Christian leaders would prefer to replace
missionary professors with less highly trained national teachers. Usually this is impossible because the missionary has
come "free" to the seminary because his support has been raised
in the homeland. The problem is to include in the seminary
budget the salary of a national professor.

Unfortunately cultural dislocation continues to be a problem even in institutions with a 100 per cent national faculty.
This is true not because of the high proportion of national
faculty who have been sent to study in Europe, to the United
States or to some other country who do not choose to return
home. These expatriates are relatively few in number. Nor are
we most concerned with the cultural change which occurs in a
man trained in another country to be a professor. An equally
significant cultural change may occur in the student who comes
from a rural church to study in an urban residence program.
After becoming accustomed to a higher standard of living it is
very hard to adjust to the more primitive conditions from which
he came. Is it unreasonable for the seminary graduate to de-

sire to remain in an area which provides better educational and
medical facilities for his family? We missionaries who always
live in cities should be able to understand this.

But even if the seminary graduate were willing to return to
his people, he might not be able to fit into the situation.
His training was for an urban ministry. His very education
separates him from those who were his peers. He talks a new
language and thinks in different patterns. Many of his values
have changed. He is no longer one with those to whom he has
come back to minister. Of course the degree of cultural change
and its significance vary from one situation to another.

Consider the case of the bilingual student who comes from a
minority culture but must receive his theological training in
the language and setting of the dominant culture. Even if such
a student were able to maintain contact with his people, one
wonders what distortions occur as he learns, perhaps with imperfect understanding, in one language which is not his native
tongue and then must teach theological concepts in terms of
other linguistic and thought patterns. If linguistic experts
struggle mightily with the translation of the Bible, how must
it be for the inexperienced student with no special training to
translate philosophical concepts into their functional equiva-
lents? Can we blame such a minister if his people do not demonstrate in their lives the things which we have taught the student in another context? The poor student may not realize the
different philosophical presuppositions of the two peoples.

Communication is not the only difficulty produced by the
cultural dislocation which often occurs when a man goes away to
seminary for a considerable period of time. The man trained to
be a professional minister may be regarded in some areas as an
economic parasite since he does no materially productive work.
He does not share in the labors, the frustrations and the as-
pirations of those among whom his task is to incarnate the Gospel. His theology has been formulated in relative isolation
from the world in which the common people live and think. The
clerical mentality acquired injects a foreignness to the Christian message. If, instead of assuming that a pastor returns to
his own people on completion of his training we consider the
case of a total stranger from another region of the country who
has been assigned by a missionary or national church association, the obstacles for planting and nurturing a truly indigenous church are legion.

Improper Selection of Candidates for Training

Theological education in the traditional pattern generally
trains the wrong men. Two basic aspects of this problem appear.
One is that the seminary, of course, can not impart the pastoral vocation or spiritual gifts necessary to exercise that call-
ing. No one should expect this of the school. And yet many
times the seminary or Bible institute receives candidates for
the ministry who have demonstrated no evidence of a pastoral

gift. The sending church hopes that the institution can do
something with them. What the seminary can do is provide certain academic preparation for the ministry. Unfortunately many
congregations and individuals are deceived into thinking that
this preparation produces pastors. The result is frustration,
disillusionment and failure.

How do such men get into the seminaries in the first place?
Whose is the responsibility for these misfits who will plague
the church for years? Part of the blame must rest with the
institutions which are eager to expand their student bodies
even if it means bending the entrance requirements a little.
However, it is mainly the responsibility of the missions and
Churches which provide the scholarships and of the pastors and
congregations which recommend the students. Particularly in
interdenominational schools there is a hesitancy to offend one
of the supporting groups by rejecting or expelling one of its
students. Generally when students not apt for the pastorate
are spotted in the first year of studies the administration
cautiously decides to give the student another chance and so he
is enrolled for another year. Suspicions are confirmed that he
shouldn't be there, but after completing two-thirds of his
training it seems too late to do anything about it now. Therefore the theological qualifications of the student are certi-
fied and the denomination to which he belongs takes this as
meaning that another pastor has been formed. Even if some
leaders of the denomination recognize the lack of pastoral
gifts, they feel an obligation to use the man after he has invested three years in study and they have invested a considerable sum of money in his preparation.

The criteria for choosing pastoral candidates need to be
carefully reexamined. Young men may be chosen because they are
tall, good looking, have a good speaking voice, demonstrate an
ability to express themselves well, got good grades in school
or possess other such arbitrary qualities. It is even sadder
when men go to Bible institute because they couldn't make it
through high school or normal school. The pastorate remains
the only profession open to them and the teachers will push
them through somehow. The parents of a teen age girl once
requested the author to obtain a scholarship to send her to
Bible institute. The real reason behind this religious call-
ing was that the girl had a crippled hand and wasn't able to
do any other kind of work.

The biblical pattern is quite distinct. Most of the spiritual gifts are listed in I Corinthians 12, Romans 12 and Ephe -
sians 4. The majority of these gifts are not described as to
functions. However, we do have a job description for the pastor in I Timothy 3 and Titus 1. The picture we get is that of
a mature married man who manages his affairs well, has brought
up his children to serve the Lord, is hospitable - probably a
home owner, has a good reputation in the church and in his community, has had several years of Christian experience and has
exercised some teaching and administrative role in the congre-

gation. This doesn't sound like the young, single immature
seminary student who has never exercised leadership in his
church or community and often has not even been a Christian
for long. The author remembers three young people in one
congregation who requested baptism only because it was a requirement to enter Bible institute. In the Third World youth
is less prestigious. Maturity is more important culturally.
We could tolerate a few of these younger students in a student
body made up of mature Christian leaders. But the greatest
tragedy is that the traditional theological education system
has been set up to exclude those whom it should serve.

Age. Let us pause to document this. In England the complaint has been made that there is no provision for late vocation (Evans 1962:21a). In the Pastor's Training School for
the Marshall and Caroline Islands, since the wives of students
caused problems only students were accepted who were willing to
leave their wives and children for protracted periods (TEF
1961:53). Before 1958 most ordinands in the Solomon Islands
were older men who had demonstrated their ability as catechists
for several years before entering formal ministerial training.
However, after that year a new policy restricted enrollment
mainly to younger men and in 1961 all students must have been
unmarried (TEF 1961:55). This may appear to some to be a
useful test to see if a man really loves the Lord more than
family or friends. It is more likely to attract only those
who will irresponsibly leave their family and other obligations for a chance at a period of free formal education.

One of the barriers to ministerial candidates is age. Because of family and other obligations the man who has demonstrated his Christian maturity is unable to attend seminary if
this means three or more years in a residence program. When
this restriction is lifted we find more older men entering the
ministry. Although other factors are involved we find in the
Chilean pentecostal churches where formal training is not required and may even be scorned that men become pastors later.
This is illustrated in Figure 1 below.

Conflict has arisen in many churches because the society
will not accept the leadership of young men who have been to
seminary. We are reminded that Jesus did not begin his public
ministry until the age of thirty. In some societies leadership
roles are assigned only to those whose grey hair indicates
maturity of judgment. In other societies a single man is not
accepted as a full adult. The prestige placed on age is not a
phenomenon only of primitive societies. In Japan a young inexperienced person is not accepted as a leader and to impose him
upon a congregation is detrimental to church growth (Vander
Bilt 1972:6). It would appear that in order to train men who
will be accepted as leaders we may have to wait until they have
already become leaders before offering them special theological education. This would also allow the possibility for a man
converted when no longer young to develop his pastoral gift.
In Japan and Korea most of the seminary students came from

AGE OF PASTORS IN CHILE

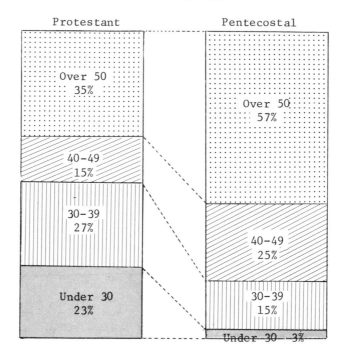

Figure 1

Source: Lalive 1967:186)

Christian homes which may indicate that for a man converted
after preparing for another profession it was less possible to
seek theological education (Commission on Theological Education 1967:17).

   Education. A second barrier to potential pastors is the
formal education required before beginning theological training. Few traditional training programs are able to cope with
more than two different educational levels. The tendency is
to upgrade step by step the entrance requirements until a substantial proportion of the population is excluded. This is
felt to be consonant with the rising educational levels in most
lands today and the need for highly trained men who can win the
respect of educated urban congregations. Fortunately we don't
have to choose between ministering to the better educated minority or to the unschooled masses. But we do have to choose
between a traditional type of theological education which ministers only to one group and an alternative form of pastoral
preparation which is more flexible in its entrance requirements. The fact we need to face is that the functional pastors,

the men who must minister to people in the name of Christ week after week in countless congregations, are not able to take advantage of the traditional theological education offered. In a survey taken at the World Vision Pastors Concference in Colombia in 1967 it was revealed that a third of those who attended had not finished primary school and that a third more had achieved only that level of education (Winter 1967c:12). Probably the educational level of those who did not attend but serve congregations would be even lower. Again in Chile we find that the Pentecostals have found to be effective pastors, at least for the numerical increase of their congregations, those whose educational attainments would exclude them from most institutions. The contrast between educational levels of pastors in the two types of churches is seen in Figure 2.

EDUCATIONAL STANDARD OF PASTORS IN CHILE

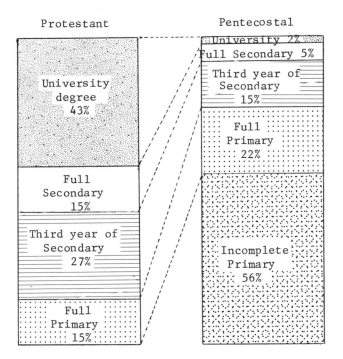

Figure 2

Source: Lalive 1967:186

The basic issue behind the problem of age and of education,
since it is less likely that older men will have completed as
much formal schooling, is whether a pastor should be trained
full time for a full time profession. It has been noted that
economic productivity may be essential for recognition of leaders in some communities. Can it be true that the Bible schools
are primarily dedicated to turning out

> ... more paid workers whom the Church cannot pay, while
> neglecting the training of the laity, the cultivation of a
> spirit of voluntary service and the promotion of advanced
> knowledge of the Bible among the most educable parts of the
> population ..." (Welch 1964:175).

On one hand the traditional system of candidate selection ad-
mits those who see the pastorate as their only chance to become a professional and enjoy a more prestigious and lucrative
occupation than the alternative of farm worker, factory em-
ployee or unskilled worker. On the other hand it excludes the
successful business or professional person who could lend prestige to the ministry and whose abilities and knowledge of the
secular world would bring relevance to the problems of the
congregation and the bearing of biblical truth upon them. The
pattern of full time pastors has been self-defeating in Iran.
The churches say that they cannot support a pastor and therefore men are dissuaded from training for the pastorate since no
one will support them when they graduate (Webster and Nasir
1962:17).

In most areas of the world the advance of the Church has depended on the laity or an unpaid ministry. There are never
enough pastors to go around and even if there were they might
not be the most effective agents of evangelism. Among the
Methodists in Brazil it has been demonstrated that lay preachers frequently are more effective evangelists than are ordained
ministers (Webster 1964:8). However, it is not the purpose of
this study to compare the merits of a full time or voluntary
ministry but only to note that traditional theological education does not provide for the training of the self-supporting
pastor or leader if such a pattern were found to be desirable.

Inferior Quality of Instruction

The educational methods used in most seminaries and Bible
institutes are bad enough for adolescents, but completely inadequate and inappropriate for adults. Much dependence on the
lecture system bores adults who are used to learning in the
give-and-take situations of real life. The cultural background
of many men who serve as pastors does not permit them to understand the abstract thinking often involved in lectures. It
would be an interesting experiment for seminary teachers, particularly at lower academic livels, to read the notes which students have taken in their courses. Since lectures seldom per-

mit effective two-way communication, the misconceptions are
never discovered and corrected. To ensure that the basic facts
are grasped the teacher may resort to rote memory. This is an
extremely distasteful way for an adult to learn and only ensures that he will be able to parrot back a list of facts on
the exam without revealing any conceptual knowledge at all.

Seminary curricula around the world are generally elaborated in imitation of the courses of study in the European or
United States seminaries from which the professors have come.
The seminary determines what a pastor should know (or rather
what a western pastor might be expected to know). Little attempt has been made to determine what a pastor in the local
situation needs to know. Therefore a large percentage of the
courses offered are irrelevant and discouraging to the student.
The study of Greek or Hebrew usually has no more permanent
value for a pastor than the study of Morse code does for a ham
radio operator's license. Its primary function is to deter
more people from getting a license. If the old members of the
club had to pass these entrance requirements, why should they
make it any easier for anyone else? Unfortunately seminary
professors who have specialized in certain subjects are always
interested in finding disciples for their narrow field of knowledge and dare not ask the significance of what they are teaching for pastors of national churches. This would be threatening to their own position or at least might require them to
make a costly and painful transformation of the whole seminary
program. Therefore seminaries and Bible institutes go on year
after year believing that as men pass the examinations and complete course assignments they have been prepared in the best
possible way for the Christian ministry. Pastoral failure or
stagnation and biblical ignorance in the churches can not be
their fault, they insist.

Even if the right subjects were taught, conventional tests
of progress toward an effective future ministry are inadequate.
A study of professional education in the United States indicates that there is very little relationship between course
grades and occupational success (Jencks and Riesman 1968:205).
Few final examinations even reflect the goals stated in the
course descriptions printed in the school catalog. Examinations show little about the student's ability to apply truth
in his local church situation (Miller 1969:101).

There is hope that some institutions involved in theological
education will heed the recommendations made in the last few
years about the type and quality of training which they give.
Some of these recommendations are indicated here. Inductive
Bible study is needed to combat the pattern of rote learning
(Mulholland 1961:59). Instead of teaching methods to study different types of biblical literature and working out hermeneuti-
cal principles which will be a useful guide later, Bible institutes are too prone to try to teach all the basic concepts and
doctrines in Scripture lest the student independently arrive at
a wrong conclusion regarding some doctrine or question the ap-

plication of certain proof texts in favor of a denominational
point of view.

Seminaries need to live up to their name by including more
seminars, research projects and independent study (Hopewell
1967:162). It would be much more helpful to print the lecture
notes and then discuss them instead of dictating (TEF 1965:36).
Guided discussions which permit group interaction are more effective learning devices in East Africa (Miller 1969:100). The
pastor needs to learn to work as a member of a team (Krusche
1967:165). He needs to learn to articulate his ideas and also
to accept criticism in a group study which is open and accept-
ing but which will not permit any fuzzy thinking. The traditional seminaries and Bible institutes are not providing enough
of this kind of educational experience. Curriculum studies are
needed to eliminate present deficiencies.

The student who has learned by the lecture method will teach
in the same way. He may in some cases tend to be dictatorial
and dogmatic in his teaching ministry in the church. Unable to
listen to the questioning of truth or his interpretation of it
he will feel threatened by questions or attempts at discussion
in Sunday School or Bible studies. Nothing of group dynamics
has been learned and therefore is not available for application in the local church or home Bible study. Poor teaching
methods, used by men who have never been trained to teach, in
the seminaries and the insistence on traditional courses of
study instead of preparation for the functional needs of a
pastor, combine to inflict upon the church the products of inadequate ministerial training. We can only thank God that many
men have learned and developed their pastoral gifts in spite of
systems organized to impede their exercise of an effective and
fruitful indigenous ministry.

POSSIBILITIES OF THEOLOGICAL EDUCATION BY EXTENSION

Theological education by extension seeks to solve all the
problems encountered in traditional approaches to ministerial
training. Nevertheless, it too is faced with problems and
limitations, some the same and others peculiar to TEE. These
problems will be discussed in a later section. At this point
we will mention only those advantages of extension programs in
regard to the difficulties enumerated for the residence type
of schools.

Flexibility

Theological education by extension is decentralized. This
means that not everyone must be brought together for instruction. One of the problems of a residence program is that different levels of students can not effectively be taught in the
same classroom. Even when all students have met equal prere-
quisites, teachers are always hindered by differences in back-

ground and learning ability. Tedious explanation for the slower learner becomes boring for those who got the idea the first time it was presented. But to speak to those who need to be challenged with more difficult subjects on a conceptual level is to leave others far behind with no understanding. This problem is not eliminated entirely in extension, but the local centers can operate at any one or more of the various recognized levels. Five such levels are defined by the Latin American Association of Institutions and Theological Seminaries by Extension (ALISTE) as follows:

Certificate B - persons who read and write with difficulty
Certificate A - persons who read and write with some facility but have had less than full primary school
Diploma   - Persons who have completed full primary school
Bachiller   - persons who have completed at least the basic course of secondary school, that is, at least nine years of formal education or its equivalent
Licentiate   - persons who have completed full secondary education or in some areas have completed at least two years of university level studies

Not only does the extension student study at his own level, but he is able to go at his own pace at that level. The content of the course is not transmitted through lectures in which all students must scribble frantically to record some impressions of what was said without having an opportunity to digest them. The extension student gains his knowledge of the subject as he studies in his own home the materials or text assigned. If he is a rapid learner he may complete the assignment, calculated at five hours' work, in three hours or less. If he is a very slow reader it may take him eight. Both students may master the same material and be able to discuss it at the weekly meeting. Even when different educational levels have been united at times in extension centers, discussion has been fruitful because each student can contribute something from his experience which is valid and illuminating for the rest.

This flexibility of levels has reached down to the church leaders who are barely functionally literate but still have the responsibility of sharing Christian truth with those even less instructed. In Honduras George Patterson has prepared materials which look much like comic books. They contain only a few pages and are abundantly illustrated. Each booklet is for a week's study and covers just one subject. It is amazing how much basic material can be reduced to a few simple points and assimilated by men highly motivated to learn in the only way available to them.

At the other extreme of the academic spectrum we find men

who would not waste their time in most residence programs because levels are inferior to their educational attainments and
capacities. Such men do not need simple step-by-step explana-
tions, but rather to be assigned reading which will require
them to examine critically their faith and the world around
them. A center in Guatemala City has attracted professional
men with excellent academic preparation. In India a large number of college graduates, including nearly a dozen with doctorates, are studying by extension.

The flexibility of TEE is such that it spans the whole range
of educational levels and also allows it to cross cultural
barriers. Cultural diversity has been largely neglected in
traditional theological education. In order to study men have
had to learn a second language, perhaps Spanish, English or
French. TEE not only permits a man to remain in his own community while he learns; it enables him to learn much more effectively in his own language. This is an area which is only
being explored. Materials are being developed slowly because of lack of time on the part of the relatively few men
capable of their preparation. A half-way point has been
reached in the case of students who must use texts written in
a language which they do not speak in their homes, but who are
able to relate their experiences and clarify concepts and apply them to their own lives in the weekly meetings held in the
vernacular. A few materials are being developed in Aymara and
Quechua. Most of the teachers in the *Seminario Bíblico Unión*
in Ecuador are Quechuas who teach their own people. Programmed
instructional materials which have been printed first in English in India and some areas of Africa will later be adapted
and translated into regional or tribal languages. The use of
local pastors, school teachers or other church leaders as extension professors is possible since this system does not require an expert in subject content, but one who is capable of
eliciting the contribution of each member of the group. Such
teachers know the people and their problems much better than
does the instructor in the residence school far away in another
culture.

TEE is able to adapt its structure to the local situation.
Normally classes are held weekly, but if geographical or other
considerations do not permit this sessions may be held for
longer periods every two weeks. Students may even meet with
their professor for two days once a month if that seems to be
the most viable solution. Centers are organized for the day,
time and place which are most convenient for the majority of
the students. This may be in a local congregation during the
hour before midweek prayer meeting begins so as not to multiply
the number of nights that students and teacher must be out.
All sorts of possibilities may be considered if our purpose is
not to maintain an institution but rather to do everything within the reach of our resources to train men and women for a more
effective use of their spiritual gifts within the Church of
Christ.

Comparison with Other Methods

Stated in negative terms TEE was conceived to correct some of the deficiencies of traditional theological education. The reconsideration of those factors and TEE's answer to them will introduce the purposes of the extension seminary. TEE is one of the ways to reach men and women whom residence seminaries can not serve. It is not the only way, but has some advantages over the alternative methods. Correspondence courses, for example, are available to those with an efficient postal service. Even if that factor did not exclude many people, the lack of personal contact with a teacher for interaction and stimulus would discourage most potential students. By the time the student receives his corrected lesson the wrong answer is already fixed in his mind and since he has continued with another lesson or two he may not even care to note the correction. Most correspondence courses are superficial, are prepared only for one level of student and cannot be applied to the local situation. The teacher does not even know the circumstances in which the student lives, works and serves his Lord.

Evening courses are popular, particularly in Latin America. It is reported that in 1961 35,000 men and women in Brazil were studying the principles of Marxism six nights a week (Benton 1962:34). In most urban centers throughout Latin America students receive university, high school or even primary school education in the evening. Language institutes, secretarial and other trade schools attract many students after normal working hours. Mario Gálvez University in Guatemala, an evangelical school, and the University of Honduras are examples of institutions which hold classes only in the evening (Mulholland 1971:55). Other schools such as the University of Medellín (Colombia) offer classes as early as six o'clock in the morning.

Although evening classes tend to attract more mature students, they suffer from some of the same defects as the day time residence programs. Instruction depends on lectures and permits even less independent study and research. In the evening school in Los Angeles in which the author taught, the students worked all day and attended classes from six to eleven four nights a week. Taking into consideration the time spent in driving from home to work to school to home, there remained very little time during the week to do home work. However, if quality of instruction is maintained and students are able to take only one or more courses according to the time at their disposition to study, evening classes can provide theological training for church leaders who live in the urban centers where facilities are available for evening study.

Short term institutes, on the contrary, are more likely to be convenient in rural areas where agricultural work is seasonal and there is no economic hardship in leaving work and family for a short period of time. The inspirational value of such

institutes is very high but there is some question as to the
amount of material that a student can assimilate in a short
period. Another disadvantage of such courses is that contact
with a teacher and actual study is very infrequent. For most
of the year the church leader receives no preparation and has
no guidance in treating matters which arise each week. The
values of short term institutes are incorporated into some extension systems in monthly and quarterly meetings where there
is opportunity for fellowship and inspiration and where special
courses may be offered and topics of general concern may be
treated.

Some kind of apprenticeship can also be a valuable adjunct
of extension studies. Alone, however, it is very difficult to
standardize the level of instruction received. It is also preferable that the student be exposed to more than one teacher
or source of information so that he may be able critically to
evaluate what is presented to him. Apprenticeship requires
the student to be almost constantly present with his mentor to
observe his manner of dealing with every kind of situation.
Although the leader of the weekly class can not be expected to
have all the answers, he should be able to help students in
working out together the application of biblical truths to
situations which the student cannot handle alone. In this way,
perhaps, the greatest value of the apprenticeship system is
served.

Expenses. Expenses for extension studies can be greatly
reduced from those which have raised the cost of traditional
theological education. An extension program can be operated
out of an office or home without the need for expensive facilities or equipment. Coordination of a large program may require
full time attention and the production of materials is extremely time consuming. However, at the local level classes
which meet in a church or other rent free location and which
are taught by men who may or may not be paid for their services, do not have large budgetary requirements. Generally
students pay for texts and other materials and also are charged
a small fee for registration and tuition. This may vary according to the economic possibilities of the students. But already there is a tremendous shift from being paid to study to
having to pay at least a little in order to study. Men who
sacrificially pay for their education are more likely to try to
get their money's worth.

Student fees are not likely to finance extension programs in
most situations. For some subjects it may be necessary to subsidize the cost of expensive texts. Programmed and provisional
materials are expensive to produce for the present small market. Transportation costs may be high, particularly if the
teacher must fly to another island as in the West Indies or to
another valley as in one Bolivian program. However, as materials are developed and standardized creating larger markets
for superior products, prices may go down. The training of local pastors and leaders as teachers will eliminate in the future

much of the transportation costs which are necessary now. Even though expenses connected with the training of one student continue for a longer period, the cost per student in extension programs is considerably less than that for traditional programs and is more likely to decrease than to increase.

Candidate Selection. Candidate selection is clearly superior for TEE. Extension seminaries do not attract young men who are searching for an attractive career with job security. There is no offer of free education and living expenses for three years while a man decides whether he really wants to be a pastor or not. Extension studies draw men who have nothing to gain financially, but who feel a need to prepare themselves for more effective service.

TEE does not have a drop out problem. It welcomes a high attrition rate. In fact it could well serve as a screening process for residential schools. If students were required to study by extension before receiving a scholarship to complete their training in residence, not only would the churches and missions be saved the cost of a year or more of studies completed in extension, but would eliminate those candidates whose sense of vocation was not great enough to take advantage of a local training program at their own expense. Then too, we shouldn't expect every student to be interested in every course. A Sunday School teacher or superintendent may take courses which he feels are important for his ministry and then drop out until something else is offered which he feels he must have. Most students may not care about getting a degree eventually.

The selection of courses introduces another possibility. That is the recognition that the church requires the exercise of various spiritual gifts and that these are not all found in one individual. It may be possible to develop a multiple ministry in which different members perform different functions in the body. The five categories named by John Taylor were pastor, evangelist, prophet, teacher and apostle (1967:150-5). A similar scheme has been functioning for some time in Venezuela. The Juan de Frías Institute presents three programs of studies. One is for catechists and Sunday School teachers. Another is for deacons, administrators and other church leaders and a third is for evangelists, lay preachers and those charged with the leadership of neighborhood meetings. Those who study for the pastorate should take most of the courses prescribed for evangelists and some of the courses in the other two categories. The value of the options of this program is that men can seek to discover what gift they have been given and develop it for a ministry within the congregation without having to follow a general course of study. Perhaps many potential students feel that they haven't been called to be pastors and that therefore theological training is not for them. By implication the seminary which prepares only pastors may indicate that only men who think they have one particular gift should develop it through further study.

Cultural Relevance. Although materials used in extension

studies have not all been adapted for the cultures in which
they are used, the cultural dislocation is minimal in comparison with that which occurs in many residence seminary programs.
Classes are held within the community in which men live and
work. Discussions are related to activities within the local
church. Practical work is not artificial, but that which moti-
vates the course work. In most cases teachers will be men
from the same culture who know the people and their problems
and have had experience in confronting the same issues in their
work and in their studies. Churches need not fear that a pastor from outside whose ways are different will be imposed upon
them. The leaders of the church will arise within the congregation and if one is selected to be pastor it will be through
the recognition of his gifts and the other qualities mentioned
in the Bible that the servant of God should demonstrate.

By keeping theological education within the church we are
reminded that the seminary exists for the church and not vice
versa. To a certain extent the seminary is obligated to offer
what the church wants and feels it needs in order to function
more effectively. Courses should contribute to the growth of
the church as the gift of evangelist is developed and others
learn to do their part in contributing to the church services.
The quality of the life of the body is improved as teaching of
the Word becomes more systematic, more comprehensible and more
penetrating. As men gain confidence in their understanding of
biblical truth they will share in the decision making regarding
the application of Christian standards to every area of their
lives. Extension education may make a significant contribution
toward the development of a truly indigenous church.

Quality of Instruction. As the seminary moves into the local church and seeks to meet the needs of that church for theological education, there may well be some concern over the
quality of instruction given. It is certain that the local
leaders wouldn't ask for many of the subjects in most seminary
catalogs. Nevertheless the seminary which teaches by extension,
as well as that which teaches those who live within its grounds,
maintains control over educational methods and standards. Regional and nationwide administration and associations of extension institutions can require that certain standards and procedures be met. Standard examinations ensure that course content is mastered. Frequent quizzes and review in the weekly
meetings force the student to keep up with his studies more
than do less frequent exams and no reviews in residence studies.

Most important, however, is that educational achievements
are measurable in the lives and ministries of the students. A
well-taught lesson or a well-conceived sermon represents a more
meaningful measure of learning than does the grade on a written
examination. Extension education can force educators to fix
and test measurable behavioral goals. As local pastors become
teachers of extension courses their effectiveness can readily
be seen in the amount of learning which their students are able

to achieve. And it is undeniably easier to replace a poor extension teacher than a teacher in a residence school.

The elimination of the lecture method in favor of group discussion, the independent study and critical thinking developed through extension, and the combination of cognitive input and field experience integrated in weekly seminars are all important contributions which extension studies will make toward the improvement of the quality of education. These certainly are characteristics of what professional education should be. Nevertheless, the great innovation to theological education which has come through the promoters and producers of materials for extension is programmed instruction.

Programmed Instruction. Programming is concerned with the ordering of materials and the sequence of learning in a systematic way so that at every point the student has all he needs to understand that which is being taught and there is continuous feedback (Emery 1973). The types of programming, educational principles involved and techniques to be employed in the preparation of programmed instructional materials are described elsewhere. Probably a small percentage of those involved in the extension movement will write programmed materials. But even if they never do, the application of its insistence on fixing and measuring goals and working systematically toward reaching them in appropriate steps may transform the classroom teaching of those professors who attend a workshop on programming. Not all extension materials will be programmed in the sense of the linear technique which most people identify with the method. But the acquaintance with programming principles and the criticism of those who use the materials will compel a constant striving for excellence on the part of those who write materials for extension studies. Growing awareness of what quality education is should help to guarantee it as a goal of extension programs.

2

The Emergence
of a Movement

Theological education by extension came into being in Guatemala in 1963. It was the creation of James Emery and Ralph Winter, two men whose preparation in anthropology, education and theology uniquely qualified them for such an undertaking. In elaborating this new form of pastoral training they were assisted by capable nationals on the staff of the Evangelical Presbyterian Seminary of Guatemala and by Ross Kinsler who arrived a year after the project had been launched. Several other factors contributed to this innovation in theological education. Ralph Winter has told the story in some detail, partly by means of some of the early documents of the movement (1969:Book I) and so only a brief summary will be included here.

THE GUATEMALA EXPERIMENT

A form of on the job training had been used by the Presbyterians in Guatemala for more than a quarter of a century. National workers were assigned books to study. Every six months they were tested on their mastery of the materials studied and then were assigned further work. On completion of the entire study program in twelve to fifteen years the men were ordained, recognized as full pastors, and began to supervise the studies of the younger men (Peters 1940:370). Ordained men could continue their studies toward a degree through correspondence courses. Short term institutes were also held to encourage men in their studies (Peters 1940:372). This system of in-service training through individual study was still used in the rural presbyteries when Emery and Winter appeared on the scene and may have helped some of the Church leaders accept the idea of a decentralized school. However, the accepted pattern of preparation for the more respected urban ministry was determined by the residence seminary established in the capital in 1938.

All of the problems of traditional theological education which were discussed earlier in this study could be found in the Presbyterian Seminary. Not enough pastors were being produced for the growing church. Most of the congregations could not achieve the status of a recognized church because they did not have an ordained pastor. Meanwhile student enrollment in the residence school varied between six and twenty. The needs of the Church were not being met.

Because of the small student body the cost per student was quite high. Emery estimated it at $3,000 per year when the number of students was reduced to six (Winter 1969:89). In 1963 when the residence and extension programs operated simultaneously 70 per cent of the personnel and 80 per cent of the budget were assigned to the training of the five residence students while the rest of the resources of the institution served the sixty-five students in the extension program. This is not the only case of imbalance. In 1972 the United Biblical Seminary of Colombia spent more on the preparation of a dozen residence students than it did on more than 300 extension students.

In an article written for *Practical Anthropology* in 1963 James Emery mentions particularly the factors of cultural dislocation and candidate selection and Ralph Winter's mimeographed article "The Extension Seminary Plan in Guatemala" (Winter 1969:11-28) written later the same year supplements these observations. Diversity within the Presbyterian Church was extreme because of work among Indian tribes with at least two major languages and the differences even between the rural and urban presbyteries of the Spanish speaking believers.

Emery points out in his article that it would have been natural for the elders of the community to fulfill the same leadership function in the church as they became believers. However, indigenous leadership patterns were not always understood or observed. Seminary students were younger, immature men who had not proven themselves in the community or in the church. Perhaps for this reason few of those who graduated from the seminary are serving the Church as pastors today (Emery 1973).

The men in rural presbyteries who studied individually suffered no cultural change which hindered their communication of the gospel in their communities. But the level of instruction which they received was inferior and uneven. This criticism might be leveled at the residence program also. Because of the diverse backgrounds of the students a compromise level of education was followed at the seminary. The lecture methods employed permitted the students to complete their studies without having acquired good study habits or the ability to continue their education in a meaningful way once they have left the presence of those who had painstakingly imparted knowledge to them. Dissatisfaction with classroom teaching was one of the compelling factors in the search for a better way to train pastors for the churches (Winter 1969:90).

The Guatemala experiment was underway and the basic structure was elaborated which has been much discussed and often
copied. Classes were held weekly to discuss what the students
had studied during the week in texts and manuals prepared
especially to guide them in their preparation at home. Monthly meetings which united students from more than one center
offered special studies and provided fellowship and stimulus.
Step by step the bugs were worked out of the system. Enrollment for the first years was 1963:50, 1964:88, 1965:90, 1966:
143 (*Evangelical Seminary* 1967:1:3).

OTHER EARLY EXTENSION PROGRAMS IN LATIN AMERICA

The success of the new method of theological education in
Guatemala attracted the attention of others. One of the first
to note the emergence of this new program was James Hopewell,
then a director of the Theological Education Fund. He learned
of the program in late 1963 and visited Guatemala about a year
later to see it first hand. Hopewell's article in the April,
1967, *International Review of Missions* spoke favorably of this
innovation and undoubtedly influenced others to consider it
seriously.

Pioneer Programs

The Berea Bible Institute operated by the Friends Mission in
Chiquimula, Guatemala was the second institution to adopt extension studies. During the last quarter of 1965 it opened
four centers which were attended by thirty-three students. In
1966 the program was extended to fourteen centers with a total
enrollment of ninety (*Evangelical Seminary* 1967:1:3).
    The Center of Theological Studies (CET) sponsored by the
United Evangelical Church in Ecuador probably has not received
due recognition as a pioneer institution in extension. This
may be because of geographical isolation, but more likely is
because its levels of study and materials have not fit into the
pattern of the other institutions. The leaders of the Church
expressed the same concerns for the training of pastors and
lay leaders that have been mentioned earlier, and in May, 1966
they met with James Hopewell and with Plutarco Bonilla who represented ALET, the regional association of theological schools.
As a result of recommendations made at that meeting, CET initiated its extension program in October, 1966, in three centers with a total of fifty-five students. The second semester
saw a slight decline to fifty-two, twenty-two students having
dropped their studies and nineteen new ones having enrolled
(CET nd:15).
    One of the difficulties in the program of CET, in the opin-
ion of the author who studied in one of the first centers, was
the wide academic and cultural range within those gathered in
a single center. No distinction was made as to levels of study.

Of the total of seventy-four students during the first year of studies, thirty-seven had completed less than primary school, eighteen had completed primary and nineteen had studied at least one year of high school. Of this last group three had had some university education. Five Quechua Indians were included in the student body, of whom two finished the year successfully (CET n.d.:15,16).

Extension programs in Guatemala served only one denomination because of geographical separation of the missions through comity agreements. In CET, however, students came from three denominations and four independent congregations. A course for pastors in Quito attracted men from four evangelical groups other than the United Evangelical Church. Later other denominations were invited to participate in the administration of the program as well.

In 1967 extension seminary programs were initiated by the West Indies Mission, the Evangelical and Reformed Church in Honduras, the Conservative Baptist Association in Honduras, the Evangelistic Institute of Mexico (soon to be suspended), the United Evangelical Center in Mexico and the Methodist Theological Seminary in Costa Rica. An excellent description of the work in the West Indies has been written by Sam Rowen (1967) and an even more detailed study of the extension movement in Honduras has been prepared by Ken Mulholland (1971).

New Structures

It was after the workshop held in Armenia, Colombia in September, 1967, that the number of institutions and students in extension really began to multiply. During 1968 at least eight new extension programs were begun. The Armenia workshop was sponsored by the Latin American Association of Theological Schools (Northern Region) which will be more simply referred to as ALET. The proceedings of that workshop were published as pamphlets in English and Spanish and constituted one of the major documents of the extension movement until their later inclusion in the definitive history of extension written by Ralph Winter (1969).

Rather than duplicate the material which appears there, suffice it to say that the meeting was very significant not only for the stimulus to various extension programs but also because of the organizations conceived during or shortly after that meeting. UNICO (Union of Theological Institutions of Grand Colombia) was in a sense the parent organization. As an association of theological schools in the sub-region of Panama, Colombia, Venezuela and Ecuador it was a very loosely organized body. An official list of members never existed. At the infrequent meetings delegates were those who showed up. However, it did serve the function of convening workshops and consultations and promoting extension throughout its region. Its main continuing function was serving as a channel through which monies from the Theological Education Fund were distributed to

CATA.
CATA (Advisory Committee on Self-teaching Texts) was made up
of technical advisors for the production of extension materials. During the latter part of its five year existence, Ross
Kinsler was international coordinator, and Peter Savage, Vernon Reimer and James Emery were regional coordinators. Their
job was to stimulate and aid authors in the production of materials and one of their most important projects was that of
Intertexts. CATA also established a curriculum for the diploma
or post-primary school level studies which has been followed,
sometimes with variations, by many institutions.

After establishing a curriculum which included thirty-six
courses of three hours credit each, authors were assigned to
prepare texts or manuals for the teaching of those subjects in
extension studies. The books to be produced were called Intertexts because of use by institutions of various denominations
on an international basis. Once an Intertext had been prepared
and had met the technical standards of the CATA advisors as to
format and content, it could be recommended to the other important organization which grew out of the Armenia workshop, CLATT.

CLATT, (Latin American Committee on Theological Texts) was
administered by its *ad hoc* secretary, Peter Wagner, It con-
sisted of certain Latin American seminaries or Bible institutes which sponsored extension programs. CLATT invited these
institutions to become members and limited itself to a group
which was representative both geographically and doctrinally.
The purpose of Wagner's work was to ensure that there would be
a market for the books produced since preliminary editions were
to be sent to the members of CLATT for their approval before
final revision and preparation for printing. Wagner also obtained the agreement of some of the major evangelical publishing houses in Latin America to handle the printing and distribution of the Intertexts.

Most of the authors assigned to write the Intertexts never
began and there was some talk of looking for new writers. Meanwhile provisional materials were produced in several institutions. One of the obstacles to greater progress was that the
introduction of programmed instruction techniques demonstrated
that the process was much more complex than originally anticipated. Potential writers had to put aside manuals they had begun and learn a whole new and difficult strategy for presenting
the material. Although Ted Ward was able to suppress the word
"semi-programmed" it was agreed that Intertexts should be programmed at least in part. By the time CATA and CLATT were dissolved in January 1973 only one official Intertext had been published, *Principles of Church Growth*. Another Intertext, *Introduction to the Old Testament*, had received preliminary approval
from some institutions. In addition, Ross Kinsler had prepared
Intertexts in English on the books of Jeremiah and Mark, but
the Spanish editions had not yet appeared in final form.

ALISTE (Latin American Association of Institutions and
Theological Seminaries by Extension) which succeeded CATA and

CLATT decided that the Intertext project was too ambitious for the time being and determined to leave the selection of extension materials to a process of natural selection. If it appears that a manual has received general acceptance over other materials written on the same subject, the writer will be encouraged to perfect his work for printing and wider distribution.

Although the Presbyterian Seminary in Guatemala continued to be the inspiration and example for all the other extension programs, two other seminaries gained some prominence after the Armenia Workshop. They were the United Biblical Seminary of Colombia and the George Allan Seminary in Bolivia. Extension materials were produced by faculty members of both institutions, but perhaps they served more importantly as models of structure. The United Biblical Seminary is treated in detail in a later section, but we will take a brief look here at the Bolivia model.

The George Allan Theological Seminary in Cochabamba, Bolivia is like the other institutions described earlier in that it serves a single denomination. The Evangelical Christian Union combined into one denomination the churches formed by the Andes Evangelical Mission (formerly the Bolivian Indian Mission) and the Evangelical Union of South America. Total membership for the denomination is over 14,000 and some 180 congregations have been organized (Covell and Wagner 1971:78). The added complication of theological education in Bolivia is the large Indian population. In order to meet the needs for pastoral training throughout the whole denomination, provision must be made for urban and rural Spanish speakers and for the major Indian populations which speak Quechua, Aymara and Guaraní. Cultural distance as well as academic preparation provide a wide range of persons to be served.

Peter Savage, who happened to be also the regional coordinator of CATA, was named rector of the new seminary. Under his leadership plans were drawn up to add an extension program to the already existing residential programs. The George Allan Seminary began operation in 1969 with a continuation of the residence studies formerly under two Bible institutes plus the extension department. Two vice-rectors were named, one for the urban program which was all in Spanish and one for the rural program which included work in Quechua and Aymara. Under these two divisions eight departments were organized, two of which were residence and the rest extension. The extension departments each had one or more centers under their administration for a total of thirteen centers (Covell and Wagner 1971:79). Savage was also named coordinator of a Theological Education Commission which placed all ministerial training under the control of the national Church.

In Brazil a new structure emerged, an association of institutions engaged in extension programs. This was AETTE (Evangelical Theological Association of Training by Extension). In some areas, such as the production of programmed texts, the Brazil-

ian counterpart to the Intertext program has advanced far more
than has the work in Spanish speaking Latin America. Perhaps
this is to be expected since more than two-thirds of all evangelicals in Latin America live in Brazil and coordination within a single country has been easier. Nevertheless, AETTE, like
all the other programs mentioned, learned about extension from
the Guatemala base.

Ralph Winter was invited to present the extension seminary
concept at a meeting of theological educators in Sao Paulo in
1968. The desperation of those men to find a resolution of the
crisis in ministerial training for a rapidly expanding church
was evidenced by the turnout of sixty-five persons. Two
months later forty-three delegates from all of Brazil arrived
in São Paulo for the formation of AETTE. Richard Sturz of the
Baptist Theological Seminary in São Paulo was named executive
secretary. At that time Peter Savage was present and Prof.
Nelson Rosamilha of the University of São Paulo presented the
concept of programmed instruction. At another meeting in April
of the same year Peter Savage was invited again to help AETTE
formulate objectives and curriculum. The initiation of the
program of extension studies was set for 1970 but a few promoters of the movement were unable to wait that long and opened
a few centers with the few provisional materials ready in
Portuguese during the second semester of 1969. Within two
years at least twenty-seven of the eighty-five theological institutions in Brazil had decided to join this new movement.
The tremendous growth is seen in the following graph.

GROWTH OF THE EXTENSION MOVEMENT IN BRAZIL

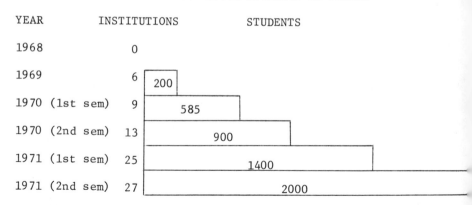

YEAR	INSTITUTIONS	STUDENTS
1968	0	
1969	6	200
1970 (1st sem)	9	585
1970 (2nd sem)	13	900
1971 (1st sem)	25	1400
1971 (2nd sem)	27	2000

Figure 3

Source: Sturz 1972:3

AETTE has placed priority on the preparation of programmed texts. Ted Ward held two workshops in Brazil in September of 1969 with a total attendance of twenty-five persons. In May of 1971 Leroy Ford held two more workshops on programming with total attendance of fifty-two persons. At the annual meetings of AETTE authors were assigned to write the various courses included in the curriculum. Many of the materials produced need much revision, but they have been used successfully in the participating institutions until more adequate materials can be perfected. By the end of 1971 some twenty programmed texts had been made ready for use and it was hoped that ten more would be ready by the end of 1972.

Many examples could be given of the greatly enlarged student bodies of the institutions which adopted the extension system. The Presbyterian Bible Institute Edward Lane had between sixty and eighty students in its residence program in the past. With the opening of extension centers throughout its region of Brazil, residence enrollment has dropped to forty, but extension students now number over 700.

Worldwide Interest in Extension

Theological education by extension passed out of the experimental stage by 1968. Five years of experience in Guatemala and the growing acceptance of the concept in many parts of Latin America convinced the rest of the missionary world that this was a program worth looking into. One of the important agencies in promoting the extension seminary movement was CAMEO (Committee to Assist Missionary Education Overseas), a joint committee of the Evangelical Foreign Missions Association and the Independent Foreign Missions Association.

In April, 1968 a meeting was called by CAMEO in Philadelphia which was attended mainly by mission executives and professors of missions. During the two day consultation a presentation was made by Sam Rowen as outlined in *The Resident-Extension Seminary: A Seminary Program for the Dominican Republic* (1968). Don Luttrell explained the operation of the Recorded Lecture Bible Institute. C. Peter Wagner reported on developments in TEE in Latin America, including the functions of CATA and CLATT. Each of these presentations was discussed by those who attended. On the basis of this introduction to the idea of the extension seminary, plans were made for a workshop to be held during the month of December.

The Wheaton workshop sponsored by CAMEO was held on December 19-21. One hundred twenty-one persons attended representing thirty missions. Topics discussed were those presented earlier, such as the relative merits of residential and extension studies and the inability of traditional theological education to meet the needs of a rapidly growing church for ministerial training. Programmed learning was introduced and its application to the preparation of extension materials was explained. Delegates divided into area interest groups for part of the

time to consider possibilities of extension studies in the
various geographic areas of the missions represented. The CATA
curriculum of thirty-six subjects for which Intertexts were to
be prepared had been worked out in Mexico just a few days earlier and was presented at the workshop.

J. Allen Thompson of the West Indies Mission brought the
Bible messages on the following themes: The Nature of Mission
and Its Relationship to Ministerial Training, The Nature of the
Church and Its Relationship to Ministerial Training, The Nature of the Ministry and Its Relationship to Ministerial Training (Winter 1969:269-274).

C. Peter Wagner gave a report on "The Crisis in Ministerial
Training in the Younger Churches." He explained the problem of
the 60,000 functional pastors in Latin America who had not been
able to benefit from traditional theological education. Instead of extracting these potential students from their responsibilities in the church and community, extension studies
could prove to be a culturally relevant solution (Winter 1969:
275-281).

Ralph Winter spoke on "Theological Education in Historical
Perspective." He stated the necessity of learning from the
past but without necessarily copying structures designed for
another era. One of the structures of great importance to missions was the monastic system and there is a certain parallel-
ism between that system and the Bible institute of our own
times. Since structures are subject to decay through various
factors they must be renewed or redesigned to meet new situations and new purposes (Winter 1969:295-306).

Winter also presented the case study of the Evangelical Presbyterian Seminary in Guatemala. He spoke of the resolution of
the problems with which the Church was faced in training pastors. In the process of wrestling with the problems some un-
expected discoveries were made. They are summarized as
follows: (Winter 1969:307-310)

1. Students and faculty not noticed before became available.
2. Extension could reach higher as well as lower academic
   levels.
3. By training men where they were five sub-cultures were
   served.
4. TEE was tougher and screened out men without self-
   discipline.
5. More younger men than ever studied although the average
   age was higher.
6. Extension students did better work mainly due to greater
   maturity.
7. The program cost far less per student.
8. With no increase in funds or personnel enrollment increased from 7 to 200.
9. Extension studies can serve men not planning on ordination.
10. Extension studies take longer and may foster a permanent
    study habit.

11. Through decentralized studies it is possible to teach indirectly the laymen in the entire Church.
12. Weekly meetings may be shared with other missions leaving denominational emphases for the monthly meetings.

Ted Ward gave a presentation on "Programmed Learning Techniques" in which he expressed the advantages and disadvantages of applying this educational tool to the preparation of extension seminary materials. During two workshop sessions Ward explained the types of programming and their use of different media and also described the preparation or qualities necessary for writers of programmed instructional materials (Winter 1969: 311-326).

Harold Alexander led two sessions on "The Use of Teachers in an Extension Program." The role of the teacher in the weekly meeting is mainly that of catalyst. However, when necessary he must summarize, serve as a resource person, stimulate the students and ensure that they understand the material. For these duties a teacher needs a general knowledge, mental agility and honesty. It is possible to work with three academic levels at the same time by adding questions which require a knowledge of concepts for the upper level students (Winter 1969: 326-339).

In a panel on existing programs of seminary extension training the four panelists explained briefly the operation of the institutions with which they had had experience in extension studies. Peter Wagner described the organization of the George Allan Seminary which coordinates ministerial training for the Evangelical Christian Union in Bolivia. Allen Thompson described the work of the West Indies Mission in the Dominican Republic and also on the islands of Guadeloupe and Martinique. Don Luttrell, director of Missionary Radio Station WIVV explained that station's activity in the training of pastors and laymen in Puerto Rico. Ralph Winter discussed some of the problems and results of the pioneer program in Guatemala. There was also a description by Wally Rehner of plans for an extension seminary program of the United Biblical Seminary in Colombia (Winter 1969:351-369).

After the Wheaton workshop extension programs continued to multiply in Latin America. It took a little time for the idea to be assimilated in the other areas, however. Men representing missions in Africa and Asia carried the ideas home with them, but it needed some time to germinate and bear fruit. In 1969 *Theological Education by Extension* was edited and published by Ralph Winter. This was the first complete survey of the extension movement from its beginning up to the time of printing. It included many of the important documents prepared by the organizers of this movement and tied the theory together with a description of the pioneer programs. It was quickly recognized as the standard (and only) text on theological education by ex-

tension. A few months later, in 1970, *Programmed Instruction
for Theological Education by Extension*, written by Ted and
Margaret, appeared. This book dealt with the essential process of preparing adequate materials for the extension students.
Although TEE does not depend on programmed instructional materials and in fact operated for several years without them,
it is generally acknowledged that the level of instruction de-
sired can only be reached through the application of programming principles to the preparation of study guides and texts.
These two books were instrumental in introducing the concepts
involved in extension to those who had not been able to attend
the workshops.

Workshops have been very important in the spread of the movement. In 1970 this alternative to traditional theological education was proposed in Africa and Asia through workshops organized in key cities on those two continents. Workshops were
valuable, not only for the information imparted on the concepts
of extension theological education and programming, but also
because of the committees which were set up in some cases. The
continuing committees have coordinated further workshops and
the production of materials, and have been the basis for the
associations of institutions working in extension which have
been formed. It is no longer necessary to invite some one from
the Caribbean or Latin America to direct the workshops yet to
be held since men and women from other areas of the world have
now become "experts," partly through their participation in
workshops and consultations.

Workshops varied in length and purpose. Some were of two or
three days length to acquaint those who attended with the principles and methods employed in theological education by extension. Longer workshops were particularly oriented toward the
training of professors for extension. Still others, the longest workshops, were for the introduction of programmed instruction and later for helping those who have already begun to work
in this area to perfect their skills. Generally it has been
the countries with the most and longest workshops which have advanced most in this movement, although it could as easily be
said that initial interest was responsible for scheduling longer workshops.

Men and women trained in the workshops and elsewhere have begun to produce extension materials in many languages and in
many lands. Benefiting from the experience of those who
learned by trial and error in Latin America, writers in Africa
and Asia may soon be able to boast of a greater quantity and
quality of programmed materials than is presently available in
Latin America. In the fall of 1972 CAMEO published a catalog
of extension materials and the quantity produced in Africa,
Asia and Australia in just two years' time is quite impressive.
Perhaps it is to be expected that large, well educated Churches
with many institutions should advance rapidly in programs associated with theological education.

Theological education by extension has come a long way from

its experimental status in Guatemala. Its diffusion throughout
Latin America and the Caribbean during the first five years was
only a beginning. Today it is a worldwide movement which has
gained recognition from missionaries and nationals, from educators and evangelists, from executives and local pastors and
laymen. Associations of theological schools find that they
must take a position with regard to the movement. Denominations are forming policies and in a few cases denominational
programs for extension. Periodicals at home and abroad can
not afford to ignore this movement which has offered so much
hope for resolving, at least in part, the urgent matter of
pastoral training.

Much work lies ahead. Programmed materials must be written,
tested and rewritten. Problems of distribution must be worked
out where one piece of programmed instruction can serve those
who share a common language and culture. Associations to coordinate efforts are in a developmental stage. Many missionaries and nationals must yet be convinced of the desirability
of the extension movement and its advantages for their Church.
Curricula must be elaborated and professors trained to teach
effectively, or rather to guide effectively, in the weekly sessions. Careful evaluation must be realized so that positive
recommendations for the improvement of TEE can be put into
effect. Problems are numerous, but the possibilities are
limitless as extension principles are adapted in hundreds of
situations to meet existing needs. Ten years after the first
tentative efforts it is apparent that theological education by
extension is here to stay as one of the most important new
movements within the Church in our age.

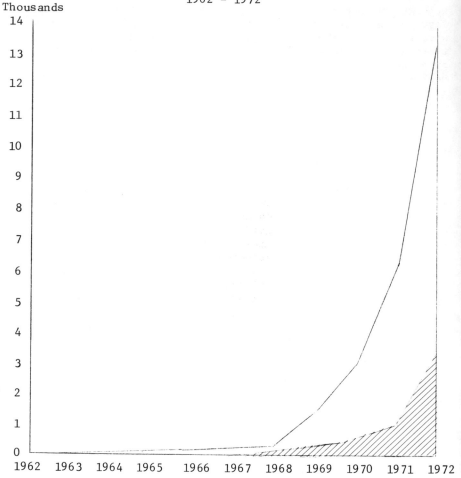

TOTAL OF EXTENSION STUDENTS
1962 - 1972

NOTE: Crosshatch area indicates the students outside Latin
America.

Figure 4

Sources: CLATT
Estimates based on partial reports from other areas.

An Evaluation of 3
Theological Education
by Extension

Theological education by extension is still quite an innovation in the eyes of most of its adherents. The great majority of institutions have had less than two years experience
with this type of training and the number of institutions com-
mencing in 1973 is quite large. Any evaluation of the movement,
therefore, will have to be very tentative. It may even be
considered a little speculative. Nevertheless, it should be
done in order to give a basis for judging the system and also
to see the dangers and weaknesses as well as the potentiali-
ties while there is yet time to avoid certain errors. The
first section of this chapter is a brief summary of the existing programs with some comparisons across the various regions represented. The second part is a case study of the
United Biblical Seminary. Because of the author's personal
knowledge of the institution it is possible to portray it in
considerable detail. And then we must close with some final
observations that hopefully will be of benefit to others engaged in extension now or those who anticipate its adoption.

THEMATIC COMPARISONS OF EXTENSION PROGRAMS

Finances

Almost every institution which operates an extension program
receives financial support through a mission based in the United States or other western countries. In a relatively few
cases there is support from the national Churches. This subsidy allows the students to pay a small proportion of their
educational costs. At this point the main item of subsidy
would be in the form of missionary personnel whose salaries
are paid overseas. The actual operating budget of many extension institutions is quite low. In a few institutions,
mainly those which serve only one denomination, the student
pays only the cost of the text which he uses. In the majority

of the institutions the student is required to pay a registration fee and tuition. This varies from approximately $0.30 to
$20.00 per semester according to the economy of the students.
The average fee seems to be about $5.00 per semester and there
is no great difference between regions in this regard.

Structure

In the Caribbean and in Latin America most of the institutions serve a single denomination or at least are operated by
only one mission board or national Church. In Asia and Africa,
on the contrary, two thirds of the institutions with extension
programs are united efforts. This difference may be due to
the commencement of extension programs in urban areas of Africa
and Asia. Some rural areas of Latin America and the Caribbean are still divided denominationally according to comity
agreements.

After the Armenia workshop and the earlier promotional workshops throughout Latin America many institutions launched
their programs. Many of them followed the pattern of Guatemala or other institutions described earlier, but no organizational structure linked them together. AETTE preceded by several years the formation of ALISTE. The Spanish speaking institutions were concerned with cooperation in the matter of
the production of textbooks and other materials, but saw no
urgent need for an association of extension seminaries.

In Africa and Asia committees were often formed at the conclusion of workshops. These committees ensured cooperation
even before programs were initiated. The institutions which
cooperated in the newly formed associations or committees all
developed at the same time. In Latin America it was possible
to use the provisional materials developed in Guatemala. In
many lands nothing could be done until materials were written
or translated. It seems strange to those who have worked in
Latin America to read of committees which have functioned for
as many as two or three years in some countries and still no
students have been enrolled for extension studies. In Asia,
in particular, there has seemed to be a reluctance to plunge
into an extension program until structures and materials have
been well developed. Even though extension is so much newer
to Asia and Africa than to Latin America there is at least as
great a proportion of teachers in Asian and African extension
programs who have prepared extension materials as in the older
programs.

Openness to Innovation

The desire to implement theological education by extension
has varied greatly from one area or country to another. The
tremendous lack of trained pastors forced the Church in desperation to try a means of training actual leaders even if it
should turn out to be a second rate program. In Korea and

Vietnam, on the contrary, no lack of trained pastors has been
felt. As was noted in reference to workshops in Japan, resistance on the part of older pastors toward any threatening
new leadership program may well be the reason why there is no
genuine extension program there. The concept of the pastor,
his role within the congregation and the degree to which tradition must be followed in his preparation are all elements
which will not be easily changed. Demonstrations of the success of extension programs in other Asian countries and in the
United States will help to break down prejudice. Meanwhile we
must recognize the opinions that exist. In Madagascar the
differences between lay theological training and pastoral preparation were stressed fifteen years ago (Ransom 1957:39).
Meanwhile it was stated in Tanzania that the ministry is the
responsibility of the whole Christian community and a tent-
making ministry was encouraged (Nyblade 1970:77). An official
of the association of theological schools in Indonesia stressed
that theological education must serve the whole Church in a
direct manner (Cooley 1970:26). In the Lutheran area of New
Guinea care was taken lest the clergy dominate the Church (TEF
1961:48). But in the Middle East there was no interest in
developing any kind of part-time or voluntary ministry (Webster and Nasir 1962:61). These attitudes account for the
acceptance or rejection of theological education by extension
and the implications for ministry in the church which general-
ized theological training brings.

One indication of a desire to preserve the distinction between clergy and laity has been the insistence that the first
area in which extension must operate is in the continuing
training of pastors. This is indeed an important function of
TEE. However, extension must not be allowed to serve as a
means for widening the gap between clergy and ministry when it
should be used for preparing new leadership as well as aiding
those already with some training.

Many institutions indicated that extension was considered
primarily to be lay training but that the possibility of ordination existed. Others stated that ordination did not depend
upon formal training and a few Churches do not have formal
ordination of functional pastors. Regional distinctions were
not significant. Of the institutions in Latin America and Africa which responded to the question as to whether extension
education would qualify a man for ordination only 12 per cent
replied that it would not do so at least under certain conditions. For Asia the slightly higher figure of 15 per cent was
registered. However, when asked about the expectations of extension students in regard to a full time ministry, a greater
difference was noted. Fewer than 13 per cent of extension students in Latin America expect to enter into a full time ministry. In Asia the percentage rises to 18 per cent and it
doubles to 36 per cent for African extension students. This
does not indicate necessarily that a greater proportion of men
studying there will fulfill pastoral roles. It merely reflects

REGIONAL DISTRIBUTION OF EXTENSION STUDENTS 1972

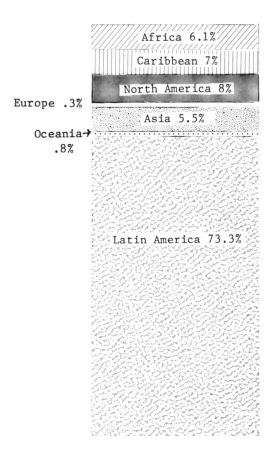

Figure 5

Sources: Estimates based on partial reports.

the fact that in Africa the pattern has been established for a full time paid ministry while a tent-making ministry is more common elsewhere.

Teachers

The student-teacher ratio was not significantly varied among the Latin American, Asian and African programs. In each case it was approximately eleven to one. Probably the average class is considerably smaller than that, however, since many teachers listed by an institution will teach more than one class during the week. Notable differences appear in the following table showing the percentages of national and full time teachers in the extension institutions.

	National Teachers	Full Time Teachers
Latin America	66%	15%
Caribbean	50%	20%
Africa	44%	47%
Asia	66%	25%

The differences in the case of Africa perhaps find their explanation in the assigning of missionary personnel to full time organization of TEE and preparation of materials in this introductory stage of development.

Academic Levels

The greatest difference noted on comparing the extension programs of the four major regions is that the academic levels of Asia are much higher. The other three regions have pretty much the same proportions of students in each of the four categories. Three factors may be possible solutions for the disparity in the case of Asia. One is that the general academic level of the leadership in the Churches there is higher. A second factor is that several institutions have decided to begin their extension studies first as continuing education of pastors. Perhaps the most influential factor, however, is that it has been necessary to begin extension programs with the use of materials in English. This has limited the student body to those whose command of English as a second language is sufficient to make their studies profitable. Such a requirement restricts studies to the higher academic levels. When extension materials are translated or written in the vernacular languages of each country a considerable lowering of average level of students will occur. A shift to rural centers and to regional or tribal languages will produce a great increase in the numbers of certificate and diploma level students. But it will

DISTRIBUTION OF STUDENTS BY ACADEMIC LEVELS

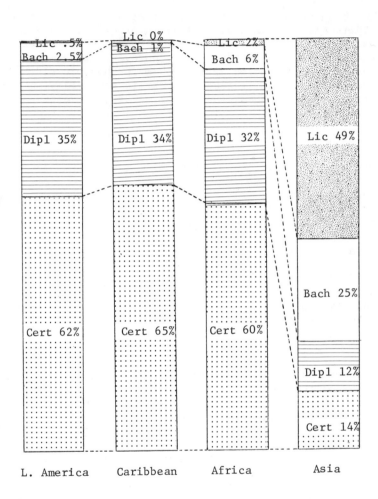

L. America   Caribbean   Africa   Asia

Figure 6

Sources: Reports from institutions.

not change the fact that a greater number of college level students have been attracted to TEE in Asia than in other regions.

AN EVALUATIVE CASE STUDY
THE UNITED BIBLICAL SEMINARY OF COLOMBIA

One of the schools which received a good deal of attention
after 1968 was the United Biblical Seminary of Colombia. While
the extension programs organized earlier had been limited to
one denomination and a relatively small geographical area, the
United Biblical Seminary which was to have four extension divisions covered the major part of the nation of Colombia and
elicited the cooperation of more than a dozen evangelical missions and Churches. Would it be possible to cooperate on extension programs not only in the looser organizations of CATA
and CLATT but even in a single seminary which could offer a
large number of interdenominational centers?

After closing down the residence program in Guatemala to
experiment with extension education, pressure from the National Church forced the reopening of the more traditional program
for a short time. In Colombia, however, there was never any
general intention to close down the residence studies in Mc-
dellín. The issue, rather, was what relative importance to
give to the two programs. Should the residence program be
considered the center from which academic standing could be
transferred to the extension studies, or should increasing emphasis be given to the extension divisions where 95 per cent
of the students were?

What were the practical benefits of extension? Did it
really help the churches to grow and increase the level of
spiritual life and biblical knowledge in the congregations?
Were the real leaders being trained or did extension studies
also mainly attract the younger unproven members of the churches? It is still too soon to evaluate theological education by
extension, but some tentative observations can be made from
this institution in which the writer worked for four years.

The Organization of the Seminary

The United Biblical Seminary of Colombia was founded in 1944
by the Interamerican Missionary Society (Oriental Missionary
Society). For some time the Wesleyan Methodist Mission also
cooperated officially in the school. Student enrollment was
never large. During the first twenty years only thirteen men
and one woman graduated from its degree program, although a
much larger number of men and women received lower level preparation there. Of the graduates five are now serving churches
in Colombia.

From its beginning the Interamerican Biblical Seminary accepted students from other denominations. In February of 1967,
after many years of non-official cooperation with other groups,

the United Biblical Seminary of Colombia was officially founded
by representatives of the following groups:

Christian and Missionary Alliance
General Conference Mennonite Church
Interamerican Missionary Society
Latin America Mission
Mennonite Brethren Mission
Overseas Crusades

Later that year the Evangelical Covenant Mission in Ecuador
offered to cooperate by transferring one of its missionary cou-
ples from Ecuador to work in the seminary.

The seminary is located in Medellín, the industrial capital
of Colombia. It is a modern city of over one million population with a very moderate climate. Medellín has traditionally
been a very conservative Roman Catholic city and the missions
which served there had experienced slow growth prior to 1967.
There has been a small evangelical community locally from which
the seminary could draw potential students.

In southern Colombia, and particularly in the city of Cali,
the Church had grown much more rapidly. In early 1967, three
of the missions working there, the Christian and Missionary
Alliance, the Gospel Missionary Union and the Mennonite Brethren Church discussed the possibility of uniting in a seminary
to serve their section of the country. The Gospel Missionary
Union had closed its Bible institute after many years of operation. The Christian and Missionary Alliance had decided to
move its Bible institute from Armenia to Cali and upgrade it
to seminary level or teach on both levels. The Mennonite
Brethren felt they were unable to train the mature leaders,
especially married, employed men, in the Emmanuel Bible Institute which they sponsored in the city of Cali.

TEE Introduced. An important event occurred during this
period of transition and indecision. ALET, the Latin American
Association of Theological Schools for the northern region,
sponsored a meeting in Armenia, Colombia from September 4 to
9. This meeting has been described elsewhere. Many of the delegates were from institutions in Colombia. Since Wallace
Rehner, the regional secretary for ALET and also the Executive
Secretary for UNICO, Union of Theological Institutions of Grand
Colombia, was also the academic dean at the United Biblical
Seminary, the effect of this meeting on the seminary is to be
imagined. Plans were soon underway for investigating and ex-
perimenting with this new form of theological training. Copies
of the manual for the study of Mark were run off in Medellín
as well as a workbook to accompany the study of the Capacitation Manual for leaders in the Evangelism in Depth movement
soon to be launched. These were to be the first extension materials used in the Medellín based seminary.

Meanwhile, in Cali the Mennonite Brethren closed down the
residence program of the Emmanuel Bible Institute at the end of

the 1967 school year and switched entirely to extension. Vernon Reimer, director of the Institute, had studied this approach to leadership training at the Fuller School of World Mission earlier in 1967. That year became an experiment in a dual program with the result, based on a self-study, that residence studies were eliminated. This self-evaluation revealed that the extension program had been more effective in training the real leaders of the local congregations. It appeared also that the cost per student in extension was approximately one-third that of the residence program.

Divisions Formed. At the time the Mennonite Brethren began their extension program, the other denominational groups working in Cali were not ready to join them in this experiment. However, shortly before the board meeting of the United Biblical Seminary in November, 1968, Wallace Rehner met with the Mennonite Brethren leaders in Cali to discuss the possibility of merging with the United Biblical Seminary to form the Cali Division. Later, interest in such a program was stimulated in a meeting attended by leaders of the Christian and Missionary Alliance, the Gospel Missionary Union, the Mennonite Brethren and the Cumberland Presbyterians.

The Board of Directors of the United Biblical Seminary, representing the cooperating church groups, voted at its Annual Meeting in November, 1968 to form three new divisions for extension studies - Medellín, Bogotá and Cali - in addition to the residence program in Medellín. The four divisions would operate under one Board of Directors. The former rector of the residence school continued as rector of the overall program and the Board named four vice-rectors, one for each of the divisions. The vice-rector in Cali was Vernon Reimer of the Mennonite Brethren Mission. The Bogotá Division was headed by G. Burton Biddulph of the Interamerican Missionary Society (OMS) who also served as rector of the overall program. The Medellín extension division was headed by Wayne Weld of the Evangelical Covenant Mission, who also taught in the residence program. The distribution of students is shown in the figure below. Plans were already underway for adding additional centers and enlisting the cooperation of other denominations.

UNITED BIBLICAL SEMINARY 1969

DIVISIONS	EXTENSION CENTERS	PROFESSORS FULL-TIME	PART-TIME	STUDENTS DIPLOMA	BACHILLER
Medellin (Res.)		3	2		14
Medellin (Ext.)	1	0	2	5	1
Bogota	3	0	7	23	7
Cali	21	5	10	102	4
TOTALS	25	8	22	130	26

Source:Winter 1969:212   FIGURE 7

The Board of Directors of the United Biblical Seminary was composed almost entirely of missionaries, few of whom had any orientation to extension studies. Therefore, little attention was given to the problems and possibilities of this new program in comparison with concern for the continuance and improvement of the residence program. Several of the board members had no contact with extension other than its mention at Annual Meetings. The overall board was dominated by the residence program and those interested primarily in it.

However, in November, 1968 a two-day seminar on theological education by extension was held at a conference center near Cali. The discussions were attended by some sixty pastors, lay leaders and missionaries of the Christian and Missionary Alliance, Cumberland Presbyterian, Gospel Missionary Union, Mennonite Brethren and SEPAL (Overseas Crusades). At this meeting the executive committee for the Cali Division was named and plans were made for its operation. It is to be noted that some groups participated in the Cali Division which did not participate in the overall program centered around the residence seminary in Medellín.

This wider cooperation in extension was also experienced in Bogota. In the capital city interest in the program was demonstrated by General Conference Mennonites, the Lutheran Church in America, the United Presbyterian Church and the Worldwide Evangelization Crusade in addition to the Interamericans and Latin America Mission already represented in the United Biblical Seminary Board. However, no general seminar on theological education has been held there as in Cali. In Medellín the extension division never received wide support and has limped along as a weak adjunct to the residence program.

Residence. Let us turn now to the residence program briefly because one of the interesting features of the United Biblical Seminary has been the relationships between residence and extension divisions within a single institution. At the same meeting in 1968 in which the extension divisions were created, the Board also decided to raise the entrance requirements, to reduce the residence program from four years to three, and to change from a quarter system to a semester system in order to facilitate coordination of curriculum between residence and extension. Previously residence students were admitted into two programs which roughly paralleled the *bachiller* and diploma levels. By requiring of all students full high school or the basic four years in the case of those twenty-five years of age or older, it was felt that the preparatory courses could be eliminated and almost every theological course squeezed into three years. The economic advantages in terms of scholarships, etc., were also obvious in the shorter period.

Every effort was made to make the two programs complementary. At the residence division in Medellín studies were offered leading to a B.Th. degree and it was hoped that a higher level program might be offered at a later period. Those who were excluded from residence studies by the higher entrance require-

ments could still study at the diploma level through extension.
All three extension divisions offered classes at the *bachiller*
and diploma levels. Some missions considered extension as a
good selection system for determining those who were really
interested and able to benefit from theological studies. A
chance to finish one's studies by residence in Medellín would
be a strong incentive to begin by extension. The requirement
that men complete at least one year by extension before entering the residence program not only would demonstrate student
motivation but would reduce the cost of education by one year.
It should be pointed out here that almost all the residence
students in Medellín are there on a full scholarship for the
three years needed to complete their studies. To facilitate
transference of credits from one program to another, the curriculum adopted for *bachiller* studies in the extension divisions was the same as that used in residence.

Multiplication and Division of the Extension Program

Let us turn now to the extension divisions and examine them
one by one. The first and largest was that of Cali. The Mennonite Brethren purchased a centrally located property which
provided space for a multi-purpose conference room, library,
three offices and several classrooms. This building took the
place of the building housing the former Emmanuel Bible Institute and served as the administrative center for the twenty-
one extension centers operated within the division. These
centers held classes in the division headquarters, in local
churches and in other facilities throughout the area. One full
time national instructor spent four days each week traveling by
boat, bus and foot to visit centers in isolated areas of the
coast. However, most of the centers were served by local missionaries and pastors.
    Figure 8 shows the overall organization of the United Bib-
lical Seminary with details for the Cali Division. The three
major cooperating denominations shared the centers in Cali and
two of the missions cooperated in another center. However,
in most of the centers the students are of a single denomination and the denomination responsible for evangelistic work in
that area is responsible for the operation of the center. The
Gospel Missionary Union and the Christian and Missionary Alliance each paid one-third of the rent (to the Mennonite Brethren
who owned the building) of the Division office while other expenses were shared according to the number of students enrolled from each mission in the Division.
    The success of the Cali Division was in a sense its un-
doing. It became evident that the United Biblical Seminary
was meeting the needs of the churches in a way which previous
residence programs had never done. But since most of the centers were conducted by one denomination for its own students
some national leaders and missionaries no longer saw the need
to be related to the United Biblical Seminary. They could

ORGANIZATION OF THE UNITED BIBLICAL SEMINARY 1969

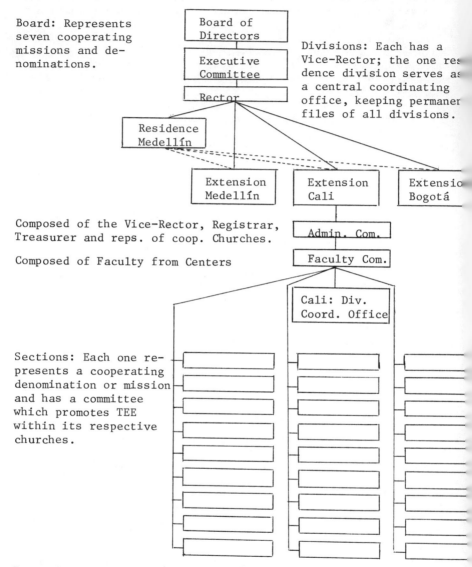

Board: Represents
seven cooperating
missions and de-
nominations.

Board of
Directors

Executive
Committee

Rector

Divisions: Each has a
Vice-Rector; the one res
dence division serves as
a central coordinating
office, keeping permaner
files of all divisions.

Residence
Medellín

Extension
Medellín

Extension
Cali

Extensio
Bogotá

Composed of the Vice-Rector, Registrar,
Treasurer and reps. of coop. Churches.

Admin. Com.

Composed of Faculty from Centers

Faculty Com.

Cali: Div.
Coord. Office

Sections: Each one re-
presents a cooperating
denomination or mission
and has a committee
which promotes TEE
within its respective
churches.

Extension Centers: Each has its director who
    1) organizes and directs the center
    2) teaches some or all of the subjects
    3) coordinates the program with the Cali office
    4) submits a monthly progress report to the Vice-Rector
    5) handles student accounts and channels monies to the Cali offi

Figure 8

Source: Winter 1969:214

offer the courses on their own and thus avoid administrative
costs. The Gospel Missionary Union withdrew some of its centers from the United Biblical Seminary. The Christian and
Missionary Alliance withdrew its centers and affiliated them
with the Bible Institute in Armenia. At present the Alliance
students on the diploma level receive credit from the Institute
in Armenia and those on the *bachiller* level receive credit from
the Alliance Bible Seminary in Guayaquil, Ecuador. Therefore
the data of Figure 9 does not represent a drop in total students so much as a change in affiliation. Although the Cali
Division of the United Biblical Seminary had only twenty-seven
students the second semester of 1971, the Christian and Missionary Alliance had 197, many of whom had previously studied in the United Biblical Seminary program.

Although other National Churches and missions cooperated in
the Bogotá Division, the major responsibility for its operation was in the hands of the Interamerican Missionary Society
and the General Conference Mennonites. Most of the centers
were within the city of Bogotá and therefore a higher proportion of *bachiller* students were enrolled than in the Cali
Division, whose students largely came from smaller towns with
fewer facilities for secondary studies. Some classes were
held in an office in the center of the city and others met in
church buildings at the extremes of the city.

In Medellín classes were held in a centrally located church.
Student enrollment was never large and after one year of offering classes at both levels the *bachiller* level studies were
not made available again. With the exception of three members
of the staff of the Interamerican Bible Institute in Cristalina,
the Medellín Division had no students outside the one center in
the city. Later the Interamerican Missionary Society did open
two centers in coastal towns which were visited by a professor
flown in from Medellín every two weeks. However, these centers were not a part of the United Biblical Seminary program
although they used materials prepared in the Cali and Medellín
Divisions.

One reason for the lack of other centers is that the first
vice-rector represented a recently arrived mission which had no
potential students to serve. Promotion was done in the city,
but no one was interested in paying his transportation in establishing centers in churches of other denominations. When
later an Interamerican Missionary Society vice-rector was
named other duties did not permit him to do the necessary
traveling and interest in the churches was generally slight.
When men are accustomed to receiving full scholarships to study by residence for three or more years it is difficult to con-
vince them to study by extension at their own expense and at
considerably greater effort than those who received scholarships. The Association of Interamerican Churches has never
been very interested in extension programs.

During the first semester of 1972 a Covenant missionary and
a Mennonite Brethren missionary offered classes in their local

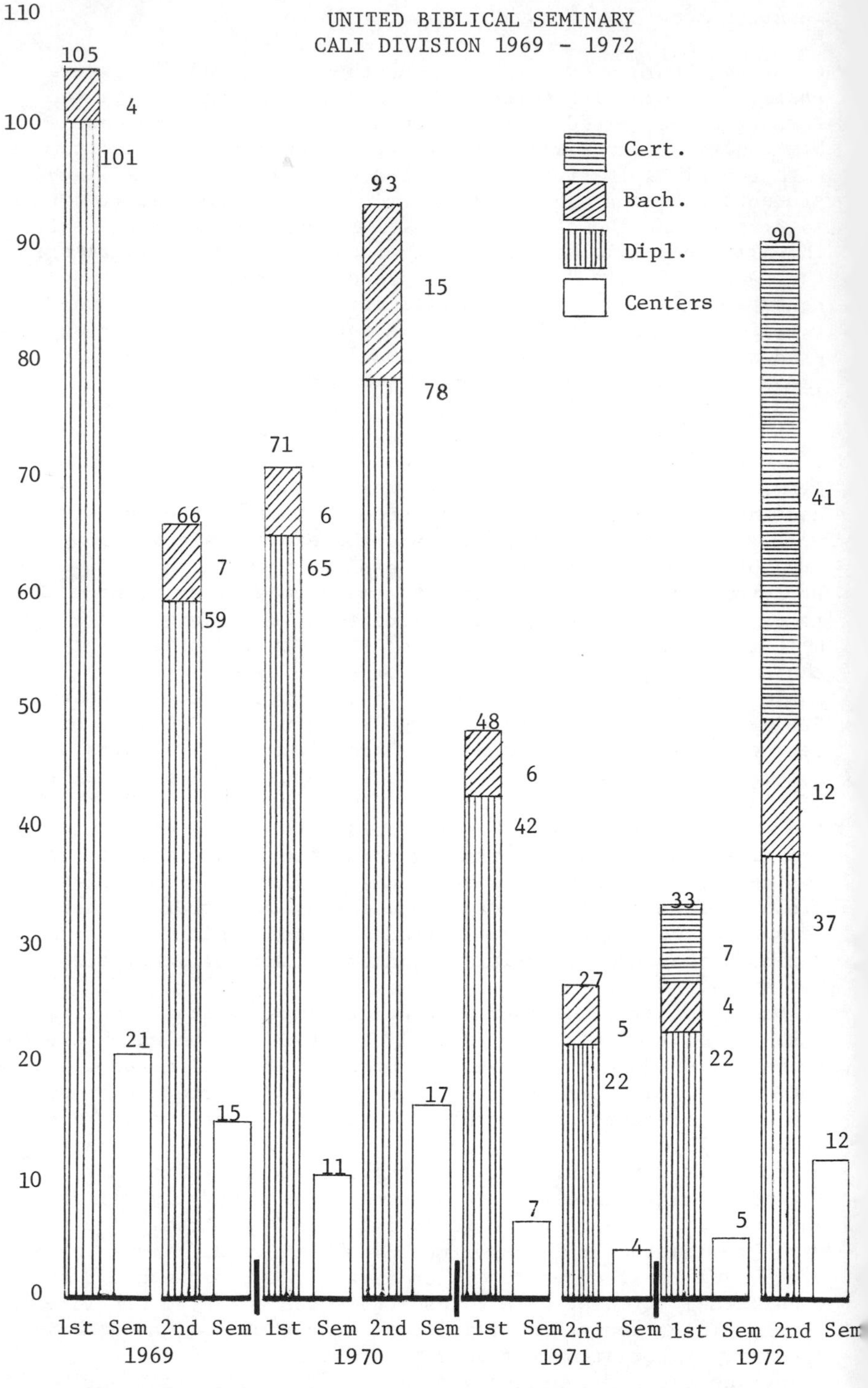

UNITED BIBLICAL SEMINARY
CALI DIVISION 1969 - 1972

Cert.
Bach.
Dipl.
Centers

1st Sem 2nd Sem   1st Sem 2nd Sem   1st Sem 2nd Sem   1st Sem 2nd Sem
   1969   1970   1971   1972

Figure 9

congregations. In these two small congregations, which still
meet in homes, they were able to enroll more students than previously they had been able to collect from all the churches in
Medellín for a centrally located center. The Cali Division also had decentralized its program to a large extent and had
moved out of the Division office to church buildings within the
city.

The Caribbean Division of the United Biblical Seminary was
added for the 1971 school year. Although nominally tied to the
United Biblical Seminary it is more closely related to the Caribbean Bible Center operated by the Latin America Mission in
Sincelejo. The centers of this division are predominantly
rural and all the classes until 1972 were held on the certificate level. For that reason it has been considered really
a denominational program which receives support and orientation
from the United Biblical Seminary, but the Seminary does not
give credit at that level.

While there are various advantages in having the extension
program tied to a residence program - visibility, accreditation,
maintenance of levels of study, a body of theological educators
to prepare materials and aid in teaching and administration -
there can also result a tug of war between the two programs.
On one hand the attendance at the residence program in Medellín diminished. This was not entirely due to competition
with extension. Part of the blame must fall on the raising of
entrance requirements. However, some missions and churches
did question the advisability of sending their students to
Medellin for three years, during which time they could contribute nothing to the work of the denomination which acquired a
large financial burden for their education.

At the same time the residence program complained of a drop
in enrollment, the extension divisions complained of the lack
of attention and coordination for the work of extension. The
Board of Directors, which theoretically was to oversee all the
divisions, devoted its time almost entirely to the problems of
residence and in particular to the means of financing the program and securing professors for it. Problems of extension
were discussed only in a very general way. Those groups involved only in extension began to ask what need they had of the
United Biblical Seminary if that institution was to be identified primarily with the residence program from which they de-
rived no benefit.

The conflict of administrative interests was resolved at the
Annual Meeting in November of 1971. In comparing Figure 8 with
Figure 10 we see that the extensions divisions have been given
equal representation on the executive committee with the residence program and that the operation of residence now does
not depend directly on the Board of Directors, but on an administrative committee in the same way that the extension divisions had previously had their financial and administrative
autonomy from the central Board. Figure 11 gives an elab-
oration of the new organization of the Cali division.

ORGANIZATION OF THE UNITED BIBLICAL SEMINARY 1972

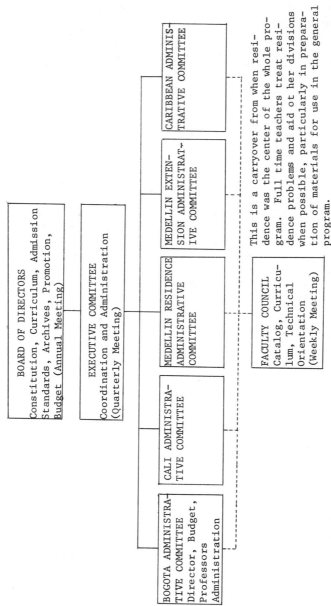

BOARD OF DIRECTORS
Constitution, Curriculum, Admission Standards, Archives, Promotion, Budget (Annual Meeting)

EXECUTIVE COMMITTEE
Coordination and Administration (Quarterly Meeting)

BOGOTA ADMINISTRATIVE COMMITTEE
Director, Budget, Professors Administration

CALI ADMINISTRATIVE COMMITTEE

MEDELLIN RESIDENCE ADMINISTRATIVE COMMITTEE

MEDELLIN EXTENSION ADMINISTRATIVE COMMITTEE

CARIBBEAN ADMINISTRATIVE COMMITTEE

FACULTY COUNCIL
Catalog, Curriculum, Technical Orientation (Weekly Meeting)

This is a carryover from when residence was the center of the whole program. Full time teachers treat residence problems and aid ot her divisions when possible, particularly in preparation of materials for use in the general program.

THE BOARD OF DIRECTORS is made up of representatives of entities that cooperate in any of the divisions. Missions or National Churches give an annual quota of at least $50.00 to the Board for the privilege of representation.
THE EXECUTIVE COMMITTEE is composed of the President of the Board, the Director and the Rector of each division. Within this group they elect a Vice-President and a Treasurer.
THE ADMINISTRATIVE COMMITTEE is formed according to the policy of each division regarding quotas and other ways of cooperation. Major contributors have greater representation, particularly in the case of the residence program.

Figure 10

UNITED BIBLICAL SEMINARY
CALI DIVISION 1972

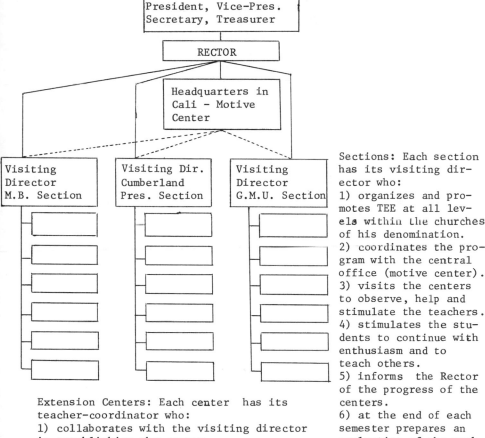

Sections: Each section has its visiting director who:
1) organizes and promotes TEE at all levels within the churches of his denomination.
2) coordinates the program with the central office (motive center).
3) visits the centers to observe, help and stimulate the teachers.
4) stimulates the students to continue with enthusiasm and to teach others.
5) informs the Rector of the progress of the centers.
6) at the end of each semester prepares an evaluation of the work of each teacher and of each center in general.

Extension Centers: Each center has its teacher-coordinator who:
1) collaborates with the visiting director in establishing the center.
2) organizes and directs the center.
3) teaches some or all the courses.
4) stimulates the students to continue with enthusiasm and to teach others.
5) controls the student accounts and sends funds to the central office.
6) submits a monthly progress report and sends reports to the central office.
7) at the end of each semester prepares an evaluation of each course and hands in the grade sheets.

Figure 11

Analysis of the Student Body

In order to evaluate the effectiveness of the extension program an attempt has been made to analyze the student body as
to age, Christian experience, occupation, role in the church
and previous education. This information was acquired mainly
from the application forms which the students filled out as
they registered for classes each semester. After a brief summary of the data for the seminary as a whole, a more detailed
breakdown for the Bogotá, Cali and Medellín Divisions is included. No data from the Caribbean Division which operates at
a lower academic level is presented. The analysis is based on
the information reported by a total of 224 students who studied one or more semesters on the diploma or *bachiller* levels.

Male: 162
Female: 62
Married of either sex: 105
Ages: 13 to 71   Mean age: 32
Education: 1 year of primary to 4 years of university
   Mean education for *bachiller:*   5 years of secondary
   Mean education for diploma: 5 years of primary
Number of students active in local churches: 195
Pastoral duties:
   21 served as pastors, 15 earned their living in that way
   24 served as lay preachers
Teaching ministry
   20 Sunday School superintendents
   78 Sunday School teachers

The Cali Division has been the largest at the higher academic levels. Its centers are located in the city of Cali,
which is approaching a population of 1,000,000, in smaller cities and in rural areas. The data below is separated between
the *bachiller* and diploma levels.

Bachiller students: 20
   Male: 15
   Female: 5
   Married of either sex: 10
   Ages: 17 to 55   Median: 26   Mean: 31
   Time as Christians: 1 to 41 years
      Median: 3 years   Mean: 6 years
   Education: 3 years of primary to 3 years of university
      Median: 4 years of secondary
   Church offices held: (some held more than one office)
      Pastor: 3   Treasurer: 2
      Lay preacher: 1   Deacon: 1
      S.S. teacher: 11   Secretary: 1
      Youth leader: 5

Secular employment:

Student: 6	Sales: 1
Pastor: 3	Public relations: 1
Teacher: 3	Policeman: 1
Factory worker: 2	Technician: 1
Colporteur: 1	Office employee: 1

Diploma students: 115
  Male: 77
  Female: 38
  Married of either sex: 47
  Ages: 16 to 71   Median: 31   Mean: 32
  Time as Christians: 6 months to 42 years
    Median: 7 years   Mean: 9.5 years
  Education: 1 year primary to university
    Median: 5 years primary   Mean: 1/2 year secondary
  Church offices held:

Pastor: 11	Visitation: 2
Lay preacher: 16	Deacon: 6
S.S. superintendent: 15	Elder: 3
S.S. teacher: 56	Treasurer: 4
Youth leader: 8	Ladies work: 2

  Secular employment:

Farmer: 13	Factory worker: 3
Housewife: 11	Carpenter: 3
Construction: 10	Accountant: 2
Teacher: 10	Cobbler: 2
Student: 10	Police: 2
Office employee: 10	Administration: 2
Mechanic: 8	Soldier: 1
Pastor: 6	Nurse: 1
Sales: 7	Tailor: 1
Secretary: 5	Dressmaker: 1

The Bogotá Division represents a much higher percentage of urban students. The city itself has a population of over 2,000,000. Centers were held at three locations in the city and in nearby towns. This accounts, at least in part, for the higher percentage of *bachiller* students.

Bachiller students: 16
  Male: 11
  Female: 5
  Married of either sex: 5
  Ages: 18 to 50   Median: 28   Mean: 32
  Time as Christians: 3 months to 14 years
    Median: 4 years   Mean: 4.5 years
  Education: 2 years of secondary to 4 years of university
    Mean: 5 years of secondary
  Church offices held:

Pastor: 3	S.S. teacher: 1
Lay preacher: 11	Youth leader: 1
S.S. superintendent: 1	

Secular employment
    Pastor: 2   Publications: 1
    Administrator: 2   Tailor: 1
    Teacher: 2   Student: 1
    Sales: 2

Diploma students: 34
  Male: 24
  Female: 10
  Married of either sex: 18
  Ages: 17 to 51   Median: 33   Mean: 33
  Time as Christians: 3 months to 40 years
    Median: 5 years   Mean: 7.5 years
  Education: 2 years of primary to 1 1/2 years university
    Median: 1 year of secondary   Mean: 5 years primary
  Church offices held:
    Pastor: 3   Deacon: 2
    Lay preacher: 4   Deaconness: 2
    S.S. superintendent: 1   Elder: 2
    S.S. teacher: 6   Counsellor: 1
    Youth leader: 5   Usher: 1
    Treasurer: 4   Ladies work: 1
  Secular employment:
    Office employee: 6   Nurse's aid: 1
    Construction: 4   Painter: 1
    Sales: 4   Barber: 1
    Pastor: 3   Administration: 1
    Dressmaker: 3   Electrician: 1
    Conductor: 2   Musician: 1
    Housewife: 2   Baker: 1
    Teacher: 1   Mechanic: 1

The Medellín Division has always been a weak sister compared to the other extension divisions. Although as many as a total of eight persons registered for classes on the *bachiller* level over the three semesters that courses were offered at that level, only one man completed a course. He is included with the diploma students for the following information. Unfortunately since a different application form was used there is no data available for secular employment or previous education.

Diploma students: 44
  Male: 34
  Female: 10
  Married of either sex: 25
  Ages: 13 to 55   Median: 32   Mean: 29
  Time as Christians: 2 months to 45 years
    Median time: 7 years   Mean: 3 Years
  Church offices held:
    Treasurer: 4   Elder: 1
    S.S. teacher: 4   Deacon: 1
    S.S. superintendent: 3   Deaconness: 1

Lay worker: 2   Counsellor: 1
Pastor: 1   Youth leader: 1

A comparison of the students in the three divisions in
various categories gives us some indication of the involvement
in extension studies of the leaders of the churches.

	Bogotá	Cali	Medellín
Mean age	33	31	29
Men	70%	67%	75%
Married	46%	42%	57%
Church offices held	78%	110%	43%
Pastor or preacher	22%	23%	7%
S.S. worker	18%	61%	14%

A questionnaire was distributed to students, mainly of the
Cali and Bogotá divisions. Of the fourteen questionnaires returned it can be noted that they represented a fairly average
section of the diploma students with the exception that they
had greater responsibilities in the church than the average
student. Six were full or part time pastors and seven were
Sunday school teachers. Because most of the students had taken only a few subjects by extension the results obtained are
inconclusive and such a study needs to be repeated at a later
date. However, some tentative observations may be made.
The courses considered most valuable by the students were
Church Growth, "I Will Build My Church," Christian Education,
Methods of Bible Study and History of Christianity. The
courses requested for future study were:

Human Relations	6	Theology	1
Homiletics	6	Church Growth	1
Music	4	Hermeneutics	1
Prophecy	2	Christian Educ.	1
Accounting	2	Grammar	1
History	1	Administration	1

Of the courses, Human Relations, Accounting, Grammar and Music
are not included in the current curriculum.
With relation to evangelism three students reported that
their studies limited the time which was available to evange-
lize. However, ten reported that studies had helped them in
this area, that they were more active and effective than before
and that extension studies had taken time away from other activities, but not from evangelism.

Five students reported that extension studies were more
valuable than residence studies because they had opportunity
to put into practice immediately the knowledge and skills acquired. Another advantage noted by five students was that because of the low cost and availability of extension studies
everyone could participate. Three students added that they
appreciated the facility of studying even while working full
time.

Disadvantages noted were the length of time required to
complete the full curriculum to receive a degree, the difficulty in obtaining all the books necessary for the studies and
the lack of contact with the teacher.

Specific criticisms of the administration of the extension
program included the need to enlist more students with experience in Christian service for their value in orienting the
younger students. Another student requested more adequate provision for those who had to miss a class for some unavoidable
reason. Two students noted that some teachers were not well
enough prepared to relate the studies to the responsibility of
the students. Merely going over the questions in class does
not help in the practical usage that students must make of the
materials studied.

Comments by Missionaries and National Leaders

Interviews were conducted with five missionaries and four
national leaders from several denominations representing three
denominational extension programs as well as the United Biblical Seminary. All of these men had experience in teaching
and/or administration of extension studies. On the basis of
their conclusions and the data presented previously, certain
recommendations can be made for greater effectiveness in extension programs.

The men questioned agree that one of the greatest needs of
the Colombian Church today is the training of full and part
time leaders. In a rapidly growing Church which forms many new
congregations each year and adds more preaching points, an increasing amount of responsibility must be placed on lay leaders.
The inadequate training of leaders in the past, even of those
who were able to attend residence studies, is shown in the
superficial level of Bible knowledge in the congregations and
the inability to relate Christian truth and standards to contem-
porary situations. Extension can help remedy this situation
not only through the training of lay leaders for more active
and effective participation in the work of the church, but
also through continuing education for those now serving churches.

The majority of those actually studying by extension are
leaders in some capacity in the churches. In the *bachiller*
level in Bogotá perhaps 90 per cent have some office in a local
church. In the certificate level in northern Colombia 80 to
90 per cent of the students are church leaders. In other areas

the percentage has not been as high. Only in the Caribbean Division operated by the Latin America Mission do most of the church officials study. Many leaders in other areas do not feel a need or see the value of participation in the extension program.

In only one case has a student who began in extension transferred to the residence program. However, other residence students may have become aware of the United Biblical Seminary through extension. In the case of the Caribbean Division, the students are brought in to the Bible Center of the Caribbean (a certificate level residence school) at least once a semester and on one occasion attended the regular classes for a day. This stimulated four or five to leave their congregations in the hands of others for a school year in which they accelerated their studies in residence.

The Colombian leaders in particular asked for more practical courses. The actual leaders of the churches need to learn some fundamentals of music and in particular how to lead congregational singing. They need to be taught how to organize and conduct a worship service. Courses offered so far have not met the needs of the Sunday School teachers or those who have administrative duties. A simple course in how to set up the financial records for a congregation would be helpful. Some practical course in Christian Education would be of value to the pastors as well as to the Sunday School teachers and superintendents. Again, Human Relations was named as one of the most needed subjects.

Courses should be geared more directly to the needs of the students. This requires flexibility in the curriculum. In particular the extension students should not be held to the same plan of studies designed for the residence program. If we are to compete with commercial and language study programs available in most cities we must offer something more attractive on the *bachiller* level. However, it appears that in most cases when students on this level have dropped out in order to pursue other studies, it has been the younger students who have done so and those who were not really functional leaders in their congregations.

Greater coordination between the subjects taught and the activities of the local church must be achieved. In some cases students need to be required to do some practical work. At least the teacher should consult with the pastor so that some meaningful church experience can be obtained and the congregation benefit indirectly from the studies. In some cases the pastors feel threatened by the capabilities of lay leaders and have not allowed these students to participate as widely as the students were willing to. At this point the pastor must be shown the need to continue his own education and should be interested in the possibility of a multiple ministry in his church through the various gifts given to the members. The pastor could be encouraged to concentrate in those areas where he has gifts instead of trying to do everything by himself.

This may require some changes in the role which he plays in the church. All this is possible only when the extension program is officially backed by the denomination and is considered its own program for leadership training. This has been one of the great weaknesses of an interdenominational program, particularly in the Bogotá and Medellín Divisions.

Costs for registration and tuition have been kept down to about $1.15 and $2.55 per semester at the *bachiller* level and $0.66 and $1.75 at the diploma level. However, for some of the courses the cost of the text was a great obstacle. Operating as an interdenominational seminary with no control over the students we found that it was necessary to charge the full price of the manuals and texts when handed out on registration day. For Church History on the *bachiller* level that could add up to more than $10. Denominational subsidy of the United Biblical Seminary or scholarships to the students would help to remove this financial barrier to many potential students.

A common complaint was that some courses were superficial. Due to the provisional materials used this was to be expected, although lamented. Another weakness was in regard to the teachers and directors of centers. Some of the teachers had had no preparation and some of those with experience in residence teaching were not able to shift over satisfactorily to a different philosophy of teaching. They tended to lecture, supplementing or repeating the information given in the workbook.

Monthly meetings of students from various centers within a division have been helpful where realized. The student needs to feel that he is part of a big and important program and that many others are struggling with the same problems and are studying to resolve them. Monthly meetings might be denominational, but at least once a quarter a larger interdenominational gathering should be held.

Recommendations

These suggestions have to do with the program of the United Biblical Seminary of Colombia, but they may be applicable to extension programs in other areas and different types of situations. Even within the structure of a single seminary it is difficult to make general recommendations which would fit all the divisions, the denominations involved and the circumstances which vary from urban to rural centers.

1. The denominations must be sold on theological education by extension. Promotion may be carried out at annual conventions, pastors' retreats or other occasions as well as in individual contacts among denominational leaders. If extension is regarded as a second rate program which is sufficient for laymen but which could never lead to ordination, the potential leaders of congregations are not going to waste their time with it. Extension must become at least one of the official pastoral and lay training programs of the denomination. It may be

that denominations should provide funds to subsidize travel expenses of teachers and the cost of textbooks, at least for some courses.

2. One way of relating extension training to the work of the denomination is the organization of centers in local congregations. This ensures that studies are related to local problems and possibilities. Experience in Cali and Medellín shows that a much greater number of students can be reached if they are taught within the program of their own congregations. When a congregation knows which of its members are studying and which are not there may be a subsequent consideration of this factor in selecting men for church offices and responsibilities. The congregation is entitled to expect greater performance of the men and women who have had this opportunity to develop their spiritual gifts.

3. We should not be too concerned with numbers. A 50 per cent drop out rate is perfectly acceptable as long as the right people are being attracted to and maintained in extension studies. Young people should not be coerced into studying just because they have the intellectual capacity to do so, but have assumed no responsibility in the church. What is more important is giving a few leaders - elders, deacons, Sunday school teachers and superintendents the training they need for more effective ministries.

4. Pastors should be encouraged to continue and renew their theological education in this way. If they feel threatened by attending the same class with the members of the churches it might be good, at least initially, to offer a special section for pastors in some of the larger churches. But ideally pastors should be encouraged and guided to become the teachers of the extension studies in their own congregations. This will develop their teaching ability in all the services of the church.

5. Even if the pastors can not always be enlisted, greater dependence on national teachers is necessary. A school teacher or one of the members of the church who has shown some gift for teaching, a seminary student or someone who has made a special study of some subject may be enlisted for at least one course. Nationals must assume the administration and promotion of the program also and it is to be hoped that a few good men will appear who will be able to write or revise extension materials or adapt them to local needs.

6. Workshops for teachers are essential. This has been one of the great weaknesses of some extension programs. Perhaps too much dependence has been placed on the programmed instruction or workbooks prepared to transmit the content of the course. It is true that the teacher need not be an expert in the subject. In fact, the temptation to lecture may be too great if he is. More important is that he have some training in group dynamics. The workshop is a time when men can work through some of the lessons of the course they will be directing. After they have done their homework there should be a

demonstration of how to lead a class and each potential teacher
should have the experience of guiding the discussion and having
his work criticized in a contructive way by other teachers and
by the "expert" conducting the workshop.

7.   The monthly meeting must be stressed.   The fellowship
and corporate worship with others who share the same life and
studies is important.   This meeting may be regional, city-wide
or denominational according to the circumstances.   However, at
least once a semester there should be a meeting which provides
for wider interdenominational fellowship.   Special courses may
be offered at this time and it may be used also to give some
orientation to the teachers and to help them with any problems
that have arisen.

8.   In order to encourage students who see completion of
studies as a very distant goal, intermediate goals may be set
up.   Perhaps the first twelve subjects completed will qualify
a man as a Sunday School teacher, the next twelve as an evangelist and the full course as a pastor.   It may be that such
goals are not so important for the mature leaders of the churches, but they may be a stimulus for some.

9.   Greater flexibility in the curriculum is essential.
Some compromise between the sequence of studies set forth by
the seminary and the needs of the local congregation must be
reached.   Perhaps some short non-credit courses could be offered occasionally if a special need is evident in the congregation.   Realizing that not all men have the same gifts, we
must allow them to prepare for different ministries in the
church.   Students must be allowed to develop their gifts for
teaching, preaching, personal evangelism, administration or
any other ministry without all being expected to take the same
classes.

10.   In an effort to show that TEE is academically respec-
table perhaps insufficient attention has been given to the certificate or lowest level studies.   This is where most of our
church people are.   Because only diploma level studies have
been offered, many of the less educated leaders have dropped
out.   Even those who have completed primary school education
might profit more on the certificate level.   Perhaps this experience would capacitate them to study at the higher level
later.   *Bachiller* and diploma level studies must not be cut
back unnecessarily, but our goal must not be primarily to
award a certain number of academic degrees, but to train the
men and women who most need our help and can profit by it.
This means doing much more on the certificate level.

FINAL OBSERVATIONS

Theological education by extension has demonstrated its
grand potential for giving quality training to ever larger numbers of actual leaders in the churches.   Yet there are some
dangers inherent in the system which must be pointed out in or-

der that they be avoided. From its beginning in Latin America
the movement was dominated by missionaries. Through development of new structures and the filling of old positions by national leaders this problem is being resolved to a large degree. Conscious continual effort must be made to indigenize
extension programs wherever possible. This is necessary in administration, teaching and preparation of materials. The
AEBICAM workshop procedure of teaming a national with a missionary seems to be quite satisfactory. As national leaders
improve their skills in the techniques of writing programmed
instructional materials through workshops and experience, the
inadequacies of translated materials may be overcome.

Another kind of workshop which is greatly needed is that
for teachers. Every national pastor should be considered a potential teacher in this system, although many may not yet demonstrate gifts in this area. In these workshops prospective
teachers may work through materials they are to teach, receive
some orientation as to group dynamics and have an opportunity
to practice with the group and receive its criticism and suggestions for more effective teaching. The Christian and Missionary Alliance Bible Institute in Colombia now requires its
residence students to gain experience in extension teaching as
a part of its curriculum. It is to be hoped that other institutions will follow this example.

Extension seminaries have been criticized (Sapsezian 1971:
266) for having less contact between the professor and the student. While I think it may be affirmed that the quality of
contact is likely to be better in the interaction of discussion
in a weekly extension class than in a daily lecture class, the
criticism is valid. One of the potential values of the residence seminary is the sense of fellowship and the force of example that the student enjoys with the teachers with whom he
lives in community. In practice, however, the resident student
may seldom see his professor outside the classroom and it is
even less likely that he will engage with him in any evangelistic outreach or church participation. On the other hand
where an extension teacher is a local pastor or a missionary
who works with the church or in the same city, a great opportunity exists for the extension student to see how teachings
are applied in real situations. This is one of the distinct
advantages of extension classes being part of a local congregation's regular activities. Church growth will likely be promoted if the center is a denominational program and the students are integrated into the evangelistic outreach of the
church.

Flexibility is desirable in the curriculum of the extension
seminary. Alternate courses for distinct ministries within the
church should be offered. Local needs must be considered. Contextualization is one of the major considerations in theological education for this decade. Yet there are two dangers of
which we must be aware in too great flexibility and local de-
termination of curriculum. One is a fragmentation which leaves

great holes in a wide and liberal education of church leaders.
Although great freedom in the order of subjects taught and in
the content of those subjects may be permitted, some balance
must be maintained. A master plan should be maintained so that
areas covered are indicated and some provision can be made for
introducing opportunely courses not yet presented.

The other danger toward which excessive flexibility draws us
is that of the encroachment of secular studies in the curriculum. It would be very easy for an extension center which finds
increased enrollment for classes in public relations, accounting and grammar to lose sight of its purpose. In North American Bible institutes pre-theological courses were added to the
ministerial training programs until they became liberal arts
colleges which soon dwarfed the theological studies. In all
of these circumstances a proper balance must be maintained and
the primary goal of training functional leaders for the churches must remain central in the program.

Only limited specialization is possible in extension programs. This is good in that it seems unlikely that a shift in
emphasis may occur which will follow the common trend in traditional theological education to prepare men more for theological scholarship than pastoral duties. In this sense extension
seminaries can never completely replace residence studies.
They don't have the facilities for the research and specialization which a theologian must seek. On the other hand, let us
not criticize extension programs for producing pastors, not
scholars.

It may actually be a great danger for extension to attempt
to approximate as much as possible the kind of education available in traditional theological seminaries. One of the great
values of TEE is that it has caused a reexamination of educational psychology and pedagogy. The weaknesses of the lecture
method have been revealed. Programmed instruction has arisen
as a great tool in the hands of competent educators. It can
well become an instrument of indoctrination. Let us not forget
the menaces of behaviorism from which programmed instruction
sprang. We have often criticized Bible schools for spoon
feeding denominational policies and doctrines. Programmed
instruction becomes a most effective tool for this kind of
approach. Those who prepare extension materials, particularly
in the area of theology, must be very careful to provide
enough points of view and source materials so that the student
may critically evaluate his own position and that of others.
Linear programming must be supplemented with a good number of
open ended questions which require the student to reflect and
critically examine the issues.

Programming and other techniques used in extension studies
may allow us to teach more effectively than before, but we may
still be teaching the wrong things. A tremendous benefit has
come to all theological education through the programmer's emphasis on setting goals which are measurable in behavior or
performance. It will be a tragedy, however, if the programmer

is satisfied with success in reaching certain goals without also asking if they are the right and relevant goals. It may be
time to scrap the curricula of our seminaries and begin all
over again by considering the functions which a church leader
must perform in his culture and context. The extension seminary curriculum and program can become as content-oriented as any
other.

The use of programmed instructional materials makes it very
easy to present a package of teachings to the student and tell
him to take it or leave it. If, on the other hand, our goal
is not to run a pastoral training program or to duplicate the
education which we have received, but rather to produce leaders
for the churches, we must begin with the student, not the
teacher or his course. We must ask what the student needs to
know, not what we have to teach him. The goal of the student
must be competency, not the completion of a course of studies
or the reception of a degree. Study must be related to life,
all of life, and to ministry in a given context.

A less formal and more holistic approach to theological education may be achieved partly through administrative procedures and preparation of materials. More important is the
orientation of teachers. They are the persons responsible for
relevancy. Only at the local level is it possible to achieve
an integration of theory and practice, spiritual and social,
individual and group participation. This means that priority
must be given to training teachers and perhaps a manual for
their direction should be prepared by someone competent in the
field of educational psychology and philosophy.

Theological education by extension is just beginning outside
the Caribbean and Latin America. It is exciting to see the
rapid rise of numbers of students enrolled during this decade.
But, as in everything else, our concern must be for quality as
well as quantity. Even those who have worked in extension for
several years can not be satisfied with flourishing programs.
There is much to be done in the production of ever better materials. In the midst of many activities on behalf of theological education by extension it is most important that we be
aware of dangers and weaknesses in the system and that we constantly strive to serve the whole Church, both directly and
indirectly, through the equipment of leaders who will ensure
its growth in membership and in maturity in Christ.

PART TWO

Directory

Introduction 4
to the Use of
this Directory

GENERAL SUGGESTIONS

The directory which constitutes the major part of this book
contains an alphabetical listing of all the extension programs
of which the author has knowledge. The institutions and countries are not divided into regions as in the regional index
which follows. A strictly alphabetical order should eliminate
any confusion as to the classifications of a given country.
It should be pointed out that in the regional listings and totals some arbitrary divisions have been made. Central and
South America are included together since they all operate under the umbrella of ALISTE or AETTE. The Dominican Republic
and Puerto Rico have been included in Latin America, but
Guyana has been placed in the Caribbean section because of
linguistic differences.

The standard format has not been followed for the United
States and Europe since the programs are so varied and generally distinct from those associated with the Latin America model
of extension that it would be rather difficult to fit the programs into the same categories. Therefore, only a brief description in more narrative style is given. Even for other
areas some arbitrary assignment to academic levels has been
made. It is to be hoped that the injustices done in this way
will be forgiven by those affected.

Approximations are included when complete data are not
available. However, these approximations are based on some report, whether incomplete or older. Unless otherwise noted,
data are from the questionnaire submitted by each institution.
Undoubtedly many institutions have been left out inadvertently.
This is because they have not come to the attention of the author or because they have not responded to his questionnaires.
For most areas coverage is quite complete. For a few regions,
such as Brazil, only a small proportion of the extension seminaries known to exist are described. This is despite repeated
efforts to obtain the information. One would like to persist

until every institution and every student is accounted for, but
complete success would be possible, if every, only after the
first data had grown quite old.

Many seminaries and Bible institutes or colleges are launching their extension programs in 1973. Where sufficient information has been available these programs are reported. Nevertheless, the figures are not included in the country or regional
totals. For uniformity the data represent extension programs
in operation in December 1972 or shortly before that date.
Since questionnaires were sent out over a period of over four
months as new institutions were identified and as old ones did
not respond to the first questionnaire, some inaccuracies as
to the period represented are inevitable. But as a matter of
policy the data are for the end of 1972.

Although many commendable efforts are being made to extend
the programs of ministerial training schools to otherwise un-
reached church leaders, short term courses and evening schools
which depend largely on the lecture method are not included in
this survey. "Extension" is reserved for those programs in
which the student masters and applies the subject content during the week and meets with a professor and other students
periodically for sharing and discussion. This is not meant as
a value judgment, but as an arbitrary means of defining a certain type of program.

Data from extension programs and other sources were being received up to the time of preparation of the manuscript for
printing. When possible this new information has been included on the page for the program. It will not appear in the regional summaries, however. When information for a new program
was received after summaries and indices had been completed a
page for the program has been included at the end of the directory.

At the conclusion of the listing of institutions for each
region there is a regional summary. This page is a review of
the information found in the country summaries following the
listing of institutions for that country. For each country
and each institution the information indicated includes the
number of centers, teachers and students. Teachers are further
distinguished as to full time, part time, missionary and nationals. The categories for students are certificate (less
than full primary), diploma (full primary), *bachiller* (nine
years or more of formal education, and licentiate (two or more
years of college). These categories have been selected since
they are those used in Latin America where the majority of the
students represented in this survey are found and they are the
levels with which the author is most familiar. Where other
terms are used outside of Latin America an attempt has been
made to fit them into these categories according to educational level, not by the terms used in other areas.

REGIONAL INDEX
Statistics as of 1972

Institution	Cent	Teach	Students				
			Cert	Dipl	Bach	Lic	Total
General Conference Baptists Casilla de Correo 30 Santiago del Estero Argentina	3	3	30	0	0	9	20
						Page	*166*
Instituto Bíblico Edén Soldini, Provincia Santa Fe Argentina	2	4	0	17	0	0	17
						Page	*167*
Seminario Bautista Evangélico Argentino Casilla de Correo 364 Tucumán, Argentina	5	6	20	31	1	0	52
						Page	*168*
Seminario Internacional Teológico Bautista Ramón L. Falcón 4080 Buenos Aires, Argentina	4	27	0	220	0	0	220
						Page	*169*
Seminario por Extensión Anglicano Santiago 1862 S.M. Tucumán, Argentina	30	35	120	10	0	0	130
						Page	*170*
ARGENTINA TOTAL	44	75	160	278	1	0	439
						Page	*165*
Instituto Bíblico Berea Santa Cruz, Bolivia						*Page*	*175*
Seminario Teológico Bautista Casilla 86 Cochabamba, Bolivia						*Page*	*176*
Seminario Teológico Jorge Allan Cajón 514 Cochabamba, Bolivia	20	28	165	45	12	0	222
						Page	*177*
Seminario Teológico Luterano en Bolivia Casilla 266 La Paz, Bolivia	9	7	28	8	7	0	43
						Page	*178*
BOLIVIA TOTAL	29	35	193	53	19	0	265
						Page	*174*

Institution	Cent	Teach	Students				
			Cert	Dipl	Bach	Lic	Total
Extension Course of the Presbytery of Cuiaba Caixa Postal 41 78000 Cuiaba, MT., Brazil		1	150	80	20	0	250

Page 180

Faculdade de Teología da   1   1   0   12   0   0   12
Igreja Metodista Livre
Rua Domingos de Morais, 2518
04036 São Paulo, SP., Brazil   *Page 181*

Instituto Bíblico Apostol
Paul "IBAP"
Caixa Postal 77
36.800 Carangola, MG., Brazil   *Page 182*

Instituto Bíblico Batista de 15   10   10   30   80   6   126
Campinas
Caixa Postal 995
13.100 Campinas, SP., Brazil   *Page 183*

Instituto Bíblico Betel   3   85
Caixa Postal 30.498
01.000 São Paulo, SP., Brazil   *Page 184*

Instituto Bíblico Eduardo Lane 43 32   700   0   20   0   720
Caixa Postal 12
38740 Patrocinio, MG., Brazil   *Page 187*

Instituto Bíblico de Maringa 3   20
Caixa Postal 384
87.100 Maringa, PR., Brazil   *Page 185*

Instituto Bíblico do Brazil
Caixa Postal 18078, Aeroporto
01.000 São Paulo, SP., Brazil   *(Program begins 1973 - no data)*

Instituto Bíblico do Norte   90
Caixa Postal 66
55.300 Caranhuns, PE., Brazil   *Page 186*

Instituto Bíblico Maranata   6   13
Caixa Postal 431
60.000 Fortaleza, Ceara
Brazil   *Page 189*

Institution	Cent	Teach	Students Cert	Dipl	Bach	Lic	Total
Instituto Bíblico Wesleyano Caixa Postal 444 69.000 Manaus, AM., Brazil	1						2

Page 190

Instituto Cristão de Educacão E Cultura Caixa Postal 1099 74.000 Goiania, Goias, Brazil	12						37

Page 191

Instituto e Seminario Bíblico Irmãos Menonitas Caixa Postal 2445 80.000 Curitiba, Parana, Brazil	20						120

Page 192

Instituto e Seminario Bíblico de Londrina Caixa Postal 58 86.100 Londrina, Parana, Brazil	6						32

Page 193

Seminario Evangélico do Río Grande do Sul Caixa Postal 2350 90.000 Porto Alegre, RS., Brazil	3	7	30	15	17	0	62

Page 194

Seminario Teológico Batista Caixa Postal 269 13.100 Campinas, SP., Brazil	8						

Page 195

Seminario Teológico Batista Equatorial Caixa Postal 88 66.000 Belem, Pará, Brazil							

Page 196

Seminario Teológico Batista do Nordeste Caixa Postal 2 Floriano, Piaui, Brazil	11	32	69	100	0	0	169

Page 197

BRAZIL TOTAL							

Page 179

Seminario Bíblico por Extensión Moneda 1898 Santiago, Chile	9	7	0	60	10	0	70

Page 200

CHILE TOTAL	9	7	0	60	10	0	70

Page 198

Institution	Cent	Teach	Cert	Dipl	Bach	Lic	Total
Estudios Teológicos por Extensión Apartado Aéreo 786 Santa Marta, Magdalena Colombia	9	2	52	17	0	0	69 *Page 202*
Gospel Missionary Union Apartado Aéreo 244 Palmira, Colombia	10	9					89 *Page 203*
Instituto Bíblico Betel División Extensión Apartado Aéreo 516 Armenia, Quindío, Colombia	20	20	150	42	18	0	210 *Page 204*
Instituto Bíblico de Ocaña Apartado Aéreo 1 Ocaña, N. de S., Colombia	6	1	70	13	0	0	83 *Page 206*
SELITE Apartado Aéreo 53005 Bogotá 2, Colombia	6	6	0	33	4	0	37 *Page 207*
Seminario Bíblico Unido Apartado Aéreo 1141 Medellín, Colombia	51	60	366	88	19	0	473 *Pages 47-65, 208*
Seminario Teológico Bautista Internacional Apartado Aéreo 6613 Cali, Colombia	4	15	20	56	0	22	98 *Page 210*
COLOMBIA TOTAL	106	107	658	249	41	22	1059 *Page 201*
Seminario Bíblico de la Iglesia Evangélica Misionera Dajaban, Dominican Republic	5	2	15	2	8	0	25 *Page 212*
Seminario Evangélico Unido de la República Dominicana Apartado 506 Azua, Dominican Republic	8	6	30	60	10	0	100 *Page 213*
DOMINICAN REPUBLIC TOTAL	13	8	45	62	18	0	125 *Page 211*

Institution	Cent	Teach	Students				
			Cert	Dipl	Bach	Lic	Total
Centro de Estudios Teológicos Casilla 455 Quito, Ecuador	9	7	87	37	38	3	165
					Pages	*30,*	*215*
Centro Interamericano de Estudios Teológicos Casilla 860 Guayaquil, Ecuador	3	4	0	40	7	0	47
						Page	*216*
Seminario Bíblico Alianza Apartado 2006 Guayaquil, Ecuador	4	6	20	24	10	0	54
						Page	*217*
Seminario Bíblico Unión Casilla 269 Latacunga, Ecuador	49	54	380	18	4	0	402
						Page	*218*
Seminario Luterano de Extensión Casilla 1334 Cuenca, Ecuador	1	2	2	6	0	0	8
						Page	*219*
ECUADOR TOTAL	66	92	489	125	59	3	676
						Page	*214*
Instituto Bíblico "Berea" Apartado 8 Chiquimula, Guatemala	21	7	125	0	0	0	125
					Pages	*30,*	*227*
Instituto Bíblico Quiché San Cristóbal, Toto, Guatemala	14	10	115	0	0	0	115
						Page	*229*
Instituto Superior Teológico Bautista Apartado 322 Guatemala, Guatemala	12	9	40	110	12	0	162
						Page	*230*
Seminario Evangélico Presbiteriano Apartado 3, San Felipe, Reu. Guatemala	18	9	0	198	42	0	240
						Page	*231*
GUATEMALA TOTAL	65	35	280	308	54	0	642
						Page	*226*

			Students				
Institution	Cent	Teach	Cert	Dipl	Bach	Lic	Total
Instituto Bíblico de	18	10	48	0	0	0	48
Extensión							
Apartado 164							
La Ceiba, Honduras					*Page 239*		
Institutos Bíblicos Inter-	4	7	35	0	0	0	35
americanos							
Apartado 97							
La Ceiba, Honduras					*Page 240*		
HONDURAS TOTAL	22	17	83	0	0	0	83
					Page 238		
Departamento de Extensión	5	2	35	15	0	0	70
La Buena Tierra							
Apartado 407							
Saltillo, Coah.							
Mexico					*Page 263*		
Departamento de Extensión	5	6	0	44	0	0	44
Seminario Luterano Augsburgo							
Apartado Postal 20-416							
Mexico 20, D.F., Mexico					*Page 264*		
Instituto Bíblico "Vida y	7	4	11	8	5	0	24
Verdad"							
Apartado 196							
H. del Parral, Chih., Mexico					*Page 265*		
Seminario Teológico Bautista	20	41	75	245	10	0	335
Mexicano							
Corregidora 1333 Ote.							
Torreón, Coah., Mexico					*Page 266*		
Seminario Teológico por Ex-	8	20	112	15	3	0	130
tensión del Sureste							
Calle 61/529							
Mérida, Yucatán, Mexico					*Page 267*		
MEXICO TOTAL	45	74	253	327	18	0	598
					Page 262		
Seminario Bethel	6	4	0	36	0	0	36
El Amanecer							
La Chorrera, Panama					*Page 276*		
PANAMA TOTAL	6	4	0	36	0	0	36
					Page 275		

			Students				
Institution	Cent	Teach	Cert	Dipl	Bach	Lic	Total
Centro Teológico de San Martín Misión Evangélica Tarapoto, San Martín Peru						*Page 278*	
Instituto Bíblico Bautista de Iquitos Casilla 231 Iquitos, Peru	17	15	90	105	6	0	201
						Page 279	
Seminario de Extensión Teológica Iglesia del Nazareno Apartado 85 Chiclayo, Peru						*Page 280*	
PERU TOTAL	17	15	90	105	6	0	201
							Page 277
Instituto Bíblico Menonita Apartado 146 Aibonito, Puerto Rico 00609						*Page 287*	
PUERTO RICO TOTAL							
							Page 286
Seminario Evangélico Menonita de Teología Avenida Millan 4392 Montevideo, Uruguay	1	10	0	10	41	0	51
							Page 312
URUGUAY TOTAL	1	10	0	10	41	0	51
							Page 311
Instituto Teológico "Juan de Frías" Apartado Postal 216 Puerto Ordaz, Estado Bolivar Venezuela	4	4	0	20	2	0	22
							Page 314
Seminario Local Cruzada Mundial Evangélica Apartado 501 Barquisimeto, Venezuela	6	4	0	25	0	0	25
							Page 315

Institution	Cent	Teach	Students Cert	Dipl	Bach	Lic	Total
Seminario Teológico Bautista de Venezuela Apartado 27 Los Teques, Venezuela	9	15	100	50	0	0	150

Page 316

VENEZUELA TOTAL		19	19	100	95	2	0	197

Page 313

REGIONAL TOTAL - LATIN AMERICA

Argentina	5	44	75	160	278	1	0	439
Bolivia	4	29	35	193	53	19	0	265
Brazil	28	132	83	959	237	147	0	1578
Chile	1	9	7	0	60	10	0	70
Colombia	7	106	107	658	249	41	22	1059
Dominican Republic	2	13	8	45	62	18	0	125
Ecuador	5	66	92	489	125	59	3	676
Guatemala	4	65	35	280	308	54	0	642
Honduras	2	22	17	83	0	0	0	83
Mexico	5	45	74	253	327	18	0	598
Panama	1	6	4	0	36	0	0	36
Peru	3	17	15	90	105	6	0	201
Puerto Rico (est.)	1			120			10	130
Uruguay	1	1	10	0	10	41	0	51
Venezuela	3	9	15	100	50	0	0	150
	72	564	575	3430	1900	414	35	6103

(Estimates include 10 institutions and 5,000 students more)

Institution	Cent	Teach	Students				
			Cert	Dipl	Bach	Lic	Total
Seminaire Evangelique des Antilles Francaises B. P. 228 Pointe-a-Pitre, Guadeloupe, F.W.I.	4	2					57

Page 225

GUADELOUPE TOTAL	4	2					57

Page 224

Lutheran Church of Guyana	6						145

Page 233

GUYANA TOTAL	6						145

Page 232

Ecole Biblique Par Extension Box 458 Port-au-Prince, Haiti	6	8	0	75	0	0	75

Page 235

Extension Bible School of Eastern Haiti Box 1096 Port-au-Prince, Haiti	7	4	135	10	0	0	145

Page 236

Institut Biblique Lumiere Boite Postale 71 Aux Cayes, Haiti	19	21	150	150	1	0	301

Page 237

HAITI TOTAL	32	33	285	235	1	0	521

Page 234

Jamaica Theological Seminary Box 121 Kingston 8, Jamaica							40

Page 254

United Theological College of the West Indies	2						20

Page 255

JAMAICA TOTAL	2						60

Page 253

Institution	Cent	Teach	Cert	Dipl	Bach	Lic	Total
Nazarene Training College P. O. Box 1245 Port of Spain, Trinidad	3	3	4	22	5	0	31 *Page 306*
Open Bible Institute P. O. Box 82 San Fernando, Trinidad	2	6	1	18	0	0	19 *Page 307*
TRINIDAD TOTAL	5	9	5	40	5	0	50 *Page 305*

REGIONAL TOTAL - CARIBBEAN

	Cent	Teach	Cert	Dipl	Bach	Lic	Total
Guadeloupe	1	4	2				57
Guyana	1	6					145
Haiti	3	32	33	285	235	1	0	521
Jamaica	2						60
Trinidad	2	5	9	5	40	5	0	50
	9	47	44	290	275	6	0	833

REGIONAL TOTAL - NORTH AMERICA

United States 1193
Page 308

REGIONAL TOTAL - EUROPE

England 50
Page 220

Institution	Cent	Teach	Students Cert	Dipl	Bach	Lic	Total
Mekane Yesus Seminary P. O. Box 1247 Addis Ababa, Ethiopia	5	11	95	25	0	0	120 *Page 222*
ETHIOPIA TOTAL	5	11	95	25	0	0	120 *Page 221*
Iran Extension of the Near East School of Theology P. O. Box 1505 Tehran, Iran	4	4	0	0	16	10	26 *Page 251*
IRAN TOTAL	4	4	0	0	16	10	26 *Page 250*
Kima Theological College P. O. Box 75 Maseno, Kenya	5	10	90	0	0	0	90 *Page 259*
KENYA TOTAL	5	10	90	0	0	0	90 *Page 258*
Biliri Bible Training School E.C.W.A. Biliri via Gombe N.E. State, Nigeria	11	9	35	82	0	0	117 *Page 269*
United Missionary Society Theological College Box 171 Ilorin Kwarastate, Nigeria	1	1	0	0	2	2	4 *Page 270*
NIGERIA TOTAL	12	9	35	82	2	2	121 *Page 268*
Brethren in Christ Church	4						51 *Page 289*
RHODESIA TOTAL	4						51 *Page 288*
Sierra Leone Bible College Box 890 Freetown, Sierra Leone	5	2	45	18	0	0	63 *Page 291*
SIERRA LEONE TOTAL	5	2	45	18	0	0	63 *Page 290*

			Students				
Institution	Cent	Teach	Cert	Dipl	Bach	Lic	Total
Durban Bible College P. O. Box 7 Jacobs, Natal, South Africa	3	10	0	40	22	0	62

Page 293

| Evangelical Bible Institute P. O. Box 629 Rustenburg, Transvaal South Africa | 3 | 2 | 21 | 0 | 5 | 0 | 26 |

Page 294

| Free Methodist Extension Bible School P. O. Box 1263 Witbank, South Africa | 12 | | 69 | 14 | 0 | 0 | 83 |

Page 295

| SOUTH AFRICA TOTAL | 18 | 12 | 90 | 54 | 27 | 0 | 171 |

Page 292

| Brethren in Christ Church | 8 | | | | | | 110 |

Page 318

| ZAMBIA TOTAL | 8 | | | | | | 110 |

Page 317

REGIONAL TOTAL – AFRICA

Institution	Cent	Teach	Cert	Dipl	Bach	Lic	Total
Ethiopia	1	5	11	95	25	0	0	120
Iran	1	4	4	0	0	16	10	26
Kenya	1	5	10	90	0	0	0	90
Nigeria	2	12	9	35	82	2	2	121
Rhodesia	1	4						51
Sierra Leone	1	5	2	45	18	0	0	63
South Africa	3	18	12	90	54	27	0	171
Zambia	1	8						110
	11	59	48	355	179	45	12	752

Institution	Cent	Teach	Students Cert	Dipl	Bach	Lic	Total
Concordia Theological Seminary 68 Begonia Road Yau Yat Chuen, Kowloon Hong Kong	12	20	0	0	0	52	52

Page 242

HONG KONG TOTAL	12	20	0	0	0	52	52

Page 241

The Association for Theological Extension Education (TAFTEE) 9/15 Lloyd Road, Extn. Bangalore 560006, India	13	19	0	0	10	210	220

Page 244

INDIA TOTAL	13	19	0	0	10	210	220

Page 243

Christian and Missionary Alliance Djalan H, Djakarta, Indonesia							225

Page 247

Lembaga Pembinaan Jemaat GPIB 10 Medan Merdeka Timur Jakarta, Indonesia	5	25	0	0	122	0	122

Page 248

Sumatra School of Theology Kotak Pos 289 Medan, Sumatra, Indonesia	9	7	53	34	23	1	111

Page 249

INDONESIA TOTAL	14	32	53	34	145	1	458

Page 246

Covenant Seminary 17-8 Nakameguro, 5 Chome Meguro ku, Tokyo, Japan	1	15	0	0	9	11	20

Page 257

JAPAN TOTAL	1	15	0	0	9	11	20

Page 256

Evangelical Lutheran Church of Malaysia and Singapore Lay Training Program 21 Jalan Abdul Samad Kuala Lumpur, Malaysia	15	6	0	0	100	0	100

Page 261

MALAYSIA TOTAL	15	6	0	0	100	0	100

Page 260

Institution	Cent	Teach	Cert	Dipl	Bach	Lic	Total
			Students				
The Extension Seminary of Theology 27-B Satellite Town Rahim Yar Khan, Pakistan	3	2	5	10	5	6	26
						Page	*272*
Gujranwala Theological Seminary P. O. Box 13 Gujranwala, Pakistan	2	2	0	0	6	23	29
						Page	*273*
Karachi Institute of Theology Selwyn House, Trinity Close Fatima Jinnah Road Karachi 4, Pakistan	2	8					
						Page	*274*
PAKISTAN TOTAL	7	12	5	10	11	29	55
						Page	*271*
Conservative Baptist Bible College P. O. Box 1882 Manila, Philippines	13	12	0	107	0	0	107
						Page	*282*
The International Biblical Seminary P. O. Box 66 Cagayan de Oro City L 305, Philippines	3	9	14	0	0	0	14
						Page	*283*
PHILIPPINES TOTAL	16	21	14	107	0	0	121
						Page	*281*
China Evangelical Seminary P. O. Box 28-4 Shihlin, Taipei Taiwan 111	2	3	4	2	2	0	8
						Page	*298*
TAIWAN TOTAL	2	3	4	2	2	0	8
						Page	*297*
Thailand Theological Seminary Box 37 Chiang Mai, Thailand	3	10	0	30	15	0	45
						Page	*303*
THAILAND TOTAL	3	10	0	30	15	0	45
						Page	*301*

Institution	Cent	Teach	Students				Total
			Cert	Dipl	Bach	Lic	
REGIONAL TOTAL – ASIA							
Hong Kong	1	12	20	0	0	0	52	52
India	1	13	19	0	0	10	210	220
Indonesia	3	14	32	53	34	145	1	458
Japan	1	1	15	0	0	9	11	20
Malaysia	1	15	6	0	0	100	0	100
Pakistan	3	7	12	5	10	11	29	55
Philippines	2	16	21	13	107	0	0	121
Taiwan	1	2	3	4	2	2	0	8
Thailand	1	3	10	0	30	15	0	45
	14	83	138	76	183	292	303	1029

Alliance College of Theology   3   2   0   0   30   0   30
P. O. Box 19 Rivett
A.C.T. 2611, Australia   *Page 172*

Armidale Diocesan Theological 4   5   80
   Education by Extension
c/o Rev. R.C. Smith
Box W73, West Tamworth
N.S.W., 2340, Australia   *Page 173*

AUSTRALIA TOTAL   7   7   0   0   30   0   110
                                                           Page 171

REGIONAL TOTAL – OCEANIA

Australia   2   7   7   0   0   30   0   110

COUNTRY INDEX

CITY INDEX

Santiago, Chile *200*

Santiago del Estero, Argentina *166*

Sao Paulo, Brazil *181, 184, A 5*

Sincelejo, Colombia *208*

Soldini, Argentina *167*

Taipei, Taiwan *298, A 3*

Tarapoto, Peru *278*

Tehran, Iran *251*

Tokyo, Japan *257*

Torreon, Mexico *266*

Tucuman, Argentina *168, 170*

West Tamworth, Australia *173*

Witbank, South Africa *295*

Barcelona, Spain *A 1*

Umtali, Rhodesia *A 2*

Fort Victoria, Rhodesia *A 4*

Esmeraldas, Ecuador *A 6*

Maradi, Niger *A 8*

INSTITUTION INDEX

The Free Methodist Extension Bible School   295

General Conference Baptists   166

Gospel Missionary Union   203

Gujranwala Theological Seminary   273

Institut Biblique Lumiére   237

Instituto Bíblico Apostol Paul "IBAP"   182

Instituto Bíblico Batista de Campinas   183

Instituto Bíblico Bautista   199

Instituto Bíblico Bautista de Iquitos   279

Instituto Bíblico Berea   175

Instituto Bíblico "Berea"   227

Instituto Bíblico Betel (Brazil)   184

Instituto Bíblico Betel (Colombia)   204

Instituto Bíblico de Extensión   239

Instituto Bíblico de Ocaña   206

Instituto Bíblico de la Iglesia de Dios de Guatemala   228

Instituto Bíblico do Brasil   (not included)

Instituto Bíblico do Norte   186

Instituto Bíblico Edén   167

Instituto Bíblico Eduardo Lane   187

Instituto Bíblico Maranata   189

Instituto Bíblico de Maringa   185

Instituto Bíblico Menonita   287

Instituto Bíblico Quiché   229

Instituto Bíblico "Vida y Verdad"   265

Instituto Bíblico Wesleyano   190

United Theological College of the West Indies   *255*

Escuela Evangélica de Teología de Barcelona   *A 1*

Rusitu Bible Institute *A 2*

Taiwan Theological College   *A 3*

Lund Bible School   *A 4*

Instituto Batista de Educacão Teológica por Extensão (IBETE) *A5*

Instituto Bíblico del Pacífico   *A 6*

Milate Heywar Bible School   *A 7*

L'Ecole Biblique D'Aguia   *A 8*

5 Supporting Agencies or Activities Affecting TEE

Numerous associations and other agencies have made substantial contributions to the extension movement through financial assistance, technical direction, promotion and other means. It is rather difficult to classify the agencies involved since some have had several functions. However, a general distinction can be drawn between those associations which operate or coordinate extension programs and those agencies which in a more indirect manner have encouraged the formation of those programs. In addition to the agencies, some mention must be made of the many publications which have helped to disseminate information about theological education by extension. Workshops and consultations are described in a separate section. Some overlapping of these categories will be inevitable in order to show the relationship between various organizations and activities.

TECHNICAL AND FINANCIAL ASSISTANCE

CAMEO

The Committee to Assist Missionary Education Overseas (CAMEO) is a joint committee of the Evangelical Foreign Missions Association (EFMA) and the Interdenominational Foreign Missions Association (IFMA). It was organized in 1964 with a Steering Committee made up of representatives of the two associations which meets two or three times a year. Raymond B. Buker, Sr. was appointed Co-ordinator of CAMEO in the spring of 1967. One of the projects in which CAMEO has been deeply involved has been the promotion of TEE throughout the world. Its major contributions to this movement are listed below.

July 1966	A workshop on Bible institutes was sponsored at the Central American Mission Bible Institute in Guatemala City which was attended by thirty-four delegates from eighteen Bible institutes and seminaries. Some delegates visited the Presbyterian Seminary and were introduced to the extension concept. Among those were James Clark, who began the extension program in Honduras for the CBFMS, and Samuel Rowen, who prepared for the West Indies Mission the booklet on the Resident-Extension Seminary (Winter 1969:122).
April 1968	A consultation was called in Philadelphia which was attended by mission executives and professors of missions. After hearing presentations on TEE, plans were made for a workshop in December.
1968	*CAMEO Release No. 1.*
December 1968	The Wheaton workshop was an important milestone in acquainting 121 persons representing thirty missions with TEE. Programmed instruction was presented as a means of presenting quality instruction in extension studies. Various programs, problems and possibilities were discussed. Continental group sessions considered TEE for areas of the world outside of Latin America.
Spring 1969	*Theological Education by Extension,* edited by Ralph Winter, which has been the definitive sourcebook on TEE, was distributed by CAMEO. The book contains 120 pages on the workshop in Wheaton.
February 1969	The CAMEO Coordinator presented TEE at the conference of the AEAM (Association of Evangelicals of Africa and Madagascar) in Limuru, Kenya. AEBICAM (Association of Evangelical Bible Institutes and Colleges of Africa and Madagascar) which is a subsidiary of AEAM set up a workshop at which the CAMEO Coordinator reported on the Wheaton workshop.
May 1969	*CAMEO Release No. 2.*
September 1969	CAMEO sponsored workshops for the preparation of writers in Recife and São Paulo, Brazil, in Cochabamba, Bolivia, and in Medellín, Colombia.
December 1969	*CAMEO Release No. 3.* CAMEO financed Ted Ward's trip to the Bogotá CATA meeting.

Spring   Distribution of *Programmed Instruction for Theologi-*
1970   *cal Education by Extension* by Ted and Margaret Ward.

January   Workshop in Wheaton on PI.
1970

August   TEE workshops organized in Nigeria, Ethiopia, and
1970   Rhodesia.

September   TEE workshops organized in Kenya, Taiwan, Vietnam,
1970   Indonesia and India.
              CAMEO Release No. 4.

January   Workshop on TEE in London.
1971

March   Workshop on TEE in Spain.
1971

May   *CAMEO Release No. 5.*
1971   Bibliography for TEE which included books on pro-
              gramming and materials for extension studies avail-
              able in different areas of the world.

August-   TEE workshops in Liberia, Ivory Coast, Zaire, Zambia,
September   West Pakistan, Thailand, Hong Kong, the Philippines
1971   and Japan.

Winter   Distribution of reports on the above workshops in a
1971   fifty-five page booklet.
              CAMEO Release No. 6.

May-   Workshops on programmed instruction at Fort Worth,
June   Texas.
1972

October   *CAMEO Release No. 7.*
1972

March   Bibliography of some 100 programmed texts in various
1973   languages and countries.
              Workshop on programmed instruction at Wheaton.

May   Report on TEE of the CAMEO Coordinator to NAE.
1973

CATA

Comité Asesor de Textos Autodidácticos - Advisory Committee
on Self-teaching Texts (CATA) was eventually formed from the
idea at the Armenia workshop for an organization to give technical assistance in the production of texts. Although it took

nearly two years for a permanent committee to be formed, the
provisional members of this organization had an important role
in the development of extension programs and materials. As
pioneers it was their task to feel their way through the planning of workshops, testing of preliminary materials and adaptation to the new technique of programmed instruction. These
men were not experts when first named, but they grew with their
responsibilities and are generally recognized worldwide as
"experts" on extension along with others who worked through
different channels.

Obviously the activities of the members of the CATA committee have been numerous. However, their meetings have been
very infrequent. Therefore, these meetings and the decisions
taken will be reported in some detail and the reader will have
to understand that much of the work of CATA was carried on by
correspondence between meetings.

September   At the Armenia workshop the idea for CATA was con-
1967   ceived. The textbook advisory committee was to con-
            sist of the UNICO President Dr. Ulises Hernández,
            Vice President Vernon Reimer and Secretary-Treas-
            urer (Executive Secretary) Wallace Rehner. Addi-
            tional members named were Mrs. Louise Walker, Ross
            Kinsler and William Wonderly.

January   In a letter to Wallace Rehner, Ralph Winter proposed
1968   a *Comité Técnico de Formato* (Technical Committee on
            Format) to be composed of Peter Wagner (Peter
            Savage alternate), Louise Walker, James Emery (Ross
            Kinsler alternate) and José Fajardo (Alfonso Lloreda
            alternate). Such a committee was never formed.

April   The UNICO Executive Committee (Hernández, Reimer and
1968   Rehner) met in Miami with the additional advisors
            Ralph Winter, James Emery, Peter Wagner, Louise Wal-
            ker and Loren Triplett. The statement of purpose in
            the minutes was as follows:

            This meeting was called with an idea to complete
            organizational structure and name the working
            committees for the production of the inter-text
            series of theological books on the diploma in
            theology level, as stated by A.L.E.T., to be pro-
            duced within the next two years for all of
            Spanish-speaking Latin America (UNICO Minutes,
            April 21-24, 1968).

            It was decided that CLATT would have no organiza-
            tional relationship with UNICO. CATA was to be
            named by the UNICO committee and be considered a sub-
            committee of that organization. Various persons were

suggested as members of CATA and a half-time executive secretary was to be named. Meanwhile, the Pro-Secretary would be Wallace Rehner with two assistants: Ross Kinsler in Central America and Peter Savage in Peru and Bolivia. The format and procedures for production and distribution of texts were discussed.

An authors' workshop was scheduled for August 1968 in Medellín, Colombia pending approval of funds from TEF. Materials for guidance in training authors and administration of extension centers were assigned to be written before the Medellín workshop. James Emery was named as principal advisor to CLATT and UNICO in the area of curriculum. Budgets were elaborated for the Intertext project and for UNICO.

December 1968

Since the Medellín workshop planned for August 1968 did not materialize the next meeting of CATA with UNICO was in Mexico City. The curriculum for Inter-texts was presented by James Emery and approved by CATA and UNICO. Authors were assigned to write the Intertexts and their work was to be supervised by the curriculum committee consisting of Ross Kinsler in the area of Bible, Wallace Rehner in the area of Practical Theology and Peter Savage in the areas of Church History and Theology. Since it had been impossible to obtain the services of a half-time executive secretary for CATA, Kinsler was named International Coordinator (UNICO Minute No. 5).

August 1969

Workshops for authors were held in Cochabamba, Bolivia and Medellín, Colombia by Ross Kinsler, the International Coordinator. Half of the writers assigned to prepare Intertexts as well as several other persons attended these two workshops.

December 1969

The Bogotá Congress on Evangelism was the occasion for the next meeting of CATA and UNICO at minimal expense to these organizations since most of the members were delegates to the Congress. At this time the permanent members of CATA were named: Ross Kinsler as International Coordinator and as Regional Secretaries: Peter Savage, James Emery and Vernon Reimer (Wayne Weld alternate during Reimer's furlough). Also present were UNICO members Ulises Hernández and Armando Hernández, CLATT secretary Peter Wagner, the Executive Secretary and President of AETTE Richard Sturz and Norman Anderson respectively and special guests Ralph Winter and Ted Ward.

Reports were given on the progress of Intertext writers. It was decided to concentrate on a few Intertexts since most of the assigned writers had not produced anything to date and the members of CATA were
kept so busy reviewing and revising manuscripts that
they themselves had no time to write. Programmed
Instruction was accepted as the technique to be used
in at least most of the Intertexts. It was decided
to dispense with advisors previously asked to examine
the content of Intertexts. The need to work on levels both higher and lower than the diploma level Intertexts was presented. Wayne Weld was named coordinator of *bachiller* level Intertexts with the cooperation of the CATA members as long as this did
not interfere with the emphasis on the diploma level.

The Evangelical Seminary, a quarterly bulletin published in the Presbyterian Seminary in Guatemala was
renamed *The Extension Seminary* and became the un-
official informative organ of CATA, CLATT and
AETTE (CATA Minute No. 2). CLATT also published its
own bulletin.

February   The CATA committee met in Guatemala and decided to
1972   convene an assembly of extension institutions in
           Spanish America for January 1973 in Medellín, Co-
           lombia. Papers were assigned to CATA members and
           others for presentation at that time. It was re-
           commended that a new structure be devised which
           would replace CATA and CLATT.

January   CATA Consultation in Medellín, Colombia. The fol-
1973   lowing papers were distributed to the delegates be-
           fore the meetings: (Spanish titles translated)

           The Spanish Intertext Project - Kinsler
           Orientation for Workshops - Savage
           The Problem of the Semi-literate in the Design of
               a Plan of Studies - Savage
           Financial Report and Budget - Reimer
           Report on CATA Activities - Kinsler
           The Sixteen Steps for the Production and Dis-
               tribution of Intertexts - Wagner
           AETTE Constitution
           Seminary Study Plans - Emery
           TEE: A Critique of its Development and Method - TEF
           Toward an Evaluation of Extension Studies - Savage
           The Professor-Teaching versus the Student-Learning -
               Savage
           Dialogue as a Method of Teaching - Kinsler

The meetings were attended by fifty-three delegates from some twenty countries and forty institutions. The Intertext project was suspended, although the new organization formed ALISTE *(Asociación Latinoamericana de Instituciones y Seminarios Teológicos por Extensión* - Latin American Association of Institutions and Theological Seminaries by Extension) assumed the functions of CATA and CLATT.

CLATT

Another organization to emerge as a result of the Armenia workshop was the *Comité Latinoamericano de Textos Teológicos* - Latin American Committee on Theological Texts (CLATT). The function of CLATT was to serve as a literary agent, lining up books which would be acceptable to the member institutions of CLATT and then arranging with an evangelical publishing house for the publication and distribution of the books. CLATT was embodied in the person of C. Peter Wagner who, with the help of his wife, carried on the correspondence involved in this task and in the production of periodic bulletins and catalogs of extension materials. The major decisive points in the history of CLATT are presented below:

September 1967
At the Armenia workshop the need for such an organization was discussed. However CLATT was created separate from UNICO, the parent organization for CATA, so as not to be associated with TEF money. CLATT was financed by a donation of $600 from a foundation in the United States. Peter Wagner was named the *ad hoc* secretary.

January 1968
In a letter from Ralph Winter to Wallace Rehner a tentative list of institutions to be members of CLATT was given. These schools had been picked by Louise Walker, Winter and Wagner to give a broad geographical and doctrinal distribution within the conservative evangelical position. Of the fourteen institutions suggested only eight later became members of CLATT.

September 1968
CLATT Boletín No. 1.
News items regarding extension were shared and the levels for the production of texts were announced.

December 1968
Mr. Wagner met with members of CATA and UNICO in Mexico City. A pert chart was worked up for the writing, testing and revision of Intertexts. The publishing houses which agreed to handle CLATT books were:

Editorial Vida – Assemblies of God
Nazarene Publishing House
Southern Baptist Publishing House
Moody Press
Editorial Caribe – Latin American Mission

February   *CLATT Boletín No. 2.*
1969   It contained a list of provisional extension mater-
           ials in Spanish.

April   *CLATT Boletín No. 3.*
1969   It included a list of the authors assigned to write
           Intertexts and also the names of content specialists
           in the CLATT institutions who would check the books.

September *CLATT Boletín No. 4.*
1969   Additional authors were named.

October   *CLATT Boletín No. 5.*
1969   A report of workshops realized by Ted Ward was given
           as well as an article by Ross Kinsler on the Inter-
           text Project and the relationships between CATA,
           CLATT and UNICO.

January   *CLATT Boletín No. 6.*
1970   It contained a graph of the number of extension stu-
           dents in Latin America from 1963 to 1970. The fol-
           lowing members of CLATT were listed:

           Asambleas de Dios – Servicio de Educación Cristiana
           Iglesia del Nazareno
           Instituto Bíblico Bautista (ABWE) *Iquitos, Perú*
           Instituto Evangelístico de México
           Seminario Bautista Evangélico Argentino (CBFMS)
           Seminario Bíblico Alianza (C&MA) *Guayaquil, Ecuador*
           Seminario Bíblico Latinoamericano (LAM) *San José,*
              Costa Rica
           Seminario Bíblico Unido (OMS, etc.) *Medellín, Co-*
              lombia
           Seminario Evangélico Presbiteriano de Guatemala
           Seminario Teológico Bautista de Cochabamba, Bolivia
           Seminario Teólogico Jorge Allan de Cochabamba, Bo-
              livia

July   *CLATT Boletín No. 7.*
1970   Announced the preliminary approval of the first Inter-
           text *(Principios del Crecimiento de la Iglesia –*
           Principles of Church Growth). A catalog of pro-
           visional materials was also published.

January   *CLATT Boletín No. 8.*
1971   Announcement of distribution of Intertext No. 1.

Intertext No. 2 was sent to CLATT members for approval (*Introducción al Antiguo Testamento*). A survey of the number of students was sent out and a new list of CLATT members was distributed.

March 1971
: *CLATT Boletín No. 9.* Results of the student survey were given. Catalog No. 2 of extension materials contained six pages of materials from thirteen institutions.

May 1971
: *CLATT Boletín No. 10.* Announcement of the moving of the CLATT office from Cochabamba, Bolivia to Pasadena, California. Data from AETTE were distributed.

March 1972
: *CLATT Boletín No. 11.* New extension materials were indicated.

September 1972
: *CLATT Boletín No. 12.* A survey of students in extension was made. A list of key persons in extension around the world was provided and a catalog of materials from sixteen institutions was given.

January 1973
: *CLATT Boletín No. 13.* The results of the student survey were given. A catalog supplement was enclosed and it was announced that CLATT would be dissolved along with CATA and its functions assumed by a new organization to be formed in Medellín.

TAP

Although the majority of the extension programs in Latin America are operated by non-conciliar evangelicals, a great deal of the financing of CATA and other projects has been with the financial help of the Theological Education Fund, which is related to the World Council of Churches. In Asia, however, considerable assistance to the development of extension studies has been given by the Theological Assistance Program (TAP) of the World Evangelical Fellowship. TAP grew out of the Asia Pacific Congress of Evangelism in Singapore in 1968. Its interest and activities have not been restricted to Asia, but the organization has been more active there. Some of its activities which have a bearing upon TEE are set forth below:

May 1969
: Vol. 1 No. 1 of *Theological News.* This quarterly bulletin has almost since its beginning carried information regarding TEE as well as other theological news around the world and has been one of the means of announcing the workshops on programmed instruc-

tion held in various areas.

June   Second Asia Evangelical Consultation on Theological
1971   Education in Singapore. At this time TAP-Asia was
            formed as an autonomous organization although a mem-
            ber body of TAP-International. TAP resolved to es-
            tablish a coordinating agency for TEE in Asia and to
            appoint an Asia Coordinator for TEE. Ian McCleary
            was named for this position. An Asia TEE Committee
            was also formed. TAP co-sponsored with CAMEO work-
            shops on programmed instruction in Singapore and
            India.

July   Vol. 1 No. 1 of *Programming News*. This TAP period-
1971   ical has published articles regarding strategies and
            principles of programming as well as indicating
            source materials for further study of the technique.

February   Ian McCleary held TEE consultations in Thailand, Ma-
1972   laysia, Singapore and Indonesia and reported on the
            progress in those areas.

April   The Executive Committee of TAP-Asia met in Seoul,
1972   Korea. The cassette ministry for application to TEE
            was supported.

August   The TEE Report was published with news of the organi-
1972   zation and progress of the movement in various areas.
            This report included minutes of TAFTEE (India),
            PACTEE (Pakistan), Sumatra TEE, PABATS-TEE (Phil-
            ippines), Thailand and Indonesia.

October   Programmed instruction workshops held in Taiwan, In-
1972   donesia, Malaysia, New Guinea, India, Philippines,
            South Vietnam, Thailand and Lebanon.

January   A report of the above workshops was published by TAP-
1973   Asia.

March   A filmstrip of 82 frames - twenty minutes prepared
1973   for distribution by TAP-Asia. The title is "TEE
            Could be the Answer."

TEF

    The Theological Education Fund (TEF) was formed in 1958 and
later formally related to the World Council of Churches. It
solicits funds from denominational and national church bodies
and realizes special studies and gives grants to promote various projects and programs of theological education around the
world. Its first mandate was primarily concerned with raising
academic standards and strengthening institutions. Its second

mandate had to do with relevance as seen in the production of
vernacular textbooks and the training of nationals as teachers. The third mandate which extends until 1977 focuses attention on reform and renewal. It is interested in faculty
development, associations of theological schools and in alter-
natives in theological education. In this last category theological education by extension has received and can expect
to receive help from TEF in developing its programs and materials. TEF has already made substantial contributions to the
extension movement.

1964   A $5,000 grant was given to the Presbyterian Semi-
            nary in Guatemala for the production of workbooks
            for extension.

1965   TEF director James Hopewell visited the Guatemala ex-
            tension program and referred to it favorably in a
            mimeographed paper "Preparing the Candidate for
            Mission," which was later printed in shorter form
            in the *International Review of Missions* in 1967.
            This encouragement from a well recognized authority
            on theological education was influential. A sur-
            vey of theological schools showed the need for an
            alternate type of ministerial training.

1966   A reference library, visual aids and furniture were
            given to each of the extension centers in Guatemala.

1967   The Armenia workshop which was sponsored by ALET was
            largely financed by TEF funds.

1968   UNICO was formed and funds were distributed through
            UNICO for the work of CATA. The TEF paid for Ralph
            Winter's transportation to the Bolivia workshop on
            extension.

1969   Various extension programs in Latin America were
            assisted financially in order to provide library
            facilities and help with other projects.

1972   Publication of *Ministry in Context: The Third Man-
            date Programme of the Theological Education Fund*
            (1970-77). Chapter 4 (pages 34-43) is entitled
            "Theological Education by Extension: A Critique of
            its Development and Method." It deals with the his-
            tory, principles and criticism of TEE. Guidelines
            for the support of TEE programs are listed. $245,000
            was budgeted for TEE during the third mandate of TEF
            (p. 105).

ASSOCIATIONS OF THEOLOGICAL SCHOOLS NOT RESTRICTED
TO INTEREST IN EXTENSION

Theological education by extension is not just an experiment
by a few people to provide lay training. It is increasingly
recognized as an alternative to traditional ministerial training. As such it must be taken into consideration by the various associations of theological schools and the accrediting
agencies which determine the standards and equivalences of
theological education. Many of the institutions of theological instruction around the world look to the United States for
guidelines in preparing programs and in setting norms for ministerial candidates. Perhaps it will come as a surprise to
some, therefore, that numerous extension programs are spring-
ing up in all parts of the United States, that prestigious
seminaries are turning to extension as a supplementary if not
fully alternative form of theological training and that the
accrediting agency for those seminaries has now expressed its
favorable opinion with regard to extension. Institutions and
agencies which want to be up to date in theological education
will have to follow. Otherwise they may soon find that their
policies govern the elite traditional students but have no relevance to the majority of those who are preparing for Christian service.

Most of the associations of theological schools were questioned with regard to programs or policies regarding TEE. The
few responses would indicate that the issue is still being
weighed. Many associations are not willing yet to commit themselves to a program which is so new in their area of the world.
The popular acceptance of extension should force them into
commiting themselves to this movement and helping to maintain
quality ministerial training.

AATS

The American Association of Theological Schools (AATS) formerly gave blanket accreditation to qualified schools which
covered all degrees granted by the institution. Its new policy,
however, is to accredit degrees offered by an institution.
This means that a seminary which chooses to offer credit to extension courses could be risking the accreditation of its whole
M.Div. program, for example. This consideration may be one of
the reasons for reluctance of most seminaries in the United
States to venture into this new mode of theological education.

No opposition to extension studies of excellent quality have
been expressed by the AATS. At a meeting of an AATS committee
on January 11, 1973 Ralph Winter presented a paper entitled
"The Extension Model in Theological Education: What It Is and
What It Can Do." The AATS representatives responded very favorably to the presentation and plan to devote an entire issue
of *Theological Education* to extension later in 1973.

AEBICAM

The Association of Evangelical Bible Institutes and Colleges
of Africa and Madagascar (AEBICAM) is a subsidiary of AEAM
(Association of Evangelicals of Africa and Madagascar). Since
the initial presentation of TEE to AEBICAM in February of 1969
the association has been interested in TEE and a large part of
its activities since then has been directed toward the promotion of this program. It worked with CAMEO in the organization of workshops in 1970 and 1971. In addition, it took the
initiative in conducting longer workshops for writers in 1972
and 1973. Several programmed instructional materials were begun in the workshops and in 1973 are being made ready for distribution. The members of the workshops agree to permit the
distribution of their work throughout all the AEBICAM institutions. Two programmed texts have been published so far.
The moving force behind TEE in Africa has been Fred Holland,
a missionary working in Zambia. One obstacle to the imple-
mentation of the program was the lack of men to write programmed texts in Africa. Mr. Holland returned to the United
States for an intensive study of PI and then began to train
missionaries and African nationals in this educational technique. The production of programmed texts in Africa is largely due to the instruction and coordination that he has given.
In addition to the PI workshops, AEBICAM is planning for
1973 a large number of workshops which will concentrate on the
role of the professor in TEE. Now that available materials
permit institutions to begin their TEE programs, these workshops will give the necessary orientation to those who will
teach and direct extension centers.
In April of 1972 the publication of the *AEBICAM BULLETIN*
began. Although its articles and news items are not restricted to TEE it has helped the movement by announcing workshops,
advising as to materials and giving an introduction to the concepts of TEE and PI.

ALET

The *Asociación Latinoamericana de Escuelas Teológicas* (ALET)
is the Latin American Association of Theological Schools for
the northern region of Latin America. Its jurisdiction extends
from Mexico to Ecuador and includes the Spanish-speaking countries of the Caribbean. It includes college level seminaries
and also the Bible institutes which operate at a lower academic level. ALET's members are generally conservative, but it
also has representation from ecumenical groups.
In the January 1967 annual meeting of ALET in Medellín, Colombia TEE was presented by Ralph Winter. Winter's election as
Executive Secretary of ALET may well have had some influence in
ALET's sponsorship of the Armenia workshop in September of the
same year. This workshop, described in greater detail elsewhere, was very important in promoting TEE throughout much of

Latin America. At that time the regional promoter of ALET for Grand Colombia, Wallace Rehner, was also named Executive Secretary for the new sub-regional association of theological schools, UNICO, although there was no direct connection between the two associations.

At the January 1968 meeting of ALET in Cuernavaca, Mexico TEE was again part of the program. A year later in Managua, Nicaragua, James Emery presented a paper "The Traditional and the Extension Seminary Conflict or Cooperation - Friends or Enemies." This paper and the responses to it are presented in Winter's book *Theological Education by Extension*. The reactions to the presentation indicate that not all of ALET's members consider TEE to be an answer to the problems of theological education in Latin America. Since that time TEE news has been included in the ALET publications, but no special attention has been given to it.

ASIT

The *Asociación Sudamericana de Instituciones Teológicas* - South American Association of Theological Institutions (ASIT) is concerned with the "Southern Cone" of South America. Like ALET, it does not aponsor any extension program. However, some of its member institutions do engage in TEE.

ASIT has informed its members through its bi-monthly bulletins the news regarding TEE, has had one annual workshop devoted to the subject and in other ways has helped to promote the movement. This corresponds to ASIT's purpose of not having any program of its own but rather stimulating the sharing of information and experience among its members so that they can aid one another in this area (Miguez 1973).

ASTE

The *Associacão de Seminários Teológicos Evangélicos* - Association of Evangelical Theological Seminaries (ASTE) is the Brazilian agency similar to ALET or other associations mentioned earlier. It is limited to the one country of Brazil and represents most of the higher academic level institutions in that land. It has become interested in extension because most of its member institutions have some program of extension studies, but has made no official pronouncement regarding the system. In the June, 1970 issue of *Simposio*, the periodical published by ASTE, there appear articles regarding new structures in theological education. One is an adaptation and translation of a section of *Theological Education by Extension* edited by Ralph Winter and a review of the book is also included in this issue (Maraschin 1973).

ATIEA

The Association of Theological Institutions in East Africa
(ATIEA) does not operate any extension program. At least one
of its member institutions does have such a program and more
will be developing extension studies. Although the association is interested in extension education it has not formulated a definite policy toward this mode of theological education (Franklin 1973).

PABATS

The Philippine Association of Bible and Theological Schools
(PABATS) represents the conservative evangelical institutions
in the Philippines. It is perhaps the association of theological schools not related directly to extension which has most
actively promoted and supported the extension movement. Most
of the delegates to the workshops in Manila and Cebu City in
the fall of 1971 were representatives of PABATS institutions
and the conservative committee formed had their full support.
It was called the PABATS TEE Working Committee and PAFTEE also
may be considered almost a subsidiary of PABATS.

ASSOCIATIONS OF EXTENSION INSTITUTIONS

Associations of theological schools are taking increasing
interest in theological education by extension and some of
them are finding a place for it alongside the traditional forms
of ministerial training. At the same time we have seen the
formation of associations of institutions which operate or coordinate extension programs. The first of these associations
was formed in Brazil in 1968. This organization, AETTE, as
well as its Spanish counterpart, ALISTE, have been mentioned
in the earlier historical treatment of the extension seminary
movement. Now there are several such associations and also
committees which may become associations as the adoption of
TEE grows.
The associations are important for their promotion and coordination of TEE in the countries or regions involved. They
have been responsible for organizing workshops, for publishing
catalogs of materials available, for informing others of programs and developments in TEE and in some cases in arranging
for the writing, production and distribution of extension
materials.

AETTE

The *Associacão Evangélica Teológica para Treinamiento por
Extensão* - Evangelical Theological Association for Extension
Training (AETTE) was the first and still is the largest associ-
ation. Theological education by extension principles were in-

troduced to Brazil by Ralph Winter at a workshop in São Paulo in August of 1968. The sixty-five educators present could see the possibilities of TEE for the rapidly growing Church in Brazil. As a consequence, in October of the same year, forty-three delegates gathered to form AETTE. At that time they were further instructed in TEE and in programmed instruction by Peter Savage and Nelson Rosamilha. The association is conservatively evangelical although it includes a wide range of denominational groups.

The annual General Assembly is the highest authority of AETTE. A Directive of six members administers the program, although much of the burden falls on the shoulders of the Executive Secretary. The purposes stated by the association are:

1) To provide methods of teaching by extension and also to prepare texts, manuals and other materials for this type of teaching.

2) To promote congresses, round table discussions, symposiums and interchange reports useful to the associates.

3) To publish the activities of the members of the association (AETTE Constitution Art. 2).

As plans were made and the work began on the production of programmed instructional materials, 1970 was set as the target date for the initiation of the extension programs of the various institutions. However, a few institutions opened centers in 1969 with the use of provisional materials. A graph of the growth of AETTE is presented on page 34.

By January, 1972 twenty programmed texts were in use in the AETTE institutions and several more were produced or revised during the year. Like the Intertexts of CLATT and CATA, the texts have been prepared for those who have completed primary school, since this is the level of greatest need for theological education in Brazil. However, there are hopes that some of the more capable writers who have emerged will turn their talents also to the production of texts for higher level studies (Sturz 1972).

Only about two thirds of the institutions in Brazil which offer extension studies have become full members of AETTE. Even those outside the association, nevertheless, have benefited from the programmed instructional materials prepared and the other activities of AETTE.

From the beginning AETTE suffered from a degree of missionary domination. This was due in large part to the lack of national personnel prepared in the new educational techniques. However, efforts are being made to make this a more indigenous organization.

ALISTE

The Latin American Association of Institutions and Theological Seminaries by Extension (ALISTE) was born at the consultation called by CATA in Medellín, Colombia on January 8-13, 1973. ALISTE is successor to CATA and CLATT. These two organizations

had decided that after five years of service it was time to
turn over the leadership of TEE in Latin America to new structures and persons, particularly Latin Americans. The members
of the previous organizations had been named by UNICO and were
not direct representatives of any institutions. ALISTE, on
the contrary, is an association of theological schools with
extension programs. Fifty-two delegates and observers from
fifteen Spanish-speaking countries and nearly forty institutions attended the meeting in Medellín.

Prior to the formation of ALISTE the delegates, most of whom
had some experience in extension work, discussed the problems
encountered and made several recommendations for more effective cooperation in the future. They agreed that institutions
which reproduce materials prepared elsewhere should pay a 10
per cent royalty to the author or sponsoring institution.
Standard format for materials will be eight and one-half inches
by eleven inches. Levels for extension studies in Latin America were established roughly as follows:

Bachiller - completion of full primary schooling
Certificate A - less than full primary
Certificate B - barely literate

Almost immediately after its formation ALISTE began the publication of a bulletin. In its first issue the functions were
listed and other information regarding decisions made in
Medellín were released. The functions of ALISTE will be: to
publish articles and information regarding extension texts and
other aspects of the extension movement; to provide technical
assistance and training for the preparation of programmed texts,
the administration of the extension program and teaching by extension; to maintain contact with institutions and organizations engaged in extension in other parts of the world; and to
coordinate the production of teaching materials in Spanish. It
was decided to suspend the idea of a single series of Intertexts with assigned authors. Instead, certain areas or objectives of common interest will be established. All the members
will be kept informed about available texts and those in preparation by means of the ALISTE Bulletin. The initiative for
the preparation of new texts remains in the hands of each
author and institution, and the best texts will gain acceptance
by a process of natural selection (Kinsler 1973:3).

PACTEE

The Pakistan Committee for Theological Education by Extension (PACTEE) is more like AETTE or ALISTE in its organization than like TAFTEE in the neighboring country of India. Instead of one extension program with various centers operated
under the direction of seminaries in Pakistan three institutions have their own extension programs and a fourth plans to
open one soon. However, because there are relatively few students within one country, there is closer coordination and control over materials and other standards than in Latin America.

At the CAMEO sponsored workshop on August 9-13, 1971 the
idea of TEE was new to most of the delegates. Nevertheless, at
the conclusion of the workshop a committee was formed, most of
whose ten members were missionaries. This reflected the attendance of twenty-four missionaries and twelve nationals at the
workshop. A coordinator was named and the committee made plans
to prepare for extension studies. The first coordinator was
John Meadowcraft, who had written a twelve-page paper proposing the adoption of TEE in the spring of 1970, nearly a year
and one-half before the idea met with general approval.

When PACTEE met again in August, 1972 initial plans were
formulated and a proposed syllabus was prepared. Classes began in Sealkot in English and assignments for writing and
translating of more materials were made. In November, 1972
the translation of materials permitted the opening of two centers for studies in Urdu as well as the three centers in
English.

The levels and purposes of the three institutions which operated extension programs in 1972 were not uniform. One em-
phasized the continuing education of pastors. Another offered a complete curriculum that would some day lead to the
degree of Bachelor of Theology and would be considered the
basis for ordination, depending on denominational requirements.
The third institution considered extension to be lay training.

PAFTEE

The Philippine Association for Theological Education by
Extension (PAFTEE) was organized on January 25, 1973. It represents thirteen groups which plan to cooperate in extension
programs and charter membership is left open until July, 1973.
At the organizational meeting in Cebu City thirty-nine delegates from twenty-two groups were present. The members of
PAFTEE are in general those which also figure in PABATS, the
association of theological schools in the conservative evangelical tradition. A strong doctrinal statement was included
in the constitution.

The purpose of PAFTEE is to develop and promote TEE among
evangelicals in the Philippines. The PAFTEE Board was charged
with the establishment of policies and guidelines regarding
levels of TEE texts, curriculum standards and format for each
of these levels, the development, testing, production and
pricing of TEE texts, and procedures for the adaptation of
texts into the languages of the Philippines. An Executive
Director, who is to devote at least half of his time to PAFTEE,
will be largely responsible for coordination and administration
of the TEE program.

An introduction to TEE came in the form of workshops in
Manila August 31 to September 3 and in Cebu City September 6
to 10, 1971. The workshops, conducted ably by Covell and
Winter, gathered 115 delegates from twenty-four groups and
seventy-two delegates from eleven groups respectively. Most

of the delegates were from the conservative evangelical
Churches. Two TEE committees were formed, one representing
PABATS and the other the conciliar groups. A national information office on TEE under the direction of Robert Samms was set
up by Philippines Crusades. This office was to serve all
groups. On October 13-14, 1971 PABATS met and named a seven
member committee. The national TEE office published a bulletin and coordinated information and materials for the PABATS
TEE working committee and the conciliar *ad hoc* TEE committee
(Samms 1972:2-3). PAFTEE is not restricted to PABATS members but has a strongly conservative statement of faith.

TAFTEE

The Association for Theological Education by Extension
(TAFTEE) in India functions not so much as a coordinator of
various extension programs as a separate institution which
operates its own extension program. It was formed specifically
for this purpose and is the only agency in India which operates a program which is fully extension in the sense of the
Latin American models. Funds and personnel have been assigned
to TAFTEE by the cooperating theological education institutions.
The formation of this association was remarkably rapid. At
the workshop in Yeotmal on September 14-16, 1970 TEE was first
introduced to many of the delegates. Nevertheless, by the end
of the workshop a seventeen member committee had been formed to
plan for a constitutional assembly the following January. Executive officers were elected, an Executive Director was tenta-
tively named and funds were requested for the operation of
TAFTEE. The Executive Committee met the day following the
workshop to name area coordinators and plan for a workshop on
programmed instruction.
TAFTEE was formally organized on January 14, 1971. It now
has nineteen member bodies. In addition, associate membership
is open to churches and individuals. Associate members may not
vote in assemblies, but receive reports on the activities of
TAFTEE-India. Of the fourteen members of the first Executive
Committee, over half were Indians. One of the objects of
TAFTEE as stated in its constitution is "...to give Biblical
and theological training primarily to committed Christians
for the varied ministries of the church within the context of
local church life and work in the world."
The extension program of TAFTEE began in August, 1971 with
five centers and 120 students. By November, 1972 this number
had grown to 220 students in twelve centers. Only degree or
college level courses have been given so far. Half of the
deans or instructors in the centers have been Indians and efforts are being made to obtain the services of a qualified
Indian as Executive Director.
By the end of 1972 ten courses had been developed on the degree level. However, work had begun also on the production and

translation of extension materials for the diploma level. Seven courses were promised for the end of 1973. These diploma materials will be produced in English but also translated into the four major regional languages of Marathi, Tamil, Telugu and Hindi. The goal is to have thirty courses for the degree level, eighteen for the diploma level and twelve for the certificate level. Thus it can be seen that on the lower levels at least there are no immediate plans to provide a complete theological education. At every level this is considered to be lay training.

TAFTEE has a statement of evangelical faith in its constitution, but is not restricted to one segment of the Protestant community. It is widely representative of the ecumenical as well as the conservative elements within the evangelical tradition. The Church of South India and the Church of North India are not members of TAFTEE but are represented on the Advisory Committees.

UNICO

The Union of Biblical Institutions of Colombia (UNICO) should originally be considered among the supporting agencies for extension. However, it is included here since it became in 1972 an association of theological institutions for Colombia. At that time it ceased to include the other countries of "Greater" Colombia - Panama, Venezuela and Ecuador.

The preliminary formation of UNICO came at the World Vision Pastors Conference in Medellín, Colombia in April, 1967. It was formally established, however, at the workshop in Armenia, Colombia in September, 1967. By that time it was sufficiently formed to act in some way as host of the workshop. Twelve institutions were represented at its first assembly. They made plans to work with Evangelism in Depth during 1968 and to make TEE part of that movement. They also discussed plans for the preparation of a series of pre-theological books for Colombia similar to the set produced in Guatemala. A tentative curriculum for extension studies was also approved. UNICO was formed as the umbrella agency under which CATA would work as a subcommittee. The parent organization requested funds from the Theological Education Fund for distribution to CATA. The request was to include the establishment of a library of extension materials to be the property of ALET. Travel for CATA members, the UNICO committee and authors of Intertexts was budgeted and funds were requested for the initial publication of the texts (Winter 1969:173-4).

In April 21-24, 1968 the UNICO Executive Committee met in Miami and named the members of CATA and agreed that CLATT would function independently of UNICO. The officers of UNICO met again in Mexico City on December 15-16, 1968. At that time CATA was restructured and the international coordinator and regional secretaries were named.

The second assembly of UNICO took place in Medellín, Co-

lombia on April 17, 1969. Fourteen institutions were represented. New officers were elected and the decisions of the Executive Committee regarding CATA and other matters were confirmed. Plans were made for the promotion of TEE throughout
the countries included in UNICO. Nevertheless, for the next
three years the principal function of UNICO was the distribution of funds to the members of CATA. It operated no program
beyond that of its daughter committee.

On June 22, 1972 the third assembly of UNICO was convened.
The occasion was the workshop on programmed instruction sponsored by UNICO in Medellín. Thirty-three delegates from thirteen groups were present. At that time it was decided that
UNICO would serve only the one country. CATA and CLATT would
be replaced by another structure a few months later and the
funds granted by TEF were nearly exhausted. The objectives
for UNICO were restated as follows:

1) Coordinate the preparation, publication and distribution
of programmed materials on all academic levels;

2) Promote and plan workshops for writers and teachers;

3) Communicate the techniques of programming. (*Boletín de
UNICO Vol. I, No. 1).*

UNICO has, since July, 1972, published a bulletin in which
it lists information of interest to its member institutions,
articles regarding TEE and catalogs of materials prepared in
Colombia for extension studies.

REGIONAL OR NATIONAL EXTENSION COMMITTEES

In addition to the associations of extension institutions
there also exist less formally organized committees on TEE.
Some such committees are very loosely structured and some have
not been very active. Therefore, the description of a few
committees which follows does not pretend to be exhaustive.
Ad hoc committees were formed after some workshops in Africa,
but coordination of TEE throughout that region has been primarily the task of AEBICAM. Consequently the committees mentioned below are all found in Asia.

CTEE

At the close of the TEE workshop in Djakarta, Indonesia on
September 7-11, 1970 an *ad hoc* committee was set up. This was
Panitha Pendidikan Teologia Exstensi (CTEE). Although CTEE has
had regular meetings since its formation, even after the workshop on programmed instruction in Sukabuni a year later there
was hesitation on the part of some groups to accept this new
form of ministerial training and the educational philosophy
and method which accompanied it.

Some institutions are thoroughly committed to TEE and have
already initiated extension programs. CTEE will assist these
groups by organizing further workshops, by serving as a clear-

ing house for information and by publishing a bulletin on programmed learning.

Malaysia TEE Fellowship

Malaysia was one of the later Asian countries to have its
own workshop on theological education by extension. A few delegates from Malaysia had been able to attend a workshop with
Peter Savage in Singapore in June of 1971, but for many the
workshop in Kuala Lumpur on September 18-19, 1972 was the first
introduction to TEE and PI. An *ad hoc* committee was formed at
its conclusion. The purpose of the committee was to meet every
three months in order to encourage writing of materials and
sharing of information.
        A three member committee has assumed the name of the TEE
Fellowship. One of its goals is to collect a library of useful books relating to TEE. It seeks to obtain samples of programmed texts and workbooks from other lands, but particularly
from other Asian countries. Another project of the TEE Fellowship has been the publication since January, 1973 of a newsletter concerning TEE in Malaysia.

Taiwan TEE Committee

The structure of TEE in Taiwan falls somewhere between the
unified program found in TAFTEE-India and the other committees
discussed. As a result of the TEE workshops in August, 1970,
an *ad hoc* committee was formed to develop plans for the imple-
mentation of a TEE program. It was decided to begin at the
certificate (but by Latin American standards *bachiller)* level.
The program fit most adequately into the non-denominational
structure of the newly formed China Evangelical Seminary and,
therefore, became that institution's TEE department.
        The extension classes are to be handled by regional centers
in Kaohsiung (Free Methodist Seminary), Hsi-Lo (Conservative
Baptist Theological College), Taichung (Oriental Missionary
Society Theological College) and Taipei. Although classes are
held in these denominational institutions, the regional centers
have regional committees composed of representatives from different denominations which are interested in cooperating in the
TEE program. Classes are not sponsored by the particular denomination but by the China Evangelical Seminary TEE department. Each denominational theological institution acts as a
regional center of the China Evangelical Seminary TEE department.
        The China Evangelical Seminary Board of Trustees appoints
the TEE Committee and its meetings are presided over by the
CES President. The TEE Committee:
        1) Establishes curriculum and approves basic texts
        2) Sets faculty standards, recruits and accredits TEE fa-
culty members
        3) Sets student enrollment policies, procedures and fees

4) Establishes regional centers as needed
5) Nominates Executive Director
6) Prepares annual budget for presentation to CES Board of
Trustees and recommends sources of income (Sprunger 1972).

Thai CoCoTEE

Thai CoCoTEE is the Consultative Committee for Theological
Education by Extension in Thailand. It came into being as a
continuation committee after the workshop in Bangkok on August
16-20, 1971. An eight man provisional committee met again in
October and then in June, 1972, CoCoTEE was established by representatives of nine groups. Among the groups cooperating in
TEE are the Churches of Christ in Thailand and at least one
pentecostal group. The purposes of the committee according to
the first *Thai TEE Bulletin* are:
1) to be a clearing house for collection and dissemination of TEE information and materials;
2) to suggest educational levels for uniformity in Thailand:
3) to suggest a model curriculum;
4) to seek to establish some common functional TEE termino-
logy in Thai;
5) to encourage training in TEE, such as seminars, workshops,
etc.;
6) to investigate common accreditation for TEE within Thailand.
In September of 1972 James Gustafson was elected Coordinator and a Coordinating Committee was named. Thai CoCoTEE
sponsored, along with TAP-Asia, a workshop on programmed instruction in Bangkok from September 25 to October 8, 1972. For
1973 a TEE seminar in Thai has been planned for May 30 to June
1 and one in English will be held later in the year. The committee also decided to publish a quarterly newsletter, to publish the first programmed TEE text in Thai, and to accept a
provisional curriculum of thirty courses. The text produced is
a translation from English of the Book of Acts. Thai materials
are to be prepared at the fourth grade level.

DENOMINATIONAL PROGRAMS AND POLICIES

The extension programs presented up to this point have been
cooperative ventures of several denominations or groups or they
have been denominational programs restricted to one country.
Another structure which is beginning to emerge is a denominational network of extension programs or institutions. Probably this kind of structure is not so generally useful as the
others mentioned, but it is a possibility where linguistic
barriers do not prevent it. Most denominations have not considered the formation of a committee to extend TEE on their
various fields, but some have formulated some policy toward extension studies.

In order to determine denominational programs or policies a
form letter was sent to forty-four representative mission
groups, almost all within the United States. Answers have been
received from some twenty-five of these agencies. It is to be
assumed that those who answered are more likely to be ac-
quainted with or have some opinion regarding this new form of
ministerial training. In general it may be noted that most mission boards have no policy regarding extension, but rather have
left involvement in the program up to the individual fields.
It is to be hoped that in the future more of those responsible
for deciding mission strategy will consider the implications
for church growth of this form of leadership training and that
they will actively encourage its adoption in suitable forms
wherever possible.

Lutherans

Perhaps the denomination which has done most to coordinate
the extension programs in its institutions throughout various
countries is the Lutheran Church in America. Although this denomination seems to have taken the initiative it was joined
by the American Lutheran Church, the Lutheran Church Missouri
Synod, the World Mission Prayer League and the Lutheran World
Federation in a joint effort in TEE in Latin America.
Lutherans in various countries throughout Latin America have
had some exposure to and even experience in TEE for several
years. This was shared at a meeting of representatives from
several countries in Bogotá, Colombia in April of 1971. Preliminary plans took more concrete form in the Consultation of
Lutheran Extension Seminaries in Mexico City on June 8-10,
1972. Of the ten persons present, six represented Lutheran
extension seminaries or departments. It was decided to name a
Continuation Committee of Lutheran Extension Seminaries whose
members would be the directors of those seminaries. Raymond
Rosales of the Extension Department of the Augsburg Lutheran
Seminary in Mexico City was named Coordinator, to assume his
duties in January of 1973. His responsibilities were to carry
out generally what CATA and CLATT were doing for all the extension institutions in Latin America and to maintain contact
with those organizations. Also at this meeting a curriculum of
twenty-eight subjects was drawn up and the budget was established. A request was to be made to the Lutheran World Federation. Meanwhile contributions were received from the participating synods.
The Latin American Secretaries of the mission boards of the
American Lutheran Church, the Lutheran Church in America and
the Lutheran Church Missouri Synod met in New York on August
28-29, 1972, and furthered the cooperative efforts of those
organizations. In Medellín, Colombia during the time of the
CATA Consultation, January 6-12, 1973 the Continuation Committee met again and decided to change its name to CO-EXTENSION
(Coordinating Committee of Lutheran Extension Seminaries in

Spanish America). Authors were assigned to prepare programmed texts for some courses at the diploma and certificate levels. The Coordinator was to edit a quarterly bulletin which would help to coordinate efforts as well as provide stimulation to the several extension programs.

Conservative Baptist Foreign Mission Society

Another mission which should be singled out for special attention is the Conservative Baptist Foreign Mission Society. This mission now sponsors extension programs in seven institutions in five countries and plans to begin TEE in four more institutions soon. However, perhaps its major contribution to the movement as a whole was the publishing in July of 1967 of a collection of documents and comments numbering twenty-two pages regarding the extension seminary movement. It must be remembered that this publicity of the movement took place two months before the very important Armenia workshop. After the Armenia meeting, but before the perhaps equally important Wheaton workshop, Milton G. Baker, Foreign Secretary for the CBFMS, produced the *Decentralized Seminary Bulletin* in 1967 and later two issues of the *Bulletin of Extension Seminary Training* in 1968. These brief periodicals helped to prepare many for an intelligent consideration of TEE later in Wheaton.

Most of the mission boards related to the ecumenical wing of the Church did not respond to the enquiry regarding extension. Of those who did, two are actively promoting extension, two others participate on some fields and one indicated very little knowledge of TEE. Of the nine mission boards of conservative denominations five actively promote or encourage extension, two show some interest and two demonstrated little knowledge of the program. Of the eleven independent missions which responded seven showed active interest, another some interest and two demonstrated little knowledge of TEE. One replied that extension studies are not applicable to its work among tribal Christians. In general it would seem that the independent missions have been more willing to accept this innovation in theological education. This may be due to their having less vested interest in traditional theological education or it may reflect the higher percentage of faith missions in Latin America, which has had a longer history of TEE. In any event it is encouraging to note that more than half of those who responded indicate an active interest in extension although few are promoting it as a matter of policy on all their fields and no denominational or mission program has been set up to coordinate efforts in this area.

MAJOR SOURCE MATERIALS ON THEOLOGICAL EDUCATION
BY EXTENSION

In connection with the preparation of this book permanent archives have been assembled at the School of World Mission of Fuller Theological Seminary. Most of the materials listed in the bibliography are to be found in the archives or in the library of the seminary. A very brief list of materials which follows contains only those books, mimeographed materials or periodicals which are more commonly available to the readers. The address of the periodicals is given and when known the subscription price is also listed.

Books and Manuscripts

COVELL, Ralph R. and WAGNER, C. Peter
1971 *An Extension Seminary Primer*. South Pasadena, California, William Carey Library. 141 pages.

This book was developed for and in workshops on TEE in 1970 and 1971. The biblical basis for ministerial training is considered and various forms of theological education are indicated. The history of the extension movement up to 1971 is set forth with descriptions of some significant programs.

FIELD, Vance R.
1972 "Theological Education by Extension." An unpublished M.Div. thesis, Western Evangelical Seminary. 91 pages.

The thesis explains the principles and philosophy of TEE including the mechanics of how it operates. A brief description of programmed texts is used. The experience of the Christian and Missionary Alliance in Colombia, Indonesia and on other fields with regard to TEE is related. The lack of field experience on the part of the writer limits the book's usefulness.

MULHOLLAND, Kenneth B.
1971 "Theological Education by Extension with Special Reference to Honduras." An unpublished M.S.T. thesis, Lancaster Theological Seminary.

Mulholland gives a valuable analysis of theological education in Latin America today. He also writes of the history of the TEE movement in general and particularly of its usage in Honduras. Perhaps the most interesting sections are those relating to church growth, pre-theological education, accreditation, the role of the teacher in TEE and the relationship of residence and extension.

TEF STAFF
1972 *Ministry in Context: The Third Mandate Programme of the Theological Education Fund (1970-77).* Bromley, Kent, England, TEF.

> One chapter of this book is a valuable evaluation of TEE. It presents the charges of critics, but indicates that they have overstated their case. Although not necessarily related to TEE the discussion of contextualization and the procedures for obtaining financial backing for educational projects are of practical value

WARD, Ted and Margaret
1970 *Programmed Instruction for Theological Education by Extension.* East Lansing, CAMEO.

> This book was developed in the workshops held by Ted Ward in Latin America during the summer of 1969. It is a very helpful introduction to programmed instruction and contains models and insights which will be helpful for anyone preparing this type of educational materials.

WINTER, Ralph D., ed.
1969 *Theological Education by Extension.* South Pasadena, William Carey Library. 617 pages.

> Since its publication this has been the standard work on TEE. A large part of the book is given over to the documents produced in various workshops and to influential articles and mimeographed materials which give the history of the development of the extension seminary movement. The first section is historical. The second deals with the very important CAMEO workshop in Wheaton in December, 1968. The third section is "An Extension Seminary Manual" which provides a description of the structure of TEE, the operation of the center and an analysis of curriculum. This book will be revised and brought up to date soon.

Reports

CAMEO
1971 1970 TEE Workshop Reports

1972 1971 TEE Workshop Reports

> These reports of the workshops held in Africa and Asia in 1970 and 1971 give important historical background to the development of TEE in each of the countries visited. They are available for $1.00 each from:

R. B. Buker, Sr.
CAMEO Coordinator
5010 West Sixth Avenue
Denver, Colorado 80204

STURZ, Richard J.
1972   *"Instrucão Programada no Brasil."* Mimeographed paper.

This short paper gives a description of TEE in Brazil
and a history of AETTE up to January, 1972. It is
available in Portuguese from:
Richard Sturz
Caixa Postal 30.259
SP 01000 Sao Paulo
Brazil

TAP-Asia
1972   "Theological Education by Extension Report."

This booklet contains reports of workshops in Asia in
1972 as well as lists of materials available in that
region and the names and addresses of TEE personnel who
participate in the TAP-Asia program.

TAP-Asia
1973   "Report of the Programmed Instruction Workshops for
Theological Education by Extension."

This booklet contains reports of nine workshops held
in Asia during 1972 and sample lessons from some of the
workshops. Those who want these reports as well as
other detailed TEE information from that area should
send $10.00 for TAP-Asia membership to:
Dr. Bong Ro, S.E. Asia Coordinator
TAP-Asia
33A Chancery Lane
Singapore 11

Periodicals

AETTE Bulletin

Quarterly bulletin published since 1968 by AETTE. It
has news of TEE in Brazil, catalogs of materials and
articles of interested. Published in Portuguese.
AETTE
Caixa Postal 5938
01000 Sao Paulo, S.P.
Brazil

AEBICAM Bulletin

Quarterly bulletin since April, 1972. It contains news
of TEE in Africa and particularly the activities of
AEBICAM. It is not restricted to TEE.
AEBICAM
Fred Holland
Box 131
Choma, Zambia

ALISTE Bulletin

Bi-monthly since February, 1973. It contains news of
ALISTE, schedules of workshops, catalogs of materials
in Spanish. Published in Spanish, sent air mail. In-
dividual membership in ALISTE is $6.00 per year.
Wayne C. Weld
ALISTE Treasurer
Apartado Aéreo 3041
Medellín, Colombia

CAMEO Releases

Irregular publication, roughly twice yearly since
Spring, 1968. It lists the activities of CAMEO with a
large proportion given to TEE. The releases contain
news of workshops and publications, catalogs of materials.
R. B. Buker, Sr.
CAMEO Coordinator
5010 West Sixth Avenue
Denver, Colorado 80204

EXTENSION

Monthly air mail newsletter on TEE since November,
1972. It contains a brief summary of TEE worldwide,
indicating workshops, materials available and short
articles and reports. Subscription is $5.00 per year.
EXTENSION
135 North Oakland Avenue
Pasadena, California 91101

EXTENSION SEMINARY

Formerly the Evangelical Seminary. Quarterly since
1966. This was the first and has been the most extensive periodical on TEE. It contains longer articles
as well as news of the movement. Published in English
and Spanish. It will supplement the ALISTE Bulletin
prepared by the same people.

EXTENSION SEMINARY
Apartado 1881
Guatemala, Guatemala

NEWSLETTER OF THE MALAYSIA TEE FELLOWSHIP

Since January, 1973. It contains TEE news, especially
of Malaysia.
Rev. Duain Vierow
21 Jalan Abdul Samad
Kuala Lumpur, Malaysia

PROGRAMMING NEWS

Published quarterly by TAP of the World Evangelical
Fellowship. Since July, 1971 it has offered articles
on programming and indicated source materials. $2.00
air mail per year and $1.00 surface mail per year.
John E. Langlois
Merevale, Forest
Guernsey, Channel Islands
United Kingdom

TEE BULLETIN - PHILIPPINES

Quarterly since 1972. It contains TEE news from the
Philippines and some from other areas. Some of the
articles are longer.
PAFTEE
Box 1416
Manila, Philippines

THAI TEE BULLETIN

Quarterly since February, 1973. News of TEE in
Thailand and other lands. Sponsored by Thai CoCoTEE.
It contains a bibliography of texts on programmed
instruction in the first issue. Published in English
and Thai.
Thai CoCoTEE
422/3 Suan Plu
Bangkok, Thailand

THEOLOGICAL NEWS

Published quarterly by TAP of The World Evangelical
Fellowship. It is concerned with theological educa-
tion in general, but gives considerable attention to
TEE. It demonstrates special interest in the TAP-
Asia programs. $2.00 air mail per year. $1.00 sur-
face mail per year.

John E. Langlois
Merevale, Forest
Guernsey, Channel Islands
United Kingdom

UNICO BULLETIN

Published since July, 1972. It concerns TEE in Co-
lombia and other areas. Shorter articles and cata-
logs of materials are included. Edited in Spanish.
UNICO
Vernon Reimer
Apartado Aereo 5945
Cali, Colombia

Workshops and Consultations Relating to TEE

Workshops on theological education by extension and later on programmed instruction have been very important in the expansion of the concept and methods of the extension movement. This is clearly an area in which the conservative evangelicals have taken a lead and in part this accounts for their domination of the movement in most areas. TEE was introduced in Africa and Asia by consultations sponsored by CAMEO and it has been TAP in Asia and AEBICAM in Africa which have continued the coordination of information on the new programs. After the initial impulse from outside many regions and countries are organizing their own consultations and workshops with local resource personnel largely trained in the earlier workshops.

The number of workshops has been astounding. Already by the middle of 1973 there had been a dozen workshops and requests for more are constantly being expressed. Because of the great number they can only be treated very briefly here. After a chronological list of all the workshops and consultations held so far, a brief description of their importance in each country or region will be presented. It would seem that those countries which have advanced most in the movement are those which have had more periods of instruction and orientation. Before listing them, therefore, let us consider the strengths and weaknesses of the workshops, some suggestions for further workshops and some reactions of those who have attended them.

THE CONTRIBUTION OF WORKSHOPS

The basic purpose of the earlier workshops on theological education by extension was to introduce the idea and show how this innovation in pastoral training could be relevant to the situation of the delegates to the workshop. The need for

trained leaders, the biblical concepts of the ministry and other
arguments such as those presented in the first chapter of this
book were expressed. Theological educators were made to see
the inadequacy of their own programs and curricula for the preparation of a sufficient number of leaders for the churches.
The first workshops depended heavily on the Guatemala model and
promoted the use of materials produced in the Presbyterian Seminary there since nothing else was available.

By 1969 workshops were being organized specifically for writers. With Ted Ward's four South American workshops in September and October of 1969, programmed instruction was seen as a
necessity for the production of satisfactory extension materials. From that time programmed instruction has been included
as a necessary element of the extension system. While it may
be advisable to begin studies with provisional materials, non-
programmed texts are recognized as stop-gap materials to be replaced as soon as possible. In the longer workshops it was
even possible to produce at least some lessons of materials to
be used in local programs. It was felt that at least five full
days were needed in order to get past the theory into the actual writing of programmed instruction.

Perhaps one type of workshop which will be increasingly
held with local resource people is that for professors. Administrative procedures can be worked out from the models giv-
en. Programmed and provisional materials are being constantly
produced. The element that is lacking is the well motivated
and qualified director of an extension center and those who
direct the learning experiences in the weekly seminar. Because
curriculum, administration and a myriad of other local factors
enter at this point it is of necessity that the professors be
trained locally. For this reason the organization of this kind
of workshop of one or two days duration or longer has been
carried out in many areas and will be frequent in others, but
will not attract attention of those not directly concerned.

Workshops have been limited in their effectiveness by linguistic problems. In some cases workshops had to be limited
to English with the consequent exclusion of many national
leaders. In other cases the translation has been inadequate
with resulting frustration for all concerned. This problem
will be alleviated as more and more persons, particularly nationals, master the concepts of extension and programmed instruction and work out suitable translations for technical
terms.

Another difficulty in later workshops was the wide difference in previous experience and study of extension and programming. In some cases it was advantageous to divide the
sessions into two groups. The basics of TEE were presented to
those recently aware of the program while the more advanced
group discussed curriculum, other aspects of extension or programmed instruction. In many cases this produced an unhappy
division between missionaries and nationals. The differences
in teaching experience and academic preparation of the parti-

cipants in the workshops was less important. The translation
of some of the basic materials on extension and programming
will help to narrow the gap between workshop participants.
In some cases this translation has been done for some information to be presented and has minimized the obstacle.

Despite the difficulties mentioned, workshops and consultations on TEE and PIM have made several important contributions
to the movement. First of all they have served to disseminate
the ideas of extension and its tools to missionaries and nationals in most parts of the world. In almost every country
there are persons who have indicated their intention to initiate extension programs although many groups are waiting to
do so until programmed instructional materials have been prepared.

Committees have been formed at the end of several workshops
which have served to promote and coordinate TEE nationally or
regionally on a permanent basis. Even the bringing together of
interested people for fellowship has been helpful, but at the
end of many workshops time has been set aside for local planning. Where associations or formal committees still do not
exist there is at least some provision for the sharing of information about extension.

The workshops have been conducted by men with expertise and
experience in the education of adults. The sessions themselves
have often served to introduce to the participants non-lecture
methods of teaching. Those who have attended have been forced
into the actual writing of sample frames and have learned by
experience how the weekly seminar may operate. The participants leave believing that extension can work and that it is
possible to program materials because they have done it.

In almost every workshop able persons with a gift for programming have appeared. Some of these people are already recognized now as experts. A participant in one workshop may be
asked to assist in a later workshop. This means that the high
cost of sending a few experts from the United States and Latin
America must not be continually repeated. On every continent
men and women have been prepared to continue as local resource
people for further workshops and consultation.

Many of the important mimeographed and printed papers on
extension have been prepared for workshops. Perhaps without
this target date and specific purpose many of the ideas would
not have been worked out for the benefit of many others beginning to work in extension. It should be remembered also
that a large part of Winter's book on *Theological Education by
Extension* has to do with the workshops in Armenia, Colombia and
Wheaton, Illinois. Ward's book, *Programmed Instruction for
Theological Education by Extension* was worked out through participation in four workshops in Latin America in 1969. The *Extension Seminary Primer* of Covell and Wagner grew out of their
experiences in workshops in Asia in 1970 and from the lectures
which they prepared for those workshops. These three books
have served as a basis of discussion in later workshops and

consultations, but more importantly they have provided the
background reading essential for more meaningful participation. The mimeographed materials are too numerous to mention,
but it is to be hoped that some of them will be prepared for
wider distribution among those who can profit from their study.
    With this introduction to the workshops, let us proceed to
examine the development of this phenomenon of the last few
years which has taken the concepts of theological education by
extension and programmed instruction to those searching for
a more adequate way to meet the ministerial training needs of
growing and increasingly indigenized churches. But first let
us see what the workshop participants said of their experiences.

"Amazing that so much could be achieved in so short a time."

"This workshop has been valuable in opening my eyes to a
whole area of educational techniques of which I have not heard
before."

"The writing of programmed frames has brought understanding
of what ought to be done - there is nothing like actually trying to write them."

"It has been revolutionary to realize the value of planning
the course from the students' point of view..."

"I gained an understanding of the prior questions and
foundational considerations in developing extension programs."

"I found new ways of assisting pastors in solving their own
problems."

"The workshop brought understanding of new techniques and
methods and the discovery of personal talents in doing them."

"During the workshop I gained new insight into the Western-
isms in our training programs."

"Learning to differentiate between important and peripheral
and how PI assists in this learning procedure."

"PI seemed impractical, but I change my attitude because I
actually did it."

"Never heard of PI or the extension seminary before - a new
understanding of what is possible."

"I have a new desire to produce material relevant to African
culture."

A CHRONOLOGICAL LIST OF WORKSHOPS

DATE	PLACE	RESOURCE PERSONS	PARTI-CIPANTS	GROUPS
		1966		
May	Quito, Ecuador	Hopewell, Bonilla	10	3
		1967		
Sept. 4-9	Armenia, Colombia	Winter, Kinsler, Wagner, Walker	28	15
		1968		
Apr. 25-26	Philadelphia, PA	Rowen, Wagner Luttrell	24	21
Aug.	Quito, Ecuador	Winter	25	
Aug. 3-7	Cochabamba, Bolivia	Winter	121	27
Aug. 8-9	São Paulo, Brazil	Winter	65	
Dec. 19-21	Wheaton, Illinois	Winter, Wagner, Rowen	121	30
		1969		
Jan.	Cochabamba, Bolivia	Savage	25	4
Jan.	La Paz, Bolivia	Savage	16	5
Feb.	Lamas, Peru	Wagner	25	4
Feb.	Cochabamba, Bolivia	Savage	30	
Feb.	Limuru, Kenya	Buker		
Aug. 8-12	Cochabamba, Bolivia	Kinsler	25	
Aug. 19-23	Medellín, Colombia	Kinsler	15	
Sep. 10-15	Recife, Brazil	Ward	14	
Sep. 17-22	São Paulo, Brazil	Ward	16	
Sep.25-Oct. 1	Cochabamba, Bolivia	Ward	13	
Oct. 6-10	Medellín, Colombia	Ward	7	

DATE	PLACE	RESOURCE PERSONS	PARTI-CIPANTS	GROUPS
		1970		
Jan. 5-9	Wheaton, Illinois	Ford		
July 6-17	Wheaton, Illinois	Ward		
Aug. 4-7	Jos, Nigeria	Ward, Rowen	31	18
Aug. 10-14	Addis Ababa, Ethiopia	Ward, Rowen	32	
Aug. 17-21	Salisbury, Rhodesia	Ward, Rowen	27	14
Aug. 24-28	Limuru, Kenya	Ward, Rowen	25	7
Aug. 24-26	Taipei, Taiwan	Covell, Wagner	26	17
Aug. 26-28	Taichung, Taiwan	Covell, Wagner	30	18
Aug. 31-Sep. 4	Saigon, Vietnam	Covell, Wagner	80	
Sep. 7-11	Djakarta, Indonesia	Covell, Wagner	47	15
Sep. 14-18	Yeotmal, India	Covell, Wagner	46	24
Sep. 12	Singapore	Covell, Wagner	7	3
		1971		
Jan. 5-8	London, England	Savage	40	26
Mar. 2-4	Jamaica	Buker, Alexander		
Mar. 1-6	London, England	Savage	5	
Mar. 8-12	Madrid, Spain	Savage	26	3
May	Fort Worth, Texas	Ford	15	
May	São Paulo, Brazil	Ford	31	
May	São Luis, Brazil	Ford	20	
June 14-	Singapore	Savage	30	20
June 30-July	Bangalore, India	Savage	30	15
Aug. 2-7	Monrovia, Liberia	Alexander, Bates	22	11
Aug. 9-14	Yamoussoukro, Ivory Coast	Alexander, Bates	45	18

DATE	PLACE	RESOURCE PERSONS	PARTI- CIPANTS	GROUPS

1971

DATE	PLACE	RESOURCE PERSONS	PARTICIPANTS	GROUPS
Aug. 10-14	Gujranwala, Pakistan	Covell, Winter	34	10
Aug.	Wheaton, Illinois	Ward, Rowen	(19 countries)	
Aug. 16-21	Kinshasa, Zaire	Alexander, Bates	16	7
Aug. 16-20	Bangkok, Thailand	Covell, Winter	40	13
Aug. 23-28	Bukavu, Zaire	Alexander, Bates	35	13
Aug. 23-24	Kowloon, Hong Kong	Covell, Winter	38	11
Aug. 21	Singapore	Covell, Winter	9	
Aug. 27	Taipei, Taiwan	Winter	21	6
Aug. 30- Sep. 3	Manila, Philippines	Covell, Winter	115	24
Sep. 6-10	Cebu City, Philippines	Covell, Winter	72	11
Sep. 13-14	Osaka, Japan	Covell, Winter	69	13
Sep. 15-16	Tokyo, Japan	Covell, Winter	171	8
Sep.	Manzini, Swaziland	Alexander, Holland	30	9
Sep. 7-10	Tananarive, Madagascar	Alexander, White	11	1
Dec. 2-4	Saltillo, Mexico	Finkbeiner	20	5

1972

DATE	PLACE	RESOURCE PERSONS	PARTICIPANTS	GROUPS
Jan. 24- Feb. 25	Salisbury, Rhodesia	Holland	16	9
Mar. 6- Apr. 7	Jos, Nigeria	Holland	14	5
Feb. 1-7	Asunción, Paraguay	Savage		5
Feb. 12	Bangkok, Thailand	McCleary	11	9
Feb. 14	Kuala Lumpur, Malaysia	McCleary	30	4
Feb. 16	Singapore	McCleary		3
Feb. 18	Djakarta, Indonesia	McCleary	18	6
Mar.	Iquitos, Peru	Savage	31	3

DATE	PLACE	RESOURCE PERSONS	PARTI-CIPANTS	GROUPS

1972

Mar.	Lima, Peru	Savage	40	7
Mar. 20-25	Wheaton, Illinois	Sharp		
May 29- June 9	Fort Worth, Texas	Ford		
June 7-9	Haiti	Alexander, Sauder	72	10
June 10-23	Medellín, Colombia	Savage	33	13
July 3-14	Beirut, Lebanon	Darnauer, Dainton	17	
July	Wheaton, Illinois	Ward, Rowen		
Aug. 14-31	Hualien, Taiwan	Savage	13	11
Aug.	Banz, New Guinea	McCleary, Harrison	20	
Aug. 28- Sep. 8	Manila, Philippines	McCleary, Harrison	30	
Sep. 4-18	Natrang, S. Vietnam	McCleary	8	
Sep. 3-24	Sukabuni, Indonesia	Savage, Dainton	30	7
Sep. 18-29	Kuala Lumpur, Malaysia	Savage	21	9
Sep. 25- Oct. 6	Bangkok, Thailand	Dainton	22	8
Oct.	Yeotmal, India	Savage	16	
Oct.	Tamworth, Australia	Morris		
Nov. 8-10	Torreón, Mexico	Finkbeiner	20	6
Dec. 15-17	Gujranwala, Pakistan			

1973

Jan. 10-25	Salisbury, Rhodesia	Crider	6	3
Jan. 15-20	Baguio, Philippines	Harrison	21	8

		RESOURCE	PARTI-	
DATE	PLACE	PERSONS	CIPANTS	GROUPS

1973

Jan. 22-27	Cebu City, Philippines	Harrison	41	9
Jan. 29- Feb. 3	Davao City, Philippines	Harrison	36	9
Jan. 29-30		Taiwan	21	8
Feb. 12-16	Armidale, Australia	Harrison	7	2
Feb. 19-23	Farmington, Mich.	Ward, Rowen		
Feb. 12- Mar. 9	Jos, Nigeria	Holland	32	11
Mar. 19-24	Wheaton, Illinois	Sharp		
May 14- June 9		Kenya	Holland	

WORKSHOPS BY COUNTRIES

DATE	PLACE	RESOURCE PERSONS	SPONSOR	PARTI-CIPANTS	GROUPS

AUSTRALIA

| Oct. 1972 | Tamworth | Morris | Anglican Diocese | | 1 |

This was a one day introduction to TEE for a small group of Anglican clergy and lay people (Harrison 1973).

| Feb. 12-16 1973 | Armidale | Harrison | Anglican Diocese | 7 | 1 |

It was noted that although the Christian and Missionary Alliance had the largest extension program at the time, the Anglican Church has the greatest potential in terms of areas and numbers of students. Other denominations have become interested in exrension (Harrison 1973).

| | | RESOURCE | | PARTI- | |
| DATE | PLACE | PERSONS | SPONSOR | CIPANTS | GROUPS |

BOLIVIA

| Aug. 3-7 1968 | Cochabamba | Winter | ABET | 121 | 27 |

This meeting gave an impulse to the formation of the George Allan Seminary in Cochabamba and to other TEE programs. Half of the participants in the workshop were nationals. This appears to be the first introduction of programmed instruction into the planning of TEE through the presentations of Peter Savage (Winter 1969:193-195).

| Jan. 1969 | Cochabamba | Savage | Baptists | 25 | 4 |

This workshop held at the Baptist Theological Seminary was primarily to train writers for CLATT texts. However, it served to orient the teaching staff of the institutions represented as to the principles of TEE. As a result of this workshop the Baptist Seminary launched its extension program in five centers (Savage 1969).

| Jan. 1969 | La Paz | Savage | | 16 | 5 |

The purpose was to help writers prepare certificate level books for the Aymaras. A committee for Aymara texts was formed that soon produced a bilingual book on Acts. This committee helped to initiate Aymara extension studies in two institutions (Savage 1969).

| Feb. 1969 | Cochabamba | Savage | | 30 | |

Basic orientation on TEE and PI (Savage 1969).

| Aug. 8 1969 | Cochabamba | Kinsler | CATA | 25 | |

The workshop was primarily for the ten Intertext authors who attended and drew participants from four countries. One of the results was to stimulate the desire for a later workshop among the Anglicans and Baptists of Northern Argentina (Kinsler 1969).

| Sept. 25- Oct. 1 1969 | Cochabamba | Ward | CAMEO | 13 | |

This workshop was to teach PI principles mainly to CATA authors *(CAMEO Release No. 3)*.

		RESOURCE		PARTI-	
DATE	PLACE	PERSONS	SPONSOR	CIPANTS	GROUPS

BRAZIL

Aug. 8,9   São Paulo   Winter   65
1968

This workshop gave the initial push to extension in
Brazil although a few individuals had heard of the
program earlier. Two months after the workshop
AETTE was formed as forty-three delegates gathered
and were aided by Peter Savage and Nelson Rosamilha
(Winter 1969:205).

Sep. 10-15 Recife   Ward   CAMEO   14
1969

Sep. 17-22 São Paulo   Ward   CAMEO   16
1969

Basic instruction in programming was given and this
permitted the rapid development of programmed texts
in the Brazilian extension program (*CAMEO Release
No. 3*).

May   São Paulo   Ford   CAMEO   31
1971

May   São Luis   Ford   CAMEO   20
1971

More advanced instruction and aid in the preparation of programmed instructional materials were
given. As a result of these workshops work has advanced on nearly thirty programmed texts to the
present (*CAMEO 1972:51-54*).

DATE	PLACE	RESOURCE PERSONS	SPONSOR	PARTI- CIPANTS	GROUPS

COLOMBIA

Sep. 4-9 1967	Armenia	Winter, Wagner Walker, Kinsler	ALET	28	15

This was the decisive meeting for the introduction of TEE in most of Latin America. The publication of the workshop report was the first major
source material for the study of this new movement.
As a direct result of the workshop UNICO and subsequently CATA and CLATT were formed. The workshop laid tentative plans for the operation of
these agencies set into motion (Winter 1969:148-
178).

Aug. -23 1968	Medellín	Kinsler	CATA	15	

The primary purpose of the workshop was for the
orientation and stimulation of the authors assigned by CLATT and CATA. Seven of them were
present at this workshop. However, others also
were interested in and helped to begin the writing of extension materials (Kinsler 1969).

Oct. 6-10 1969	Medellín	Ward	CAMEO	7	

Ward introduced programmed instructional principles
which were completely new for most of the CATA
authors of this region. The workshop caused a complete revision in the work done to that time on extension materials (*CAMEO Release No. 3*).

June 10-23 1972	Medellín	Savage	UNICO	33	13

General orientation to TEE, curriculum design and
other concepts in education and an introduction to
programmed instruction were given the first week.
The second week was devoted to the use of an audio
visual presentation of PI for potential authors.
At this workshop UNICO held its first assembly in
over three years and was given new direction in
activities and in limiting itself to Colombia
(*UNICO Vol. I, No. 1*).

		RESOURCE		PARTI-	
DATE	PLACE	PERSONS	SPONSOR	CIPANTS	GROUPS

ECUADOR

| May 1966 | Quito | Hopewell, Bonilla | TEF | 10+ | 3 |

Hopewell of TEF and Bonilla, then Secretary of
ALIB, which later became ALET, advised as to the
possibilities of decentralized theological education. Hopewell described the program of the Presbyterian Seminary in Guatemala. As a result of
the workshop plans were drawn up later for the in-
auguration of the Center of Theological Studies,
CET, which was one of the pioneer programs in
TEE (CET n.d.)

| Aug. 1968 | Quito | Winter | | 25 | |

Orientation as to curriculum and goals as well as
a general introduction to TEE.

ENGLAND

| Jan. 5-8 1971 | London | Savage | CAMEO | 40 | 26 |

Those who attended were mostly missionaries from
other countries. Several of them were looking for
ideas as to how to improve the TEE programs in their
own countries but others heard for the first time
about TEE. Subsequent to the workshop considerable
interest in TEE was expressed in England (Savage
1971).

| Mar. 1-6 1971 | London | Savage | | 5 | |

This introduction to PI was sparsely attended due
to the postal strike (Savage 1973).

DATE	PLACE	RESOURCE PERSONS	SPONSOR	PARTI-CIPANTS	GROUPS

ETHIOPIA

Aug. 10-14 Addis Ababa Ward, Rowen   CAMEO   32
1970

Eleven potential producers of programmed instructional materials attended the workshop. At the
end an informal association was formed of the representatives of the participating groups (CAMEO
1971:1-3).

HAITI

June 7-9   Port-au-Prince Alexander,   72   10
1972   Sauder

Although TEE had begun a year earlier this was the
introduction of many to the program. The other
church groups were able to learn from the experience of the West Indies Mission and the Missionary
Church programs as well as to learn something of
programmed instruction. Subsequent to this workshop smaller seminars were organized for teachers
in the extension program (*CAMEO Release No. 7*).

HONG KONG

Aug. 24-25 Kowloon   Covell, Winter CAMEO   38   15
1971

TEE principles and programs were explained. A
consultative committee of five members was formed.
However, many delegates believed that because Hong
Kong presents no geographical obstacles to study
the more traditional night school studies were
adequate for training those who could not attend a
residence program (CAMEO 1972:6).

| | | RESOURCE | | PARTI- | |
| DATE | PLACE | PERSONS | SPONSOR | CIPANTS | GROUPS |

INDIA

Sep. 14-18 Yeotmal   Covell, Wagner CAMEO   46   24
1970

A general orientation to TEE was given although
some were already interested in the program. The
possibility of exclusion of missionaries in the
future gives urgency to the training of national
leaders. A seventeen member planning committee was
formed which was the informal beginning of TAFTEE.
An executive director was named and funds were
sought for the operation of the program. A constitutional meeting for TAFTEE was set for January,
1971. Eighteen nationals attended the workshop
and several were named to the committee (Wagner
1970b).

June   Bangalore   Savage   TAP   30   15
1971

Programmed instruction was introduced and some
authors were assigned to prepare materials *(Extension Seminary 1971, 4:7)*.

Oct.   Savage   TAP   16
1972

The emphasis of this workshop was to encourage
those who had begun writing and to help others to
start. Curriculum planning was an important item.
TAFTEE assigned some persons to work full time in
the preparation of materials. Some of the participants were more advanced than others (TAP 1973:7).

| | | RESOURCE | | PARTI- | |
| DATE | PLACE | PERSONS | SPONSOR | CIPANTS | GROUPS |

INDONESIA

| Sep. 7-11
1970 | Djakarta | Covell, Wagner | CAMEO | 47 | 15 |

Eighteen nationals were among the participants.
After the introduction to TEE an *ad hoc* committee
was formed *(Panitha Pendidikan Teologia Ekstensi* -
CTEE) to work out a program of extension. It was
decided to upgrade the theological training of the
pastors before providing lay training (Nanfelt 1970).

| Feb. 18
1972 | Djakarta | McCleary | TAP | 18 | 6 |

Slight knowledge of TEE was manifested by some of
those who attended this consultation. Nevertheless
the Southern Baptists and the Assemblies of God
were pressing ahead with their programs (McCleary
1972).

| Sep. 3-24
1972 | Sukabuni | Savage, Dainton | TAP | 30 | 7 |

Attention was given to theological education objectives. Most of the time was spent in intensive
training of writers in programmed instruction. The
section led in English by Savage was more advanced
than the section led in Indonesian by Dainton.
This was largely due to the lack of materials in Indonesian. Extension programs of the National Council of Churches, the Southern Baptists and the Christian and Missionary Alliance were stimulated (TAP
1973:4-5).

| | | RESOURCE | | PARTI- | |
| DATE | PLACE | PERSONS | SPONSOR | CIPANTS | GROUPS |

IVORY COAST

Aug. 9-13 Yamoussoukro Alexander, Bates CAMEO   45   18
1971   Holland

Delegates included twenty-four nationals and representatives from five countries - Upper Volta,
Mali, Dahomey, Niger and Ivory Coast. Plans were
made for writing materials for Francophone Africa
and for the translation of materials from English
to French. Eight persons volunteered to prepare
courses for extension. Three persons planned to
write programmed instructional materials. Six delegates indicated plans to begin TEE programs
(CAMEO 1972:25-26).

JAPAN

Sep. 13-14 Osaka   Covell, Winter CAMEO   69   13
1971
A general introduction to TEE was given. Because
of strong professional ideas of the clergy and
pride in academic attainment the idea of extension
training for pastors was not readily accepted. It
had been mistakenly translated as lay training
(CAMEO 1972:18-19).

Sep. 15-16 Tokyo   Covell, Winter CAMEO   171   8
1971
It was felt that the two day presentation (some
were not present the first day) was too short to
give an adequate explanation of TEE. The delegates
may be classified as follows: missionaries 17,
pastors 26, laymen 18 and seminary students 110.
Greater interest was shown on the part of the missionaries than among the pastors. The older leadership was not enthusiastic but would investigate the
possibilities (CAMEO 1972:16-17).

DATE	PLACE	RESOURCE PERSONS	SPONSOR	PARTI-CIPANTS	GROUPS

KENYA

DATE	PLACE	RESOURCE PERSONS	SPONSOR	PARTICIPANTS	GROUPS
Feb. 1969	Limuru	Buker	AEBICAM	25	7

At the regular meeting of AEAM, AEBICAM set up a meeting for Buker to present TEE. Some of those present indicated the intention to begin writing programmed materials. Extension was seen as a solution first to the problem of continuing education of the pastors. Plans were made for continuing exchange of information among those interested. Representatives were present from Tanzania, Uganda and Zaire as well as the Ivory Coast *(CAMEO Release No. 2)*.

DATE	PLACE	RESOURCE PERSONS	SPONSOR	PARTICIPANTS
Aug. 24-28 1970	Limuru	Ward, Rowen	CAMEO	25

Principles of TEE and PI were presented. The goals mentioned in the first workshop were repeated (CAMEO 1971:10-12).

LEBANON

DATE	PLACE	RESOURCE PERSONS	PARTICIPANTS	GROUPS
July 13-14 1972	Beirut	Darnauer, Dainton	17	17

Participants came from Lebanon, Jordan, Egypt and North Africa. Six Egyptian nationals participated. An introduction to TEE and PI was given. The delegates were able to practice writing objectives and short programs *(CAMEO Release No. 7)*.

DATE	PLACE	RESOURCE PERSONS	SPONSOR	PARTI-CIPANTS	GROUPS

LIBERIA

Aug. 2-7 1971	Monrovia	Alexander, Bates	CAMEO	22	11

Delegates included one from Nigeria and three from the Sierra Leone Bible College. Fourteen were nationals. Eleven indicated intentions of doing TEE and two said they would write PI. The problem of illiteracy was discussed. Radio Station ELWA was willing to use radio time to broadcast PI lessons for TEE (CAMEO 1972:21-24).

MADAGASCAR

Sep. 7-10 1971	Tananarive	Alexander,	CAMEO	11	1

Plans were made for the establishment of three to five extension centers after the introduction to TEE had been made. Materials will be translated into French. The decentralized seminary program was to be sponsored by the Malagasy Baptist Association with the assistance of missionary professors. Six nationals were among the delegates (CAMEO 1972: 32-35).

MALAYSIA

Feb. 14 1972	Kuala Lumpur	McCleary	TAP	30	4

Preparations had been made for TEE but no programs existed yet (McCleary 1972).

Sep. 18-19 1972	Kuala Lumpur	Savage		21	8

TEE and PI were introduced. Eleven members of the workshop formed an *ad hoc* committee for meetings every three months to encourage writing of materials and sharing of information. Four delegates were from Indonesia. Two schools already reported attendance of 222 students in extension programs (TAP 1973:6).

DATE	PLACE	RESOURCE PERSONS	SPONSOR	PARTI-CIPANTS	GROUPS

MEXICO

Dec. 2-4 1971	Saltillo	Finkbeiner		20	5

(Extension Seminary 1972, 2:7).

Nov. 8-10 1972	Torreón	Finkbeiner		20	6

Most of those who attended were not familiar with
TEE although some programs had been in operation in
Mexico for several years. One of the results of the
workshop was a change in attitude on the part of
some denominational leaders. Materials for the
workshop had to be translated into Spanish and there
was some difficulty with technical terms (Finkbeiner
1972).

NEW GUINEA

Aug. 1972	Banz	McCleary, Harrison	TAP	20	

The workshop was held in English with the result
that participation by New Guineans was limited. It
was decided to concentrate first on the continuing
education of pastors before launching lay training
programs (TAP-Asia 1972b).

DATE	PLACE	RESOURCE PERSONS	SPONSOR	PARTI-CIPANTS	GROUPS

NIGERIA

Aug. 3-8 1970	Jos	Ward, Rowen	CAMEO	31	28

Programmed instruction methods were studied. Attention was given to curriculum planning. No immediate plans for TEE were made, but it was planned to use PI in correspondence courses (CAMEO 1971:5-6,8).

Mar. 6- Apr. 7 1972	Jos	Holland	AEBICAM	14	

This month long workshop allowed the actual production of parts of programmed materials to be used in TEE in Anglophone Africa. Seven courses were begun and would be sent to the AEBICAM office for approval, reproduction and distribution. During the workshop *Talking with God* by Fred and Grace Holland came off the press. This book on prayer was the first programmed extension text for Africa *(AEBICAM Bulletin, April, 1972)*.

WEST PAKISTAN

Aug. 9-13 1971	Gujranwala	Covell, Winter	CAMEO	34	10

This was an introduction to TEE for most of the participants in the workshop. As a result of the meetings CTEE, the Pakistan committee to continue and coordinate TEE was formed (CAMEO 1972:1-4).

DATE	PLACE	RESOURCE PERSONS	SPONSOR	PARTI- CIPANTS	GROUPS

PARAGUAY

Feb. 1-7 1972	Asunción	Savage		5	

This workshop included representatives from Chile
and Argentina. In addition to the introduction of
TEE and PI for many, there was sharing of information about programs already in operation. The Anglican Diocese of Northern Argentina and Paraguay already had a TEE program among the Matacos Indians.
The Southern Baptists were closing their residence
program in Paraguay in 1973 to go into TEE. The
Brethren *Facultad Evangélica* in Asunción initiated
TEE in 1972. The Assemblies of God were also considering TEE *(Extension Seminary 1972, 2:6).*

PERU

Feb. 1969	Lamas	Wagner		25	4

The workshop oriented the participants to TEE and
also to PI. Two of the four institutions represented made plans for beginning extension programs
in their area of the country. Two authors for
Intertexts were discovered through this workshop
(Savage 1969).

Mar. 1972	Iquitos	Savage		31	3

Mar. 1972	Lima	Savage		40	7

In both of the workshops above small group discussion was based on eight study papers. There was
an opportunity for each one to gain practical experience in programming principles and various educational methods (Extension Seminary 1972, 2:7-8).

DATE	PLACE	RESOURCE PERSONS	SPONSOR	PARTI- CIPANTS	GROUPS

PHILIPPINES

| Aug. 31-
Sep. 3
1971 | Manila | Covell, Winter | CAMEO-
PABATS | 115 | 24 |

This was an introduction to TEE for most of the delegates. Most of the delegates were from the conservative evangelical groups. Two TEE committees were
formed. Onc, representing the conservatives, is
under PABATS. The other is composed of men representing the ecumenical groups. A national office
was established. A month later, on October 13-14,
a committee was named by PABATS which was the pre-
cursor of PAFTEE organized in January of 1973
(CAMEO 1972:11-15).

| Sep. 7-10
1971 | Cebu City | Covell, Winter | CAMEO-
PABATS | 72 | 11 |

Thirty-seven nationals were present at the workshop.
This group shared in the decisions of those at the
Manila workshop earlier (CAMEO 1972:11-15).

| Aug. 28-
Sep. 8
1972 | Manila | McCleary,
Harrison | TAP | 30 | |

Half of those attending were Filipinos. Several
delegates were designated for full time work in TEE
and PI by their sponsoring groups (TAP-Asia 1972b).

| Jan. 15-20
1973 | Baguio | Harrison | PAFTEE | 21 | 8 |

| Jan. 22-27
1973 | Cebu City, | Harrison | PAFTEE | 41 | 9 |

| Jan. 29-
Feb. 3
1973 | Davao City | Harrison | PAFTEE | 36 | 9 |

These three workshops were designed to help writers
of programmed instructional materials. Miss Pat
Harrison assembled materials to produce the following three programmed instruction workshop manuals:
Book 1-Instructional Foundations (to be read before
attending the workshop as background); Book 2--
Source Book - A Selection of Readings in Programming; Book 3-Program Manual - Selected Samples of
Programmed Lessons (Harrison 1973).

| | | RESOURCE | | PARTI- | |
| DATE | PLACE | PERSONS | SPONSOR | CIPANTS | GROUPS |

RHODESIA

Aug. 17-21 Salisbury   Ward, Rowen   CAMEO   27   14
1970
Plans were made to write PI materials and to use
TEE principles in existing schools. No immediate
plans for TEE were made. Delegates attended from
Zambia, Malawi, Rhodesia and South Africa (CAMEO
1971:4-5, 9).

Jan. 24-   Salisbury   Holland   AEBICAM   16
Feb. 25
1972   Teams of nationals and missionaries were formed
where possible to work on the production of programmed materials. The courses that were complete
and tested and mimeographed for use on a provisional basis were:
    Christian Experience
    I Corinthians
Eight other courses were begun at the workshop
(*AEBICAM Bulletin April 1972*).

Jan. 10-25 Salisbury   Crider   AEBICAM   6   3

DATE	PLACE	RESOURCE PERSONS	SPONSOR	PARTI-CIPANTS	GROUPS

SINGAPORE

| Sep. 12 1970 | Singapore | Covell, Wagner | CAMEO | 7 | 3 |

In three hours of discussion TEE was introduced to those present and it was agreed that promotion by Asian leaders and more workshops in various countries would be preferable to trying to bring delegates to a central location (Covell 1970b).

| June 1971 | Singapore | Savage | TAP | 30 | 20 |

Principles of programmed instruction were presented. Delegates came from Taiwan, Vietnam, Thailand, Malaysia, Singapore, Indonesia and India (*Extension Seminary 1971, 1:7*).

| Aug. 21 1971 | Singapore | Covell, Winter | CAMEO | 9 | |

The Southern Baptists announced their intention to go entirely to extension for ministerial and lay training in Indonesia. The need was seen to train leaders among the young people who leave the established churches to have fellowships in English (CAMEO 1972:5).

| Feb. 16 1972 | Singapore | McCleary | TAP | | 3 |

Little chance of beginning TEE soon in most churches was expressed (McCleary 1972).

DATE	PLACE	RESOURCE PERSONS	SPONSOR	PARTI-CIPANTS	GROUPS

SPAIN

DATE	PLACE	RESOURCE PERSONS	SPONSOR	PARTI-CIPANTS	GROUPS
Mar. 8-12 1971	Madrid	Savage	CAMEO	26	3

The three groups represented were FIEDE - Federation of Independent Churches of Spain, TEAM, and the Plymouth Brethren. All these groups have a plan for some form of TEE (Savage 1971).

SWAZILAND

DATE	PLACE	RESOURCE PERSONS	SPONSOR	PARTI-CIPANTS	GROUPS
Sep. 1971	Manzini	Alexander, Holland	CAMEO	30	9

Four nationals attended the workshop. Delegates came from South Africa, Mozambique, Rhodesia and Swaziland. Sixteen plan to do TEE work and seven planned to write programmed instructional materials (CAMEO 1972:41, 50).

| | | RESOURCE | | PARTI- | |
| DATE | PLACE | PERSONS | SPONSOR | CIPANTS | GROUPS |

TAIWAN

Aug. 24-26 Taipei   Covell, Wagner CAMEO   26   17
1970
This was a brief introduction to TEE with translation into Chinese (Covell 1970).

Aug. 26-68 Taichung   Covell, Wagner CAMEO   30   18
1970
The workshop was held for missionaries and other
participants able to participate in English. The
decision was made to broaden the extension program
of the China Evangelical Seminary. Writers were
selected for *bachiller* level materials (Covell
1970).

Aug. 27   Taipei   Winter   CAMEO-CES   27   6
1971
For most of the delegates this was the initial introduction to TEE. Interest could be continued by
dissemination of information, but there was no
immediate plan for extension programs in new groups
(CAMEO 1972:10).

Aug. 14-31 Hualien   Savage   TAP   13   11
1972
The problem of communicating in English limited
the effectiveness of the workshop. It was organized
by Taiwan church leaders, an indication of interest
on their part. Delegates attended from Hong Kong,
Malaysia and the Philippines. Initial training was
given to programmed instructional materials writers.
Centers were reported in Kaohsiung, Hsi-lo, Taichung and Taipei (TAP 1972:3-4).

Jan. 29-30 Taichung   Liao, Shen   CES   21   8
1973
Teacher training seminar. Nine participants
indicated interest in teaching in extension.

DATE	PLACE	RESOURCE PERSONS	SPONSOR	PARTI-CIPANTS	GROUPS

THAILAND

Aug. 16-20 1971	Bangkok	Covell, Winter	CAMEO	32	11

After this introduction to TEE and PI a nine man committee was formed, the Consultative Committee on TEE (Thai CoCoTEE) (CAMEO 1972:6-9).

Feb. 12 1972	Bangkok	McCleary	TAP	11	9

It was estimated that some 350 potential students for TEE could be reached. The Central Bible School reported 200 students and the Yao Bible School reported 10 students in four centers. The Cassette Bible School informed that there were 900 machines in the country and that it would produce some 100 courses which could be used in conjunction with extension studies (McCleary 1972).

Sep. 25-Oct. 6 1972	Bangkok	Dainton	TAP	22	8

This was an introduction to TEE for some but most were able to go on and begin the writing of programmed instructional materials. Representatives came from Laos and Bangla Desh (TAP 1973: 5,6).

May 29-June 1 1973	Bangkok		CoCoTEE		

The workshop is planned for the training of Thai extension professors.

		RESOURCE		PARTI-	
DATE	PLACE	PERSONS	SPONSOR	CIPANTS	GROUPS

UNITED STATES

| Apr. 25-26 1968 | Philadelphia | Rowen, Wagner Luttrell | CAMEO | 24 | 21 |

Brief presentations were given of the Resident-
Extension Seminary, the Intertext project and the
Recorded Lecture Bible Institute. Plans were made
for the December workshop.

| Dec. 19-21 1968 | Wheaton | Winter, Wagner Rowen, Thompson | CAMEO | 121 | 30 |

This workshop was very important for the introducing of TEE to mission executives and professors
as well as field missionaries from various denominations and representing many fields of the world.
It is described in detail elsewhere (Winter 1969:
Book II).

Jan. 5-9 1970	Wheaton	Ford	CAMEO		
July 6-17 1970	Wheaton	Ward	CAMEO		
May 1971	Fort Worth, Texas	Ford	CAMEO	15	
Aug. 1971	Wheaton	Ward, Rowen	CAMEO	19 countries	
Mar. 20-25 1971	Wheaton	Sharp	CAMEO		
May 29– June 9 1972	Fort Worth	Ford	CAMEO		
Feb. 19-23 1973	Farmington, Mi.	Ward, Rowen	MISS INTERN		
Mar. 19-22 1973	Wheaton	Sharp	CAMEO		

Although no details are given for these workshops
their importance should not be minimized. Generally they were limited to thirty participants. Introduction to TEE principles was given, but the
main emphasis has been on the production of writers
of programmed materials. Men and women have come
from many denominations and fields and have returned to teach others and to put into practice
what they have learned. Missionaries trained in
the United States have helped to direct TEE programs
in various parts of the world.

DATE	PLACE	RESOURCE PERSONS	SPONSOR	PARTI- CIPANTS	GROUPS

SOUTH VIETNAM

Aug. 31-
Sep. 4
1970   Saigon   Covell, Wagner   CAMEO   80

Half of the delegates were Vietnamese, largely from the dominant denomination in Vietnam, the Christian and Missionary Alliance. TEE was seen as a vehicle for continuing education for pastors first and later to be developed for lay training. There are few pastors in Vietnam without Bible School training and there was some resistance to TEE (Wagner 1970).

Sep. 4-18
1972   Natrang   McCleary   TAP   8

Five of the eight delegates were from the tribal churches since this is an area of great need for ministerial training not available through traditional institutions. The delegates hoped to work with pastors to train laymen. During the workshop the delegates produced the book "How to Study Bible Characters." PI was studied in the day and TEE was introduced to the delegates and others who entered for the evening sessions. Plans called for ten centers in 1973.

ZAIRE

Aug. 16-21
1971   Kinshasa   Alexander, Bates   CAMEO   16   7

Five of the delegates were nationals. Four of those who attended wanted to initiate TEE programs in their Churches and two men planned to write PI. A meeting for January 1972 for further planning was cited (CAMEO 1972:27).

Aug. 23-27
1971   Bukavu   Alexander, Bates   CAMEO   35   13

This workshop served to introduce TEE for the first time to most of those who attended. Seventeen nationals were present. One came from Burundi and three from Rwanda. Plans were laid for a Decentralized Theological School. Most of the delegates expressed the intention to do TEE. A few will write programmed instructional materials (CAMEO 1972: 28-31).

WORKSHOPS ON TEE 1966-1972

YEAR	WORKSHOPS	RESOURCE PERSONS	PARTICIPANTS	WORKSHOP MAN-DAYS
1966	1	2	10+	30
1967	1	4	28	140
1968	5	4	356	1191
1969	11	4	186	655
1970	12	5	351	1946
1971	26	9	945	4318
1972	23	11	462	4094
TOTAL	79	38	2343	12,374

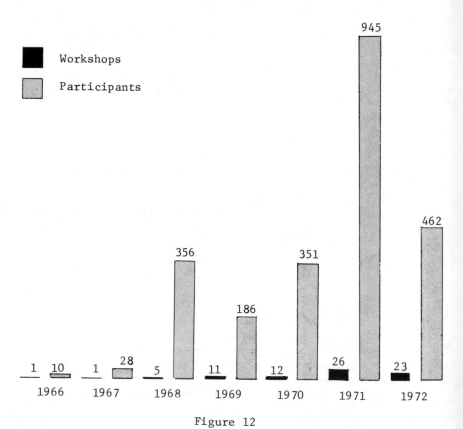

Figure 12

REGIONAL DISTRIBUTION OF TEE WORKSHOPS
1966 - 1972

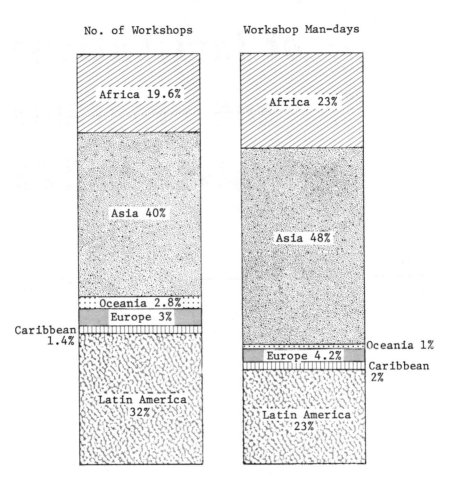

NOTE: The above figures do not include the workshops held in
the United States which served all areas since attendance was mainly by missionaries on furlough and missionary candidates. Also excluded are local or denominational workshops of which the author does not have knowledge.

Figure 13

7

An Alphabetical List of Institutions and Programs Involved in TEE

With the exception of a few non-typical programs a standard format is used in the following list of institutions and programs. Suggestions for the use of this section and indices begin on page 73. Institutions whose reports were received too late for inclusion in the alphabetical listing by countries are found at the end of this section.

ARGENTINA - Country Summary

Year	Inst	Cent	Teachers					Students				
			Full	Part	Miss	Natl	Tot	Cert	Dipl	Bach	Lic	Tot
1968	1	1							10			10
1969	1	1							10			10
1970	5	7							67			67
1971	5	10							87			87
1972	5	44	15	60	28	47	75	160	278	1	0	439
1973												
1974												
1975												

NATIONAL COORDINATOR: Terry Barratt
Seminario por Extension Anglicano
Santiago 1862
S.M. Tucuman, Argentina

AFFILIATION: ALISTE

COUNTRY: Argentina

General Conference Baptists
Casilla de Correo 30
Santiago del Estero
Argentina

		Teachers					Students			
Year	Cent	Full	Part	Miss	Natl	Total	Cert	Dipl	Bach	Lic	Total
1970											
1971											
1972	3	0	3	3	0	3	20	0	0	0	20
1973											
1974											
1975											

SPONSORING GROUPS: General Conference Baptists.

OTHER PARTICIPANTS: None.

SUPPORTED BY: Mission subsidy.

STUDENT FEES: Students pay the cost of their own materials and $2.00 for each course.

RECOGNITION OF   Certificates are given for each course com-
   STUDIES: pleted.

ORDINATION: This is considered lay training, but some students may be ordained.

CANDIDATES FOR   None at present.
FULL TIME SERVICE:

ACCREDITATION: None.

PREPARATION OF   One member of the faculty has prepared
   MATERIALS: extension materials.

PLANS: No present plans for extending the program.

COUNTRY: Argentina

Instituto Bíblico Edén
Soldini, Provincia Santa Fe
Argentina

		Teachers					Students				
Year	Cent	Full	Part	Miss	Natl	Total	Cert	Dipl	Bach	Lic	Total
1968	1							10			10
1969	1							10			10
1970	2							17			17
1971	2							17			17
1972	2	0	4	2	2	4	0	17	0	0	17
1973	3	2	1	0	3	3	0	42	0	0	42
1974											
1975											

SPONSORING GROUPS: Brethren Church

OTHER PARTICIPANTS: None

SUPPORTED BY: Brethren Church

STUDENT FEES: None.

RECOGNITION OF STUDIES: Certificates are given for courses completed.

ORDINATION: Those who complete their studies and meet other requirements may be ordained.

CANDIDATES FOR FULL TIME SERVICE: Some

ACCREDITATION: The institution is affiliated with ASIT.

CLASS FREQUENCY: Bi-weekly.

PLANS: Plans are to open other extension centers as personnel becomes available.

COUNTRY: Argentina

Seminario Bautista Evangélico Argentino
Casilla de Correo 364
Tucumán, Argentina

		Teachers					Students				
Year	Cent	Full	Part	Miss	Natl	Total	Cert	Dipl	Bach	Lic	Total
1970	5										50
1971	8										70
1972	5	1	5	3	3	6	20	31	1	0	52
1973											
1974											
1975											

SPONSORING GROUPS: Conservative Baptist
General Association of Baptist Churches
of Northwest Argentina

OTHER PARTICIPANTS: None

SUPPORTED BY: Mission subsidy and the Argentine churches.

STUDENT FEES: The student pays approximately $10.00 per month tuition plus about $20.00 for books.

RECOGNITION OF STUDIES: A certificate is given upon the completion of each course.

ORDINATION: Program is primarily for laymen.

CANDIDATES FOR FULL TIME SERVICE: 20%.

ACCREDITATION: None.

CLASS FREQUENCY: Weekly.

PREPARATION OF MATERIALS: Three members of the faculty have prepared extension materials.

PLANS: The seminary plans to open a new center in 1973 and add courses in the others.

COUNTRY: Argentina

Seminario Internacional Teológico Bautista
Ramón L. Falcón 4080
Buenos Aires, Argentina

Year	Cent	Teachers					Students				
		Full	Part	Miss	Natl	Total	Cert	Dipl	Bach	Lic	Total
1972	4	9	18	10	17	27	0	220	0	0	220
1973											
1974											
1975											

SPONSORING GROUPS: Southern Baptist Convention in the U.S.A.
                             Baptist Conventions of Argentina, Chile,
                             Uruguay and Paraguay.

OTHER PARTICIPANTS: Mennonite Church of Paraguay
                             Conservative Baptist Mission
                             General Conference Baptists

SUPPORTED BY: Mission subsidy and national churches.

STUDENT FEES: The student pays $20.00 per month per
course plus approximately $6.00 per semester for books.

RECOGNITION OF   No certificates are given until the entire
STUDIES: course is completed.

ORDINATION: The program is for lay training as well
as preparation for ordination.

CANDIDATES FOR
FULL TIME SERVICE: 10%.

ACCREDITATION: None, but the institution is seeking accreditation from A.S.I.T.

CLASS FREQUENCY: Weekly.

PREPARATION OF
MATERIALS: No member of the faculty has prepared extension materials.

PLANS: The seminary hopes to open four new centers
in 1973.

COUNTRY: Argentina

Seminario por Extensión Anglicano
Santiago 1862
S.M. Tucumán, Argentina

		Teachers					Students			
Year	Cent	Full	Part	Miss	Natl	Total	Cert	Dipl	Bach	Lic	Total
1970											
1971											
1972	30	5	30	10	25	35	120	10	0	0	130
1973											
1974											
1975											

SPONSORING GROUPS: Anglican Church
South American Missionary Society

OTHER PARTICIPANTS: None at present, but the seminary is seeking cooperation with Baptists, Biblical
Assemblies or others.

SUPPORTED BY: South American Missionary Society (British).

STUDENT FEES: The student pays for his own texts which
vary between $.10 and $1.50.

RECOGNITION OF
STUDIES: Recognition of completion of courses is
given through the giving of different positions in the church.

ORDINATION: Studies are not specifically for ordination but rather for the whole church.

CANDIDATES FOR
FULL TIME SERVICE: 1%. The denominational pattern is for the
pastors to support themselves in secular
employment.

ACCREDITATION: None.

CLASS FREQUENCY: Weekly.

PREPARATION OF
MATERIALS: Four members of the faculty have prepared
extension materials.

PLANS: The seminary hopes to triple the number of
students during 1973.

AUSTRALIA - Country Summary

			Teachers					Students				
Year	Inst	Cent	Full	Part	Miss	Natl	Tot	Cert	Dipl	Bach	Lic	Tot
1971	1											
1972	2	7	1	6	2	5	7	80	80	30	0	190
1973												
1974												
1975												

COUNTRY: Australia

The Alliance College of Theology
P. O. Box 19, Rivett
A.C.T. 2611, Australia

Year	Cent	Teachers					Students				
		Full	Part	Miss	Natl	Total	Cert	Dipl	Bach	Lic	Total
1971											
1972	3	1	1	2	0	2	0	0	30	0	30
1973											
1974											
1975											

SPONSORING GROUPS: The Christian and Missionary Alliance.

OTHER PARTICIPANTS: None.

SUPPORTED BY: Mission subsidy.

STUDENT FEES: The student pays $7.00 per subject plus the cost of textbooks and a $5.00 registration fee.

RECOGNITION OF STUDIES: Degrees granted are L.Th. (two years equivalent) and Sch. of Theology (3 years). A Christian Workers Certificate is granted after one year as an intermediate goal.

ORDINATION: The program leads to ordination but also involves lay people.

CANDIDATES FOR FULL TIME SERVICE: 25%.

ACCREDITATION: None. There is no accrediting agency in Australia.

PREPARATION OF MATERIALS: Two members of the institution have prepared extension materials.

PLANS: The institution plans to add a residence program using the TEE approach by offering a full load in one place. Also, they plan to add centers in the country areas.

COUNTRY: Australia

Armidale Diocesan Theological Education by Extension
c/0 Rev. R. G. Smith
Box W73, West Tamworth,
N.S.W. 2340, Australia

		Teachers					Students				
Year	Cent	Full	Part	Miss	Natl	Total	Cert	Dipl	Bach	Lic	Total
1972	4	0	5	0	5	5					80
1973	6	0	5	0	5	5					100
1974											
1975											

SPONSORING GROUPS: The Church of England, Diocese of Armidale, (The Diocesan Board of Christian Education).

OTHER PARTICIPANTS: The Presbyterians and Methodists also send students.

SUPPORTED BY: Funds allocated by the Diocesan Board of Christian Education and student fees.

STUDENT FEES: The student pays about $3.50 per course plus textbooks ($3.00 to $5.00 per course).

RECOGNITION OF   Certificates are given upon completion of
STUDIES: each course. A Parish Leader's Certificate and a Certificate in Theology can be earned after four and eight courses.

ORDINATION: At present this is lay training. They would like eventually to offer the standard Th.L. earned by Anglican ministers.

CANDIDATES FOR
FULL TIME SERVICE: None.

ACCREDITATION: None. There are no accrediting agencies in Australia.

CLASS FREQUENCY: Bi-weekly.

PREPARATION OF   Two members of the program have prepared
MATERIALS: extension materials.

PLANS: They hope to open new centers as personnel becomes available.

BOLIVIA - Country Summary

Year	Inst	Cent	Teachers					Students				
			Full	Part	Miss	Natl	Tot	Cert	Dipl	Bach	Lic	Tot
1969	4											115
1970	4											150
1971	4											
1972	4	29	5	30	14	21	35	193	53	19	0	265
1973												
1974												
1975												

NATIONAL COORDINATOR: Robert Andrews
                         Seminario Teologico Luterano
                         Casilla 266
                         La Paz, Bolivia

AFFILIATION: ALISTE

COUNTRY: Bolivia

Instituto Bíblico Berea

Santa Cruz, Bolivia

		Teachers					Students			
Year	Cent	Full	Part	Miss	Natl	Total	Cert	Dipl	Bach	Lic	Total
1969	2									
1970										
1971										
1972										
1973										
1974										
1975										

COUNTRY: Bolivia

Seminario Teológico Bautista
Casilla 86
Cochabamba, Bolivia

		Teachers					Students			
Year	Cent	Full	Part	Miss	Natl	Total	Cert	Dipl	Bach	Lic	Total
1969											50
1970											
1971											
1972											
1973											
1974											
1975											

COUNTRY: Bolivia

Seminario Teológico Jorge Allan
Cajón 514
Cochabamba, Bolivia

		Teachers					Students				
Year	Cent	Full	Part	Miss	Natl	Total	Cert	Dipl	Bach	Lic	Total
1969											65
1970											150
1971											
1972	20	5	23	10	18	28	165	45	12	0	222
1973											
1974											
1975											

SPONSORING GROUPS: Evangelical Christian Union.

OTHER PARTICIPANTS: Andes Evangelical Mission
Evangelical Union of South America
South America Mission

SUPPORTED BY: Subsidy from the United States and other countries.

STUDENT FEES: The student pays $.30 per course per month plus the cost of books.

RECOGNITION OF
STUDIES: Bachelor of Theology, Diploma in Theology. At the certificate level certificates are given at the end of each semester.

ORDINATION: There is no ordination other than local church recognition in this denomination.

CANDIDATES FOR
FULL TIME SERVICE: 3%.

ACCREDITATION: None.

CLASS FREQUENCY: Weekly for Spanish studies. For some Indian groups every third week is for study.

PREPARATION OF
MATERIALS: Eleven members of the faculty have prepared extension materials.

COUNTRY: Bolivia

Seminario Teológico Luterano en Bolivia
Casilla 266
La Paz, Bolivia

Year	Cent	Full	Part	Miss	Natl	Total	Cert	Dipl	Bach	Lic	Total
1969											
1970											
1971											
1972	9	0	7	4	3	7	28	8	7	0	43
1973											
1974											
1975											

SPONSORING GROUPS: La Iglesia Evangelical Luterana Boliviana
La Federacion de Iglesias Evangelicas Lu-
teranas en Bolivia
The World Mission Prayer League

OTHER PARTICIPANTS: None.

SUPPORTED BY: The World Mission Prayer League and
student fees.

STUDENT FEES: The student pays between $3.00 and $5.00
for each course.

RECOGNITION OF
STUDIES: A certificate is given upon completion of
each course.

ORDINATION: The course of study can lead to ordination.
There is a complete curriculum for ordination.

CANDIDATES FOR
FULL TIME SERVICE: None.

ACCREDITATION: None.

PREPARATION OF
MATERIALS: Three members of the faculty have prepared
extension materials.

PLANS: The seminary plans to expand according to
demand and possibilities of professors.
The new professors will be nationals.

BRAZIL - Country Summary

			Teachers					Students				
Year	Inst	Cent	Full	Part	Miss	Natl	Tot	Cert	Dipl	Bach	Lic	Tot
1969	6											200
1970	13											900
1971	27											2000
1972	28	132						83	959	237	147	0	1578
1973												
1974												
1975												

(Data from 1969-1971 Sturz 1972, 1972 data incomplete)

NATIONAL COORDINATOR: John Klassen
Caixa Postal 5938
01000 São Paulo, Brazil

PUBLICATIONS   *Boletim Da Aette*

AFFILIATION: AETTE

COUNTRY: Brazil

Extension Course of the Presbytery of Cuiaba
Caixa Postal 41
78000 Cuiaba, MT,
Brazil

Year	Cent	Teachers					Students				
		Full	Part	Miss	Natl	Total	Cert	Dipl	Bach	Lic	Total
1970	9						130				130
1971	9						200				200
1972		1	0	1	0	1	150	80	20	0	250
1973											
1974											
1975											

SPONSORING GROUPS: The Presbytery of Cuiaba of the Presbyterian
                     Church of Brazil.

OTHER PARTICIPANTS: Isolated students from other denominations.

SUPPORTED BY: The Central Brazil Mission.

STUDENT FEES: The student pays about $1.00 for workbooks.

RECOGNITION OF   Certificates are given upon completion of
   STUDIES: individual courses.

ORDINATION: This is considered to be lay training, with
                     the rare possibility of ordination.

CANDIDATES FOR   0.5%.
FULL TIME SERVICE:

ACCREDITATION: None.

CLASS FREQUENCY:

PREPARATION OF   One teacher has prepared extension mater-
   MATERIALS: ials.

PLANS: The program seeks to recruit more students,
                     possibly 500.

COUNTRY: Brazil

Faculdade de Teología da Igreja Metodista Livre
Rua Domingos de Morais, 2518
Sao Paulo, S.P. Brazil
04036

Year	Cent	Teachers					Students				
		Full	Part	Miss	Natl	Total	Cert	Dipl	Bach	Lic	Total
1971											
1972	1	0	1	1	0	1	0	12	0	0	12
1973											
1974											
1975											

SPONSORING GROUPS: Free Methodist Mission of Brazil
                      Free Methodist Church of Brazil

OTHER PARTICIPANTS: Mennonite Brethren
                      Overseas Crusades

SUPPORTED BY: Subsidy by North American mission.

STUDENT FEES:

RECOGNITION OF   Certificates are given.
   STUDIES:

ORDINATION: These studies are considered sufficient
                      for ordination in the Free Methodist
                      Church.

CANDIDATES FOR   10%.
FULL TIME SERVICE:

ACCREDITATION: None, but is a member of ASTE.

CLASS FREQUENCY: Every eight weeks.

PREPARATION OF   None prepared locally.
   MATERIALS:

PLANS: No fixed plans. The program is being
                      studied.

COUNTRY: Brazil

Instituto Bíblico Apostol Paul "IBAP"
Caixa Postal 77
36.800 Carangola, MG., Brazil

| | | Teachers | | | | | Students | | | |
Year	Cent	Full	Part	Miss	Natl	Total	Cert	Dipl	Bach	Lic	Total
1971	14										150
1972	0										0
1973											
1974											
1975											

NOTE: The program was suspended in 1972 in order to prepare materials.

COUNTRY: Brazil

Instituto Bíblico Batista de Campinas
Caixa Postal 995
13.100 Campinas, SP., Brazil

		Teachers					Students				
Year	Cent	Full	Part	Miss	Natl	Total	Cert	Dipl	Bach	Lic	Total
1969											
1970											
1971											52
1972	15	2	8	1	9	10	10	30	80	6	126

SPONSORING GROUPS: Conservative Baptist Foreign Mission
Brazilian Baptist Convention of the State
of Sao Paulo

OTHER PARTICIPANTS   Southern Baptists
General Conference Baptists

SUPPORTED BY: Mission subsidy.

STUDENT FEES: The student pays for texts and $1.00 per
month.

RECOGNITION OF
STUDIES: A diploma is given on finishing the course.

ORDINATION: Possible for some after practical work.

CANDIDATES FOR
FULL TIME SERVICE: 5 to 10%

ACCREDITATION: None.

CLASS FREQUENCY: Weekly.

PREPARATION OF
MATERIALS: One member of the faculty has prepared
extension materials.

PLANS: More centers may be opened.

COUNTRY: Brazil

Instituto Bíblico Betel
Caixa Postal 30.498
01.000 Sao Paulo, SP., Brazil

		Teachers					Students			
Year	Cent	Full	Part	Miss	Natl	Total	Cert	Dipl	Bach	Lic	Total
1970										
1971											175
1972	3										85
1973										
1974										
1975										

COUNTRY: Brazil

Instituto Bíblico de Maringá
Caixa Postal 384
Maringá, Paraná, Brazil

Year	Cent	Teachers					Students				
		Full	Part	Miss	Natl	Total	Cert	Dipl	Bach	Lic	Total
1972		0	2	1	1	2	5	10			15
1973		0	2	1	1	2	5	8	7		20
1974											
1975											

SPONSORING GROUPS: United Missionary Society
                     Missionary Church Mission

OTHER PARTICIPANTS: None.

SUPPORTED BY: Subsidy by North American missions and
                     National Churches.

STUDENT FEES: $5.00 for subjects per semester, pay for
                     texts and workbooks and $15.00 tuition.

RECOGNITION OF   Diploma in Theology and Christian Education.
   STUDIES:

ORDINATION: Some study toward this goal.

CANDIDATES FOR   15%
FULL TIME SERVICE:

ACCREDITATION: None.

CLASS FREQUENCY: Weekly.

PREPARATION OF   One member of the faculty has prepared
   MATERIALS: extension materials.

PLANS: More centers will be established.

COUNTRY: Brazil

Instituto Bíblico do Norte
Caixa Postal 66
55.300 Garanhuns, PE., Brazil

		Teachers					Students				
Year	Cent	Full	Part	Miss	Natl	Total	Cert	Dipl	Bach	Lic	Total
1972	9										90
1973	12	0	18	3	15	18					105
1974											
1975											

SPONSORING GROUPS: Presbyterian Church in the United States

OTHER PARTICIPANTS: Presbyterian Church of Brazil

SUPPORTED BY: Subsidy from the Presbyterian Mission in
                         the U.S.A. and contributions from individ-
                         uals and churches in Brazil.

STUDENT FEES: The student pays a matriculation fee of
                         $2.00 and $1.50 for each course.

RECOGNITION OF   A certificate is given upon completion of
   STUDIES: each course. A Diploma in Bible or in
                         Christian Education is awarded upon com-
                         pletion of the course of 3 years.

ORDINATION: This is considered lay training.

CANDIDATES FOR
FULL TIME SERVICE: At the present, none.

ACCREDITATION: None.

CLASS FREQUENCY: Weekly.

PREPARATION OF   One member of the institution has prepared
   MATERIALS: extension materials and another is doing
                         so at present.

PLANS: Plans are to continue forming centers and
                         extending the program.

COUNTRY: Brazil

Instituto Bíblico Eduardo Lane
Caixa Postal 12
38740 Patrocinio, MG
Brazil

		Teachers					Students			
Year	Cent	Full	Part	Miss	Natl	Total	Cert	Dipl	Bach	Lic	Total
1969	15	1	8	1	8	9	270	0	15	0	285
1970	20	1	12	1	12	13	400	0	15	0	415
1971	34	2	15	2	15	17	500	0	15	0	515
1972	43	2	30	3	29	32	700	0	20	0	720
1973											
1974											
1975											

SPONSORING GROUPS: Board of World Missions of the Presbyterian Church, U.S.

OTHER PARTICIPANTS: The Presbyterian Church of Brazil

SUPPORTED BY: Subsidies from U.S. churches and scholarships from national and U.S. churches.

STUDENT FEES: The student pays about $2.00 per semester
plus a matriculation fee of $1.50.

RECOGNITION OF
STUDIES: A certificate is given upon completion of
each course. Recognition is also given
upon completion of a "Basic Course" of
seven subjects, a "Practical Course" of
four subjects, and an "Advanced Bible
Course" of seven subjects. Upon completion of these three courses a diploma is
awarded.

ORDINATION: At the Bible institute level it is lay
training, but at the seminary level ordination is the goal.

CANDIDATES FOR
FULL TIME SERVICE: 60% of the seminary level.

ACCREDITATION: None.

CLASS FREQUENCY: Weekly or bi-weekly.

COUNTRY: Brazil

Instituto Bíblico Eduardo Lane (continued)

PREPARATION OF   Three members of the faculty have pre-
    MATERIALS: pared extension materials.

PLANS: The institution plans to open new centers
                        in cities near their headquarters.

COUNTRY: Brazil

Instituto Bíblico Maranata
Caixa Postal 431
60.000 Fortaleza, Ceara, Brazil

		Teachers					Students			
Year	Cent	Full	Part	Miss	Natl	Total	Cert	Dipl	Bach	Lic	Total
1971											4
1972	6										13
1973											
1974											
1975											

COUNTRY: Brazil

Instituto Bíblico Wesleyano
Caixa Postal 444
69.000 Manaus, AM., Brazil

Year	Cent	Teachers					Students				
		Full	Part	Miss	Natl	Total	Cert	Dipl	Bach	Lic	Total
1971	1										3
1972	1										2
1973											
1974											
1975											

COUNTRY: Brazil

Instituto Cristão de Educacão E Cultura
Caixa Postal 1099
74.000 Goiania, Goias, Brazil

			Teachers					Students			
Year	Cent	Full	Part	Miss	Natl	Total	Cert	Dipl	Bach	Lic	Total
1972	6					6					37
1973	13	1	11	7	5	12	60	70	0	0	130
1974											
1975											

SPONSORING GROUPS: Igrejas de Cristo do Brasil

OTHER PARTICIPANTS: Baptists
                     Presbyterians

SUPPORTED BY: Missionaries and national churches.

STUDENT FEES: The student pays a matriculation fee of
                     $12.00 per year.

RECOGNITION OF   Certificates are given at the end of each
   STUDIES: year. A Diploma in Theology will be given
                     upon completion of 3 or 4 years.

ORDINATION:

CANDIDATES FOR
FULL TIME SERVICE: Not known.

ACCREDITATION: None, but is a member of AETTE.

CLASS FREQUENCY: Weekly.

PREPARATION OF   No extension materials have been prepared
   MATERIALS: at the institute.

PLANS;   Plans are for more national teachers.

COUNTRY: Brazil

Instituto e Seminario Bíblico Irmãos Menonitas
Caixa Postal 2445
80.000 Curitiba, Parana, Brazil

		Teachers					Students				
Year	Cent	Full	Part	Miss	Natl	Total	Cert	Dipl	Bach	Lic	Total
1969											
1970											
1971											80
1972	20										120
1973											
1974											
1975											

COUNTRY: Brazil

Instituto e Seminario Bíblico de Londrina
Caixa Postal 58
86.100 Londrina, Parana, Brazil

| | | Teachers | | | | | Students | | | | |
Year	Cent	Full	Part	Miss	Natl	Total	Cert	Dipl	Bach	Lic	Total
1970											
1971											30
1972	6										32
1973											
1974											
1975											

COUNTRY: Brazil

Seminario Evangélico do Rio Grande do Sul
Caixa Postal 2350
90000, Porto Alegre, R.S.,
Brazil

		Teachers					Students				
Year	Cent	Full	Part	Miss	Natl	Total	Cert	Dipl	Bach	Lic	Total
1970											
1971											43
1972	3	1	6	1	6	7	30	15	17	0	62
1973											
1974											
1975											

SPONSORING GROUPS: West Indies Mission

OTHER PARTICIPANTS: Alianca Bíblica do Brasil

SUPPORTED BY: Mission subsidy and national churches.

STUDENT FEES: The student pays $3.00 per semester course.
                     He also pays a matriculation fee of $4.50
                     per semester and buys his own books.

RECOGNITION OF   A program of intermediate goals is now
STUDIES: being planned.

ORDINATION: The program can lead to ordination for those
                     who finish the course and meet denominational
                     requirements.

CANDIDATES FOR   24%.
FULL TIME SERVICE:

ACCREDITATION: None.

CLASS FREQUENCY: Weekly.

PREPARATION OF   One member of the faculty has prepared ex-
MATERIALS: tension materials.

PLANS: The institution plans to open new centers
                     in other cities.

COUNTRY: Brazil

Seminario Teológico Batista
Caixa Postal 269
13.100 Campinas, SP., Brazil

		Teachers					Students			
Year	Cent	Full	Part	Miss	Natl	Total	Cert	Dipl	Bach	Lic	Total
1973	8									
1974										
1975										

COUNTRY: Brazil

Seminario Teológico Batista Equatorial
Caixa Postal 88
66.000 Belem, Pará, Brazil

		Teachers					Students				
Year	Cent	Full	Part	Miss	Natl	Total	Cert	Dipl	Bach	Lic	Total
1970											
1971											
1972											
1973											
1974											
1975											

COUNTRY: Brazil

Seminario Teológico Batista do Nordeste
Caixa Postal 2, Floriano, Piaui
Brazil

		Teachers				Students				
Year	Cent	Full	Part	Miss	Natl	Total	Cert	Dipl	Bach	Lic	Total
1970	1		3	3			8				8
1971	4		8	8			71				71
1972	11	2	30	20	12	32	69	100	0	0	169
1973	8		5	4			45				45
1974											
1975											

SPONSORING GROUPS: Conservative Baptist Mission of Brazil
Baptist Convention of Piaui-Maranhao

OTHER PARTICIPANTS: Missionary Aviation Fellowship

SUPPORTED BY: Special projects through the C.B.F.M.S. in the United States and contributions from local Brazilian churches.

STUDENT FEES: The student pays about $5.00 for three courses per semester including textbooks. He also pays a matriculation fee of $1.00 per semester.

RECOGNITION OF STUDIES: The student receives a certificate each year indicating the subjects completed in that year of study.

ORDINATION: This is considered lay training although in special cases it might lead to ordination.

CANDIDATES FOR FULL TIME SERVICE: Some.

ACCREDITATION: None.

CLASS FREQUENCY: Weekly or bi-weekly.

PREPARATION OF MATERIALS: Seven members of the faculty have prepared extension materials.

PLANS: The institution plans to open new centers yearly.

CHILE - Country Summary

Year	Inst	Cent	Teachers					Students				
			Full	Part	Miss	Natl	Tot	Cert	Dipl	Bach	Lic	Tot
1972	1	9	1	6	1	6	7	0	60	10	0	70
1973												
1974												
1975												

NATIONAL COORDINATOR: Sergio Correa
                        Seminario Bíblico por Extensión
                        Moneda 1898
                        Santiago, Chile

AFFILIATION: ALISTE

COUNTRY: Chile

Instituto Bíblico Bautista
Casilla 96, Correo 38
Santiago, Chile

		Teachers				Students				
Year	Cent	Full	Part	Miss	Natl	Total	Cert	Dipl	Bach	Lic	Total
1973	1	0	5	5	0	5					
1974											
1975											

SPONSORING GROUPS: Gospel Mission for South America

OTHER PARTICIPANTS: None.

SUPPORTED BY: Association of Baptists for World Evangelism

STUDENT FEES: The student pays $2.00 matriculation and
                      from $5.00 to $10.00 for books.

RECOGNITION OF   A certificate is given for each of the
    STUDIES: seven divisions completed.

ORDINATION: The program is primarily lay training.

CANDIDATES FOR   Not known as yet.
FULL TIME SERVICE:

ACCREDITATION: None.

CLASS FREQUENCY: Twice a month.

PREPARATION OF   Four members of the institution have pre-
    MATERIALS: pared materials for extension.

PLANS: There are no plans for extending the program
                      as yet.

COUNTRY: Chile

Seminario Bíblico por Extensión
Moneda 1898
Santiago, Chile

		Teachers					Students			
Year	Cent	Full	Part	Miss	Natl	Total	Cert	Dipl	Bach	Lic	Total
1972	9	1	6	1	6	7	0	60	10	0	70
1973											
1974											
1975											

SPONSORING GROUPS: National Presbyterian Church
                      Presbyterian Mission for Northern Chile

OTHER PARTICIPANTS: None.

SUPPORTED BY: Mission subsidy with some help from the
                      national church.

STUDENT FEES: Vary.

RECOGNITION OF
   STUDIES:

ORDINATION: The majority of the students does not ex-
                      pect to be ordained but it would be possible
                      upon finishing the course and fulfilling
                      other denominational requirements.

CANDIDATES FOR
FULL TIME SERVICE:

ACCREDITATION: None.

CLASS FREQUENCY: Weekly.

PREPARATION OF   Two members of the institution have pre-
   MATERIALS: pared extension materials.

PLANS: The institution has the goal of extablishing
                      six new centers in the country. They are
                      studying the possibility of having classes
                      every two weeks or every month for a longer
                      duration.

COLOMBIA - Country Summary

Year	Inst	Cent	Full	Part	Miss	Natl	Tot	Cert	Dipl	Bach	Lic	Tot
1968												
1969	2	25	3	16	7	12	19	0	119	22	0	141
1970	3	23	2	24	10	16	26	0	141	30	0	171
1971	4	44	0	27	8	9	27	375	61	11	0	447
1972	7	106	3	95	27	71	98	658	249	41	22	1061
1973												
1974												
1975												

NATIONAL COORDINATOR: Vernon Reimer
Apartado Aereo 5945
Cali, Colombia

PUBLICATIONS: *BOLETIN DE UNICO*

AFFILIATION: ALISTE
UNICO

COUNTRY: Colombia

Estudios Teológicos por Extensión
Apartado Aéreo 786
Santa Marta, Magdalena
Colombia

Year	Cent	Full	Part	Miss	Natl	Total	Cert	Dipl	Bach	Lic	Total
1972	9	2	0	2	0	2	52	17	0	0	69
1973											
1974											
1975											

SPONSORING GROUPS: Evangelical Union of South America
                     Association of Evangelical Churches of Mag-
                        dalena

OTHER PARTICIPANTS: None.

SUPPORTED BY: "Work funds" from missionaries.

STUDENT FEES: The student pays about $0.25 per semester
                     course plus books. The total is about
                     $2.00 per course.

RECOGNITION OF   As yet no recognition is given for comple-
   STUDIES: tion of courses.

ORDINATION: The program is geared for laymen, but later
                     some may be ordained through regular channels.

CANDIDATES FOR
FULL TIME SERVICE: Not known.

ACCREDITATION: None.

CLASS FREQUENCY: Weekly. With the professor, every two or
                     three weeks.

PREPARATION OF   One member of the institution is about to
   MATERIALS: begin preparation of extension materials.

PLANS:

COUNTRY: Colombia

Gospel Missionary Union
Apartado Aéreo 244
Palmira, Colombia

		Teachers					Students				
Year	Cent	Full	Part	Miss	Natl	Total	Cert	Dipl	Bach	Lic	Total
1970						8					66
1971						7					75
1972	10					9					89
1973											
1974											
1975											

(Hammers 1973)

SPONSORING GROUPS: Gospel Missionary Union

STUDENT FEES: The student pays $0.50 registration fee and up to $1.00 per book.

COUNTRY: Colombia

Instituto Bíblico Betel
División - Extensión
Apartado Aéreo 516
Armenia, Quindío,
Colombia

		Teachers					Students			
Year	Cent	Full	Part	Miss	Natl	Total	Cert	Dipl	Bach	Lic	Total
1967	2	0	1	1	0	1					
1968	3	0	2	2	0	2	0	6	2	0	8
1969	4	0	4	2	2	4	0	10	5	0	15
1970	11	1	6	4	3	7	100	40	10	0	150
1971	19	1	14	5	10	15	180	47	15	0	210
1972	20	0	20	5	15	20	150	42	18	0	210
1973	16	0	16	3	13	16	121	89	14	0	224
1974											
1975											

SPONSORING GROUPS: Christian and Missionary Alliance Mission
                     Christian and Missionary Alliance National
                         Church

OTHER PARTICIPANTS: Gospel Missionary Union
                     Presbyterian Church
                     Cumberland Presbyterian Church

SUPPORTED BY: The North American missions plus student
                     matriculation fees.

STUDENT FEES: The student pays $1.00 matriculation fee on
                     the certificate level, $1.50 on the diploma
                     level, and $1.50 on the bachelor level.

RECOGNITION OF   A certificate is given upon completion of
STUDIES: each course. Degrees awarded are a Certifi-
                     cate in Theology and a Diploma in Theology.

ORDINATION: Not based on theological studies.

CANDIDATES FOR   35%.
FULL TIME SERVICE:

ACCREDITATION: None.

CLASS FREQUENCY: Weekly.

PREPARATION OF   Three members of the faculty have pre-
MATERIALS: pared extension materials.

COUNTRY: Colombia

Instituto Bíblico Betel (continued)

PLANS: Plans are for new and better courses,
                          printed materials, orientation visits,
                          regional coordinators, helps for pro-
                          fessors, an annual assembly at Betel, a
                          full-time director, a full-time secretary,
                          and that the residence students may receive
                          credit by teaching or studying in the ex-
                          tension program.

COUNTRY: Colombia

Instituto Bíblico de Ocaña
Apartado Aéreo 1
Ocaña, N. de S.,
Colombia

		Teachers				Students				
Year	Cent	Full	Part	Miss	Natl	Total	Cert	Dipl	Bach	Lic	Total
1972	6	1	0	1	0	1	70	13	0	0	83
1973											
1974											
1975											

SPONSORING GROUPS: The Evangelical Alliance Mission

OTHER PARTICIPANTS: The Association of Evangelical Churches of
                    Eastern Colombia

SUPPORTED BY: Mission subsidy and the national churches.

STUDENT FEES: The student pays $0.60 for matriculation and
                    manual every three months.

RECOGNITION OF   A certificate is given upon completion of
   STUDIES: each program of six courses. A diploma in
                    theology is given upon termination of the
                    complete course of five programs.

ORDINATION: This program can lead to ordination.

CANDIDATES FOR   Not known.
FULL TIME SERVICE:

ACCREDITATION: None.

CLASS FREQUENCY: One day every three months.

PREPARATION OF   One member of the institution has prepared
   MATERIALS: extension materials.

PLANS: The institution plans to open a new center
                    in 1973.

COUNTRY: Colombia

SELITE (Servicio Luterano de Instrucción Teológica
Apartado Aéreo 53005
Bogotá 2, Colombia

		Teachers					Students				
Year	Cent	Full	Part	Miss	Natl	Total	Cert	Dipl	Bach	Lic	Total
1972	6	1	5	0	4	6	0	33	4	0	37
1973											
1974											
1975											

(UNICO Bulletin February 1973:3)

SPONSORING GROUPS: American Lutheran Church

OTHER PARTICIPANTS: None.

SUPPORTED BY: Subsidy from North American Mission.

STUDENT FEES: The student pays $1.50 matriculation fee plus $1.50 tuition per semester.

ORDINATION: Ordination is possible upon completion of studies.

CANDIDATES FOR
FULL TIME SERVICE: Some.

ACCREDITATION: Affiliated with the Augsburg Lutheran Seminary in Mexico.

CLASS FREQUENCY: Generally once a week.

PREPARATION OF
MATERIALS: Two members of the institution have prepared materials for extension.

PLANS: Possibility of opening new centers.

COUNTRY: Colombia

Seminario Bíblico Unido
División Medellín
Apartado Aéreo 1141
Medellín, Colombia

Seminario Bíblico Unido
División Bogotá
Apartado Aéreo 5678
Bogotá, Colombia

Seminario Bíblico Unido
División Cali
Apartado Aéreo 5945
Cali, Colombia

Seminario Bíblico Unido
División Caribe
Apartado Aéreo 19-
Sincelejo, Colombia

		Teachers					Students				
Year	Cent	Full	Part	Miss	Natl	Total	Cert	Dipl	Bach	Lic	Total
1968											
1969	25	3	16	7	12	19	0	119	22	0	141
1970	23	2	24	10	16	26	0	141	30	0	171
1971	41	0	27	8	19	27	225	61	11	0	297
1972	51	0	60	10	50	60	366	88	19	0	473
1973											
1974											
1975											

SPONSORING GROUPS: Interamerican Missionary Society (OMS)
                      Evangelical Covenant Mission
                      General Conference Mennonite Church
                      Mennonite Brethren Mission
                      Overseas Crusades
                      Gospel Missionary Union
                      Cumberland Presbyterian Church
                      Latin America Mission

OTHER PARTICIPANTS: Wesleyan Mission
                      World Evangelization Crusade
                      Lutheran Church in America
                      Presbyterian Church of Colombia
                      Panamerican Mission
                      Foursquare Gospel Church

SUPPORTED BY: Subsidy from the North American Missions

STUDENT FEES: About $3.00 per semester course plus a
                      $1.00 registration fee. The student also
                      pays for all texts and workbooks.

RECOGNITION OF   A certificate is given on completion of each
STUDIES: course. Bachelor of Theology and Diploma
                      in Theology degrees are awarded upon comple-
                      tion of all studies.

COUNTRY: Colombia

Seminario Bíblico Unido   (continued)

ORDINATION: Ordination is possible, depending on
                         denominational requirements.

CANDIDATES FOR   A small proportion plan on full time
FULL TIME SERVICE: service.

ACCREDITATION: None. The seminary is a member of ALET.

CLASS FREQUENCY: Weekly except in some isolated areas.

PREPARATION OF   Six members of the faculty have prepared
    MATERIALS: extension materials.

PLANS: Plans are for a greater decentralization
                         of studies into congregations, more empha-
                         sis on certificate level studies, and a
                         greater flexibility in curriculum.

COUNTRY: Colombia

Seminario Teológico Bautista Internacional
Apartado Aéreo 6613
Cali, Colombia

Year	Cent	Teachers					Students				
		Full	Part	Miss	Natl	Total	Cert	Dipl	Bach	Lic	Total
1971	3						50				50
1972	4	0	15	9	6	15	20	56	0	22	98
1973											
1974											
1975											

SPONSORING GROUPS: Foreign Missions Board of the Southern
                     Baptist Convention

OTHER PARTICIPANTS: None.

SUPPORTED BY: Mission subsidy and the National Baptist
                     Convention

STUDENT FEES: The student pays from $2.00 to $2.25 per
                     semester course including texts and manuals.

RECOGNITION OF   A certificate is given each year indicating
   STUDIES: the courses completed. A diploma will be
                     offered upon completion of the curriculum.

ORDINATION: The majority of the students does not expect
                     to be ordained, but it will be possible in
                     the future.

CANDIDATES FOR
FULL TIME SERVICE: Not known.

ACCREDITATION: Member of ALET.

CLASS FREQUENCY: Weekly.

PREPARATION OF   One member of the institution has prepared
   MATERIALS: extension materials.

PLANS: The institution plans to organize new
                     centers in other cities.

DOMINICAN REPUBLIC – Country Summary

Year	Inst	Cent	Teachers					Students				
			Full	Part	Miss	Natl	Tot	Cert	Dipl	Bach	Lic	Tot
1971	2											
1972	2	13	2	6	5	3	8	45	62	18	0	125
1973												
1974												
1975												

AFFILIATION: ALISTE

COUNTRY: Dominican Republic

Seminario Bíblico Unido de la Iglesia Evangélica Misionera
Dajabon, Dominican Republic

		Teachers				Students				
Year	Cent	Full	Part	Miss	Natl	Total	Cert	Dipl	Bach	Lic	Total
1971											
1972	5	1	1	1	1	2	15	2	8	0	25
1973											
1974											
1975											

SPONSORING GROUPS: The Missionary Church

OTHER PARTICIPANTS: Cooperation with the Evangelical Mennonite
                     Church and the West Indies Mission.

SUPPORTED BY: Mission subsidy.

STUDENT FEES: The student pays $1.50 for registration plus
                     half the cost of the books.

RECOGNITION OF   Certificates are given for every course and
   STUDIES: there is a   diploma   for the completion
                     of 18 basic courses.

ORDINATION: This is considered lay training and few stu-
                     dents are preparing for a full time ministry.
                     The curriculum can lead to ordination.

CANDIDATES FOR
FULL TIME SERVICE: Very few.

ACCREDITATION: None.

CLASS FREQUENCY: Weekly.

PREPARATION OF
   MATERIALS: One member of the faculty has prepared ex-
                     tension materials.

PLANS: The seminary plans to open centers in the
                     larger cities.

COUNTRY: Dominican Republic

Seminario Evangélico Unido de la República Dominicana
Apartado 506
Azua, Dominican Republic

Year	Cent	Teachers					Students				
		Full	Part	Miss	Natl	Total	Cert	Dipl	Bach	Lic	Total
1971											
1972	8	1	5	4	2	6	30	60	10	0	100
1973											
1974											
1975											

SPONSORING GROUPS: Evangelical Mennonite Church
West Indies Mission
Missionary Church

OTHER PARTICIPANTS: Christian Bible Church

SUPPORTED BY: Tuition of the students.

STUDENT FEES: The student pays $2.00 for each course.

RECOGNITION OF
STUDIES: A certificate is given upon completion of each course.

ORDINATION: This is considered lay training, but they hope to make it preparation for pastors.

CANDIDATES FOR
FULL TIME SERVICE: The majority are pastors who work to support themselves.

ACCREDITATION: None.

CLASS FREQUENCY: Weekly and bi-weekly.

PREPARATION OF
MATERIALS: Four members of the institution have prepared extension materials.

PLANS: Plans are to open new centers, to include other churches and missions, and to open a residence institute.

ECUADOR - Country Summary

Year	Inst	Cent	Teachers					Students				
			Full	Part	Miss	Natl	Tot	Cert	Dipl	Bach	Lic	Tot
1966	1	3	2	1	3	0	3	55				55
1967	1	4	2	2	3	1	4	52	24	0	0	76
1968	1	6	1	1	2	0	2	94	29	0	0	123
1969	4											
1970	5											
1971	5											
1972	5	66	14	78	20	72	92	489	125	59	3	676
1973												
1974												
1975												

NATIONAL COORDINATOR: Enrique Guang T.
                         Seminario Biblico Alianza
                         Apartado 2006
                         Guayaquil, Ecuador

AFFILIATION: ALISTE

COUNTRY: Ecuador

Centro de Estudios Teológicos
Casilla 455
Calle 1509, Nueve de Octubre
Quito, Ecuador

Year	Cent	Teachers					Students				
		Full	Part	Miss	Natl	Total	Cert	Dipl	Bach	Lic	Total
1966	3	2	1	3	0	3	55	0	0	0	55
1967	4	2	2	3	1	4	52	24	0	0	76
1968	6	1	1	2	0	2	94	29	0	0	113
1969	7	3	1	4	0	4	50	25	0	0	75
1970	11	5	2	6	1	7	52	21	0	0	73
1971	11	4	7	4	2	11	40	29	0	0	69
1972	9	6	1	4	3	7	87	37	38	3	165
1973											
1974											
1975											

(1966 data CET n.d.)

SPONSORING GROUPS: United Evangelical Church of Ecuador
                      Evangelical Covenant Church of Ecuador
                      United Andes Indian Mission
                      Church of the Brethren

OTHER PARTICIPANTS: Foursquare Church
                      Various local congregations

SUPPORTED BY: North American mission boards and TEF

STUDENT FEES   The student pays an annual matriculation
                      fee of from $1.25 to $2.00 plus $0.12 for
                      each lesson of two weeks of study.

RECOGNITION OF   A certificate is given upon completion of
STUDIES: each course.

ORDINATION: The program is mainly for laymen, but
                      there is a curriculum which can lead to
                      ordination.

CANDIDATES FOR
FULL TIME SERVICE: 1%.

CLASS FREQUENCY: Generally, weekly.

PREPARATION OF   Two members of the center have prepared
MATERIALS: extension materials.

COUNTRY: Ecuador

Centro Interamericano de Estudios Teológicos
Casilla 860
Guayaquil, Ecuador

		Teachers					Students			
Year	Cent	Full	Part	Miss	Natl	Total	Cert	Dipl	Bach	Lic	Total
1970	1	0	2	2	0	2	0	12	5	0	17
1971	1	0	2	1	1	2	0	24	4	0	28
1972	3	0	4	3	1	4	0	40	7	0	47
1973											
1974											
1975											

SPONSORING GROUPS: Oriental Missionary Society International
                     Association of Interamerican Churches in
                         Ecuador

OTHER PARTICIPANTS: Gospel Missionary Union
                     Christian and Missionary Alliance
                     Foursquare Gospel Church

SUPPORTED BY: Mission subsidy and tuition

STUDENT FEES: The student pays $0.40 per semester course
                     and buys his own books and manuals.

RECOGNITION OF   A grade card is given upon completion of
    STUDIES: each course. Degrees offered are Diploma
                     in Theology and Bachelor of Theology.

ORDINATION: The program is considered appropriate as
                     lay training and also will fulfill the pre-
                     requisites for ordination of the Associa-
                     tion of Interamerican Churches.

CANDIDATES FOR   Perhaps 20%
FULL TIME SERVICE:

ACCREDITATION: None.

CLASS FREQUENCY: Weekly or bi-weekly.

PREPARATION OF   No member of the institution has prepared
    MATERIALS: extension materials.

COUNTRY: Ecuador

Seminario Bíblico Alianza
Apartado 2006
Guayaquil, Ecuador

		Teachers					Students			
Year	Cent	Full	Part	Miss	Natl	Total	Cert	Dipl	Bach	Lic	Total
1969											
1970	3						1	14	4	2	21
1971	5										60
1972	4	4	2	2	4	6	20	24	10	0	54
1973											
1974											
1975											

SPONSORING GROUPS: Christian and Missionary Alliance

OTHER PARTICIPANTS: None.

SUPPORTED BY: Mission subsidy.

STUDENT FEES: The student pays $5.00 for the cycle of six months.

RECOGNITION OF STUDIES: Certificates are given upon the completion of each cycle.

ORDINATION: The diploma and bachelor level can lead to ordination.

CANDIDATES FOR FULL TIME SERVICE: About 30%.

ACCREDITATION:

CLASS FREQUENCY: Weekly.

PREPARATION OF MATERIALS: One member of the faculty has prepared extension materials.

PLANS: Regional vice-rectors have been named for 1973 with the purpose of opening ten new centers.

COUNTRY: Ecuador

Seminario Bíblico Unión
Casilla 269
Latacunga, Ecuador

		Teachers					Students				
Year	Cent	Full	Part	Miss	Natl	Total	Cert	Dipl	Bach	Lic	Total
1969	2	0	3	3	0	3	10	9	2	0	21
1970	10	2	5	7	0	7	10	43	10	0	63
1971	13	3	4	7	0	7	15	60	15	0	90
1972	49	4	50	9	45	54	380	18	4	0	402
1973											
1974											
1975											

SPONSORING GROUPS: The Berean Mission and Gospel Missionary
                     Union.
OTHER PARTICIPANTS: None.

SUPPORTED BY: Offerings from the U.S.
                     Student fees

STUDENT FEES: The student pays about $2.50 for texts plus
                     a matriculation fee of $.40 per year.

RECOGNITION OF   A progress report is given at the end of
   STUDIES: each year.

ORDINATION: This program is considered lay training.

CANDIDATES FOR
FULL TIME SERVICE: Not known.

ACCREDITATION: None.

CLASS FREQUENCY: Weekly.

PREPARATION OF   Four members of the institution have pre-
   MATERIALS.   pared extension materials.

COUNTRY: Ecuador

Seminario Luterano de Extensión
Casilla 1334
Cuenca, Ecuador

		Teachers					Students			
Year	Cent	Full	Part	Miss	Natl	Total	Cert	Dipl	Bach	Lic	Total
1969											
1970	2						1	2	5	0	8
1971											12
1972	1	0	2	2	0	2	2	6	0	0	8
1973											
1974											
1975											

SPONSORING GROUPS: Evangelical Lutheran Mission

OTHER PARTICIPANTS: None.

SUPPORTED BY: Mission subsidy and student tuition.

STUDENT FEES: The student pays $3.00 per semester course
                     plus $0.50 matriculation.

RECOGNITION OF
   STUDIES: As yet, none.

ORDINATION: Ordination does not depend on the course of
                     study. A person who is called can be or-
                     dained after, before or during the course.

CANDIDATES FOR
FULL TIME SERVICE: None.

ACCREDITATION: None.

CLASS FREQUENCY: Weekly.

PREPARATION OF   No member of the seminary has prepared ex-
   MATERIALS: tension materials.

PLANS: There is a possibility of opening two new
                     centers.

COUNTRY: England

A workshop on theological education by extension was led
by Peter Savage in Bridewell Hall, London under the auspices of
the Evangelical Missionary Alliance on January 5-8, 1971.   Forty delegates from some twenty-six missionary societies and six
Bible colleges in Great Britain attended.   Most of those present
were interested in the application of extension outside of
England.   However, after the workshop, Savage lectured on extension at eight Bible colleges and considerable interest was
shown.   Some ten years earlier the Church of England had begun
some experiments in ministerial training which incorporate some
of the extension principles and are described briefly below.

Rochester Theological College began in 1959 to train men
from business and professional backgrounds through a group study
system.   Most of these men were between the ages of thirty and
forty.

The first scheme to provide a full training for ordination
while men remain in their existing jobs was initiated by the
Southwork Ordination Course in 1960.   In this three year course
men attend lectures two nights a week, spend one weekend a
month together and have a two week summer school session.   At
the end of the three year course there is a final six week
residential term.   Much of the teaching is done through discussion and each man is assigned a parish priest as his tutor.
About twenty men per year followed this system.

The Worcester Ordination College opened in October of 1962.
It accepts candidates between the ages of forty and sixty.   They
are trained for a shortened General Ordination Exam.   Teaching
is given by clergy from the Diocese (Evans 1963:181-2).

ETHIOPIA – Country Summary

Year	Inst	Cent	Teachers					Students				
			Full	Part	Miss	Natl	Tot	Cert	Dipl	Bach	Lic	Tot
1970	1											
1971	1											
1972	1	5	1	10	6	5	11	95	25	0	0	120
1973												
1974												
1975												

COUNTRY: Ethiopia

Mekane Yesus Seminary
P. O. Box 1247
Addis Ababa, Ethiopia

		Teachers					Students			
Year	Cent	Full	Part	Miss	Natl	Total	Cert	Dipl	Bach	Lic	Total
1970											
1971											
1972	5	1	10	6	5	11	95	25	0	0	120
1973											
1974											
1975											

SPONSORING GROUPS:	Swedish Lutheran Mission
	German Hermansburg Mission
	Norwegian Lutheran Mission
	Finnish Lutheran Mission
	Evangelical Church Mekane Yesus
	American Lutheran Mission
OTHER PARTICIPANTS:	Bethel Church
	Eritrea Evangelical Church
SUPPORTED BY:	The Evangelical Church Mekane Yesus, its synods and the sponsoring missions.
STUDENT FEES:	The student pays about Eth. 4.00 per semester course.
RECOGNITION OF STUDIES:	Certificates are given at the end of each year. Plans call for diplomas as pastors, evangelists, Sunday School teachers, workers etc., after 25 subjects have been studied.
ORDINATION:	The program could lead to ordination but it mainly aims at training laymen.
CANDIDATES FOR FULL TIME SERVICE:	25%.
ACCREDITATION:	None. The institution is negotiating with Trinity College of HSIU for recognition.
CLASS FREQUENCY:	Weekly.
PREPARATION OF MATERIALS:	12 members of the institution have prepared extension materials.
PLANS:	The seminary plans to organize new centers within several synods and congregations, beginning in September of 1973.

COUNTRY: France

No institutional program of extension has been discovered in France. Beginning in 1973 two Conservative Baptist missionaries are instructing lay leaders for more effective ministry in the church. In the city of Rouen three men on a diploma level of instruction will be instructed evenings with a full weekend retreat once a month. It is hoped that these men together will assume the pastoral leadership of their small congregation (Olsen 1973).

GUADELOUPE - Country Summary

Year	Inst	Cent	Teachers					Students				
			Full	Part	Miss	Natl	Tot	Cert	Dipl	Bach	Lic	Tot
1967	1											
1968	1											
1969	1											
1970	1											
1971	1											
1972	1	4	1	1	2	0	2	57	0	0	0	57
1973												
1974												
1975												

COUNTRY: Guadeloupe

Seminaire Evangelique des Antilles Francaises
B.P. 228
Pointe-a-Pitre, Guadeloupe, F.W.I.

		Teachers					Students				
Year	Cent	Full	Part	Miss	Natl	Total	Cert	Dipl	Bach	Lic	Total
1967											
1968											
1969											
1970											
1971											
1972	4	1	1	2	0	2					57
1973											
1974											
1975											

SPONSORING GROUPS: West Indies Mission

OTHER PARTICIPANTS: Southern Baptists

SUPPORTED BY: Mission subsidy and student fees.

STUDENT FEES: The student pays $30.00 for the first
course (including retreat fees and workbook) and $5.00 for each additional course.

RECOGNITION OF   A certificate is given for each course.
STUDIES: An intermediate diploma is given for a basic
core of studies representing about half of
the curriculum.

ORDINATION: These studies can lead to ordination.

CANDIDATES FOR
FULL TIME SERVICE: 5%.

ACCREDITATION: None.

CLASS FREQUENCY: Weekly.

PREPARATION OF
MATERIALS: Two members of the faculty have prepared extension materials.

PLANS: This year the goal of four centers was
reached and no new plans have been for-
mulated.

GUATEMALA - Country Summary

Year	Inst	Cent	Full	Part	Miss	Natl	Tot	Cert	Dipl	Bach	Lic	Tot
1963	1	7	5	0	4	1	5	0	38	12	0	50
1964	1	7	6	2	6	2	8	0	67	21	0	88
1965	1	9	8	1	6	3	9	0	67	16	0	83
1966	2	24	8	4	6	6	12	85	115	22	6	228
1967	2	24	8	4	6	6	12	100	114	26	6	246
1968	2	27	8	7	6	9	15	115	169	30	6	315
1969	3	30	7	6	4	9	13	120	191	43	6	360
1970	4	33	8	6	5	9	14	125	167	43	6	341
1971	4	33	8	6	5	9	14	130	228	43	6	407
1972	4	65	19	16	14	21	35	280	308	54	0	642
1973												
1974												
1975												

NATIONAL COORDINATOR: Jose G. Carrera
                          6 Avenida A 4-68, Zona 1
                          Guatemala, Guatemala

PUBLICATIONS: ALISTE Bulletin
                          Extension Seminary

AFFILIATION: ALISTE

COUNTRY: Guatemala

Instituto Bíblico "Berea"
Apartado 8
Chiquimula, Guatemala

		Teachers					Students				
Year	Cent	Full	Part	Miss	Natl	Total	Cert	Dipl	Bach	Lic	Total
1966	13	1	3	2	2	4	85	0	0	0	85
1967	9	1	3	2	2	4	100	0	0	0	100
1968	12	1	4	2	3	5	115	0	0	0	115
1969	15	1	4	2	3	5	120	0	0	0	120
1970	18	1	4	1	4	5	125	0	0	0	125
1971	19	2	4	1	5	6	130	0	0	0	130
1972	21	2	5	1	6	7	125	0	0	0	125
1973	18	1	7	2	6	8	129	0	0	0	129
1974											
1975											

SPONSORING GROUPS: California Yearly Meeting of Friends.
Central America Yearly Meeting of Friends.

OTHER PARTICIPANTS: None.

SUPPORTED BY: Mission subsidy.

STUDENT FEES: The student buys the manual and textbook -
an average of $3.00 per trimester.

RECOGNITION OF   A "Christian Worker's" Certificate is
STUDIES: given upon completion of the program.

ORDINATION: The program is primarily lay training, but
credit is given for these studies in the
residence program, which is the training
program for ordination.

CANDIDATES FOR
FULL TIME SERVICE: About 15%.

PREPARATION OF   Eight members of the institution have pre-
MATERIALS: pared extension materials.

PLANS: Plans are to add courses to the program for
the bachelor level.

COUNTRY - Guatemala

Instituto Bíblico de la Iglesia de Dios de Guatemala
Postal: Apartado 102, Quezaltenango
Edificio: 7a. Av. 13-41 Z. 5, Quezaltenango

		Teachers					Students				
Year	Cent	Full	Part	Miss	Natl	Total	Cert	Dipl	Bach	Lic	Total
1973		3	0	0	3	3	62	28	0	0	90
1974											
1975											

SPONSORING GROUPS: Church of God, World Missions
                     Churches of God in Guatemala

OTHER PARTICIPANTS: None.

SUPPORTED BY: Mission subsidy and national churches.

STUDENT FEES: The student pays a matriculation fee of
                     $13.50 per semester and buys his texts.

RECOGNITION OF
   STUDIES:

ORDINATION:

CANDIDATES FOR
FULL TIME SERVICE:

ACCREDITATION:

CLASS FREQUENCY:

PREPARATION OF
   MATERIALS: No member of the faculty has prepared ex-
                     tension materials.

PLANS:

COUNTRY: Guatemala

Instituto Bíblico Quiche
San Cristobal, Toto
Guatemala

		Teachers					Students				
Year	Cent	Full	Part	Miss	Natl	Total	Cert	Dipl	Bach	Lic	Total
1969											
1970											
1971											
1972	14	7	3	5	5	10	115	0	0	0	115
1973											
1974											
1975											

SPONSORING GROUPS: Presbyterian Church of Guatemala
Primitive Methodist Church of Guatemala

OTHER PARTICIPANTS: Various other churches send students.

SUPPORTED BY: Subsidy from the U.S.A. and the tuition of
the students.

STUDENT FEES: The student pays $1.00 for the manual and
the course.

RECOGNITION OF   A certificate is given upon completion of
   STUDIES: each course.

ORDINATION: This program is lay training.

CANDIDATES FOR
FULL TIME SERVICE: None.

ACCREDITATION: None.

CLASS FREQUENCY: Weekly or every two weeks.

PREPARATION OF
   MATERIALS:

PLANS: Plans are to open more centers and train
more teachers in various places according
to funds available.

COUNTRY: Guatemala

Instituto Superior Teológico Bautista
Apartado 322
Guatemala, Central America

		Teachers					Students			
Year	Cent	Full	Part	Miss	Natl	Total	Cert	Dipl	Bach	Lic	Total
1970											
1971											
1972	12	2	7	4	5	9	40	110	12	0	162
1973											
1974											
1975											

SPONSORING GROUPS: Southern Baptist Convention of the U.S.A.,
                    Board of Foreign Missions

OTHER PARTICIPANTS: None.

SUPPORTED BY: Mission subsidy and the national convention
                    of churches.

STUDENT FEES: The student pays $1.00 and buys his texts.

RECOGNITION OF   Certificates are given for completion of
STUDIES: each course and diplomas are given upon com-
                    pletion of a program.

ORDINATION: This program is considered appropriate for
                    laymen and also leads to ordination.

CANDIDATES FOR
FULL TIME SERVICE: About 12%.

ACCREDITATION:

CLASS FREQUENCY: Weekly.

PREPARATION OF   Three members of the institution have pre-
MATERIALS: pared extension materials.

PLANS: Plans are to organize new centers as needed.

COUNTRY: Guatemala

Seminario Evangélico Presbiteriano
Apartado 3
San Felipe Retalhuleo

Year	Cent	Teachers					Students				
		Full	Part	Miss	Natl	Total	Cert	Dipl	Bach	Lic	Total
1963	7	5	0	4	1	5	0	38	12	0	50
1964	7	6	2	6	2	8	0	67	21	0	88
1965	9	8	1	6	3	9	0	67	16	0	83
1966	11	7	1	4	4	8	0	115	22	6	143
1967	15	7	1	4	4	8	0	114	26	6	146
1968	15	7	3	4	6	10	0	164	30	6	200
1969	15	6	2	2	6	8	0	191	43	6	240
1970	15	7	2	4	5	9	0	167	43	6	216
1971	14	6	2	4	4	8	0	228	43	6	277
1972	18	7	2	4	5	9	0	198	42	0	240
1973	16	6	1	2	6	7	0	199	30	0	229
1974											
1975											

SPONSORING GROUPS: Presbyterian Church

OTHER PARTICIPANTS: None.

SUPPORTED BY: The Synod.

STUDENT FEES: The student pays about $20.00 per year.

RECOGNITION OF   A certificate is given upon completion of
   STUDIES: each course and diplomas upon completion of
                     the program of studies.

ORDINATION: Some students are lay leaders and others are
                     seeking ordination.

CANDIDATES FOR
FULL TIME SERVICE: 25%.

ACCREDITATION: Affiliated with ALET.

CLASS FREQUENCY: Weekly.

PREPARATION OF   Five members of the institution have pre-
   MATERIALS: pared extension materials.

PLANS: The institution plans to open new centers
                     as possible.

GUYANA - Country Summary

			Teachers					Students				
Year	Inst	Cent	Full	Part	Miss	Natl	Tot	Cert	Dipl	Bach	Lic	Tot
1971	1	6										145
1972												
1973												
1974												
1975												

COUNTRY: Guyana

Lutheran Church of Guyana

		Teachers					Students			
Year	Cent	Full	Part	Miss	Natl	Total	Cert	Dipl	Bach	Lic	Total
1971	6										145
1972											
1973											
1974											
1975											

The program was offered in connection with the United Theological College of the West Indies *(Extension Seminary* 1971 No. 4:9).

HAITI – Country Summary

Year	Inst	Cent	Teachers					Students				
			Full	Part	Miss	Natl	Tot	Cert	Dipl	Bach	Lic	Tot
1971	1											
1972	3	32	6	27	15	18	33	450	235	1	0	688
1973												
1974												
1975												

NATIONAL COORDINATOR: Centre d'Information et de Estatistique
                        Evangelique
                        B.P. 458
                        Port-au-Prince, Haiti

COUNTRY: Haiti

Ecole Biblique Par Extension
Box 458
Port-au-Prince, Haiti

		Teachers				Students				
Year	Cent	Full	Part	Miss	Natl	Total	Cert	Dipl	Bach	Lic	Total
1972	6	0	8	3	5	8	0	75	0	0	75
1973											
1974											
1975											

SPONSORING GROUPS: Unevangelized Fields Mission

OTHER PARTICIPANTS: None.

SUPPORTED BY: Mission subsidy and tuition.

STUDENT FEES: The student pays $5.00 per semester.

RECOGNITION OF
STUDIES: Certificates are given upon completion of each course.

ORDINATION: This is considered lay training. As yet there is no curriculum which is intended to lead to ordination.

CANDIDATES FOR
FULL TIME SERVICE: None.

ACCREDITATION: None.

CLASS FREQUENCY: Weekly.

PREPARATION OF
MATERIALS: Two members of the institution have prepared materials for extension.

PLANS: Plans are to open new centers in 1973 and to conduct two training seminars.

COUNTRY: Haiti

Extension Bible School of Eastern Haiti
Box 1096
Port-au-Prince, Haiti

		Teachers					Students			
Year	Cent	Full	Part	Miss	Natl	Total	Cert	Dipl	Bach	Lic	Total
1972	7	1	3	4	0	4	135	10	0	0	145
1973											
1974											
1975											

SPONSORING GROUPS: Missionary Church (World Gospel Mission, integrated in Haiti as a partner mission).

OTHER PARTICIPANTS: American Baptists

SUPPORTED BY: Mission subsidy.

STUDENT FEES: The student pays $1.00 per semester course.

RECOGNITION OF   Certificates are given for each semester
STUDIES: course completed. Plans are being formulated for future certificates at some interval or cycle of completion.

ORDINATION: This program is considered lay training.

CANDIDATES FOR
FULL TIME SERVICE: None.

ACCREDITATION: None.

CLASS FREQUENCY: Weekly or bi-weekly.

PREPARATION OF   Three members of the institution have pre-
MATERIALS: pared materials for extension.

PLANS: Plans are to organize new centers in new areas.

COUNTRY: Haiti

Institut Biblique Lumiere
Boite Postale 71
Aux Cayes, Haiti

		Teachers					Students			
Year	Cent	Full	Part	Miss	Natl	Total	Cert	Dipl	Bach	Lic	Total
1971	15	2	12	4	10	14	85	90	0	0	175
1972	19	5	16	8	13	21	150	150	1	0	301
1973											
1974											
1975											

SPONSORING GROUPS: West Indies Mission
Evangelical Baptist Mission of South Haiti

OTHER PARTICIPANTS: None.

SUPPORTED BY: Mission subsidy plus tuition.

STUDENT FEES: The student pays $6.00 matriculation and $4.00 toward books and materials per year.

RECOGNITION OF STUDIES: No intermediate certificates are given.

ORDINATION: Most students do not hope for ordination but men students with 75% average and with character for the same are eligible for the residence seminary.

CANDIDATES FOR FULL TIME SERVICE: Information not available.

ACCREDITATION: None.

CLASS FREQUENCY: Weekly.

PREPARATION OF MATERIALS: Four members of the institution have prepared extension materials.

PLANS: Plans are being made to expand to a full four year program. New centers will be opened as students apply and teachers are available.

HONDURAS – Country Summary

			Teachers					Students				
Year	Inst	Cent	Full	Part	Miss	Natl	Tot	Cert	Dipl	Bach	Lic	Tot
1967	1											20
1968	3	3							36	5		41
1969	3	4							50			50
1970	3					4			26			26
1971	2											
1972	2	22	5	12	4	13	17	83	0	0	0	83
1973												
1974												
1975												

(Data 1967–70, Mulholland 1971: 139, 167, 176, 153–159).

AFFILIATION: ALISTE

COUNTRY: Honduras

Instituto Bíblico de Extensión
Apartado 164
La Ceiba, Honduras

Year	Cent	Teachers					Students				
		Full	Part	Miss	Natl	Total	Cert	Dipl	Bach	Lic	Total
1967	2	1					15	0	0	0	15
1968	3	1					15	0	0	0	15
1969	5	1	2	1	2	3	20	0	0	0	20
1970	8	3	2	1	4	5	30	0	0	0	30
1971	11	3	2	1	4	5	35	0	0	0	35
1972	18	3	7	1	9	10	48	0	0	0	48
1973											
1974											
1975											

SPONSORING GROUPS: Conservative Baptist Mission

OTHER PARTICIPANTS: None.

SUPPORTED BY: Conservative Baptist Mission.

STUDENT FEES: The student pays less than $2.00 per year unless he wishes to buy books for his own use.

RECOGNITION OF STUDIES: Certificates are given at the end of each period.

ORDINATION: Almost all of the students are already lay pastors. They do not ordain in a formal sense.

CANDIDATES FOR FULL TIME SERVICE: About 5-10%.

ACCREDITATION: None.

CLASS FREQUENCY: Varies from once a week to once a month.

PREPARATION OF MATERIALS: Three members of the institution have prepared extension materials.

PLANS: The institution hopes to continue opening new sub-centers and sub-sub-centers. The goal of each student is to plant a church and open a sub-center in it, and make the process continue until they reach the whole field.

COUNTRY: Honduras

Institutos Bíblicos Interamericanos
Apartado 97
La Ceiba, Honduras

		Teachers					Students				
Year	Cent	Full	Part	Miss	Natl	Total	Cert	Dipl	Bach	Lic	Total
1968											
1969											
1970											
1971											
1972	4	2	5	3	4	7	35	0	0	0	35
1973											
1974											
1975											

SPONSORING GROUPS: Evangelical Mennonite Mission
Evangelical Mennonite Church of Honduras
Baptist Church

OTHER PARTICIPANTS: None.

SUPPORTED BY: Funds from sponsoring groups.

STUDENT FEES: The student pays the cost of books plus a
matriculation fee which is determined locally

RECOGNITION OF   A certificate is given upon completion of
STUDIES: each course.

ORDINATION: There is one program of studies for workers
and another for ministerial candidates, al-
though ordination is based on spiritual, not
educational qualifications.

CANDIDATES FOR
FULL TIME SERVICE: Not   known.

ACCREDITATION: None.

CLASS FREQUENCY: Varies according to the area.

PREPARATION OF   Two members of the institution have pre-
MATERIALS: pared extension materials.

PLANS: There are three new centers about to be
opened. They hope to train more personnel
in different regions to teach in a continued program.

HONG KONG - Country Summary

Year	Inst	Cent	Teachers					Students				
			Full	Part	Miss	Natl	Tot	Cert	Dipl	Bach	Lic	Tot
1972	1	12	6	14	3	17	20	0	0	0	52	52
1973												
1974												
1975												

COUNTRY: Hong Kong

Concordia Theological Seminary
68 Begonia Road,
Yua Yat Chuen
Kowloon, Hong Kong

		Teachers					Students				
Year	Cent	Full	Part	Miss	Natl	Total	Cert	Dipl	Bach	Lic	Total
1972	12	6	14	3	17	20	0	0	0	52	52
1973											
1974											
1975											

SPONSORING GROUPS: Lutheran Church, Missouri Synod

OTHER PARTICIPANTS: None.

SUPPORTED BY: Mission subsidy and student fees.

STUDENT FEES: The student pays $1.00 per credit and buys his own books.

RECOGNITION OF STUDIES: The seminary awards the following degrees: Master of Ministry, Bachelor of Divinity, Bachelor or Theology, and Teacher Education Program.

ORDINATION: All students may be ordained for a preaching or teaching ministry.

CANDIDATES FOR FULL TIME SERVICE:

ACCREDITATION:

CLASS FREQUENCY: Weekly.

PREPARATION OF MATERIALS: All the professors are working on programmed materials.

PLANS:

INDIA - Country Summary

			Teachers					Students				
Year	Inst	Cent	Full	Part	Miss	Natl	Tot	Cert	Dipl	Bach	Lic	Tot
1971												
1972	1	13	5	14	7	12	19	0	0	10	210	220
1973												
1974												
1975												

NATIONAL COORDINATOR: Rev. Ian McCleary
9/15 Lloyd Road Extension
Bangalore 5
India

COUNTRY: India

The Association for Theological Extension Education (TAFTEE)
9/15 Lloyd Rd. Extn.
Bangalore 560006, India

		Teachers					Students			
Year	Cent	Full	Part	Miss	Natl	Total	Cert	Dipl	Bach	Lic	Total
1971											
1972	13	5	14	7	12	19	0	0	10	210	220
1973											
1974											
1975											

SPONSORING GROUPS: Allahabad Bible Seminary (Oriental Mission-
ary Society)
Gurukal Lutheran Theological Seminary
Kaluari Bible School (United Fellowship of
Christian Service)
South India Bible Seminary
Southern Asia Bible College (Assembly of
God)
Union Biblical Seminary
Baptist Christian Association Work Program
Bible and Medical Missionary Fellowship
Bihar Mennonite Church
Brethren Mission
Christian and Missionary Alliance
Church of the Nazarene Mission
General Conference Mennonite Mission
Indian Baptist Mission
Mennonite Brethren Church
Regions Beyond Missionary Union
Poona and Indian Village Mission

OTHER PARTICIPANTS: Groups all over India provide tutors and
encourage students to join.

SUPPORTED BY: Overseas donations, subscriptions from member bodies and student fees.

STUDENT FEES: The student pays $10.00 per year plus the
cost of textbooks.

RECOGNITION OF
STUDIES: Degrees are granted as follows:
B.T.S. - Part I - 2 years
Part II - 3 years
Dip. R.K. - Part I - 2 years

ORDINATION: This is considered lay training and not intended to prepare for ordination.

COUNTRY: India

The Association for Theological Extension Education (TAFTEE)
   (continued)

CANDIDATES FOR
FULL TIME SERVICE: 5%.

ACCREDITATION: Member of the Board of Theological Educa
                      tion.

CLASS FREQUENCY: Weekly.

PREPARATION OF   One member of TAFTEE has prepared extension
   MATERIALS: materials.

PLANS: Plans are to add more courses at both levels,
                      the translation of courses in vernaculars,
                      the beginning of certificate courses and
                      the opening of new centers at each level.

INDONESIA - Country Summary

			Teachers					Students				
Year	Inst	Cent	Full	Part	Miss	Natl	Tot	Cert	Dipl	Bach	Lic	Tot
1972	3	14	6	26	2	30	32	53	34	145	1	458
1973												
1974												
1975												

NATIONAL COORDINATOR: G. Kamphausen
                         Djalan H
                         Djakarta, Indonesia

COUNTRY: Indonesia

Christian and Missionary Alliance
Djalan H
Djakarta, Indonesia

		Teachers					Students			
Year	Cent	Full	Part	Miss	Natl	Total	Cert	Dipl	Bach	Lic	Total
1972											225
1973											
1974											
1975											

(Savage 1972)

COUNTRY: Indonesia

Lembaga Pembinaan Jemaat GPIB (Institute for churchmen education
                           development of the Protestant
                           Church in Western Indonesia)
10 Medau Merdeka Timur, Jakarta

		Teachers						Students			
Year	Cent	Full	Part	Miss	Natl	Total	Cert	Dipl	Bach	Lic	Total
1973	5	4	21	1	24	25	0	0	122	0	122
1974											
1975											

SPONSORING GROUPS: Division of Overseas Ministries, New York

OTHER PARTICIPANTS: Students from three other Indonesian evange-
                    lical churches and some students from the
                    Army chaplaincy.

SUPPORTED BY: Division of Overseas Ministries
                    Local church.

STUDENT FEES: The student pays at least $10.00 per year.
                    Some give more as a contribution.

RECOGNITION OF   Bachelor of Theology and Diploma in Theology
   STUDIES: with no intermediate goals at the present
                    time.

ORDINATION: This is both lay and ministerial training.

CANDIDATES FOR
FULL TIME SERVICE:

ACCREDITATION: The Bachelor degree and the Theological
                    Diploma will be given by the Theological
                    Seminary at Ujung Pandang and is therefore
                    accredited.

CLASS FREQUENCY: Weekly and bi-weekly.

PREPARATION OF
   MATERIALS: All twenty-five faculty members prepare
                    extension materials.

PLANS: A special conference on theological educa-
                    tion by extension, organized by the Associ-
                    ation of Indonesian Theological Schools will
                    be held in April, 1973.

COUNTRY: Indonesia

Sumatra School of Theology
Kotak Pos 289 Medan
Sumatra, Indonesia

		Teachers				Students				
Year	Cent	Full	Part	Miss	Natl	Total	Cert	Dipl	Bach	Lic	Total
1971											
1972	9	2	5	1	6	7	53	34	23	1	111
1973											
1974											
1975											

SPONSORING GROUPS: Assemblies of God

OTHER PARTICIPANTS: Independent Pentecostal Churches of
Northern Sumatra
Lutheran Church

SUPPORTED BY: Subsidy from U.S. mission.

STUDENT FEES: The student pays $0.55 per month plus a
registration fee of $0.15.

RECOGNITION OF
STUDIES: Certificates are given upon the completion
of each course. A diploma in Theology will
be given after the completion of 15 year
long units.

ORDINATION: This is considered ministerial training,
but the details of ordination have not yet
been worked out. It depends upon the cooperation of the residence schools and the
national church.

CANDIDATES FOR
FULL TIME SERVICE: 53%.

ACCREDITATION: None.

CLASS FREQUENCY: Weekly.

PREPARATION OF
MATERIALS: One member of the faculty is now preparing
an extension course.

PLANS: Plans include extension programs operating
in connection with each of the four residence
schools on four different islands in the
Indonesian Archipelago.

IRAN - Country Summary

Year	Inst	Cent	Teachers					Students				
			Full	Part	Miss	Natl	Tot	Cert	Dipl	Bach	Lic	Tot
1970												
1971												
1972	1	4	1	3	3	1	4	0	0	16	10	26
1973												
1974												
1975												

COUNTRY: Iran

Iran Extension of the Near East School of Theology
P. O. Box 1505
Tehran, Iran

		Teachers					Students			
Year	Cent	Full	Part	Miss	Natl	Total	Cert	Dipl	Bach	Lic	Total
1970											
1971	2	1	1	2	0	2	0	0	7	5	12
1972	4	1	3	3	0	4	0	0	16	10	26
1973	4	1	3	3	0	4	0	5	9	12	26
1974											
1975											

SPONSORING GROUPS: Evangelical Church of Iran
United Presbyterian Church in the U.S.A.

OTHER PARTICIPANTS: Episcopal Church of Iran
Philadelphia Church of Iran (Assembly of God)
Armenian Apostolic Church (Orthodox)
Roman Catholic Church (Dominican)

SUPPORTED BY: Student fees
An endowment fund of the Evangelical Church
of Iran for Theological Education
United Presbyterian Church in the U.S.A.

STUDENT FEES: The student pays $40.00 per course plus all
books. Auditors pay $7.50 per course.

RECOGNITION OF   The institution grants a Bachelor of Theo-
STUDIES: logy degree.

ORDINATION: The program is primarily lay training but
fulfills requirements for ordination for
those desiring it and so selected by the
church.

CANDIDATES FOR
FULL TIME SERVICE: 15%.

ACCREDITATION: The N.E.S.T. is accredited by A.T.E.N.E.

CLASS FREQUENCY: In Tehran - two evenings a week.
In the provinces - 4 days once a month.

PREPARATION OF   No member of the institution has prepared
MATERIALS: extension materials.

PLANS: Plans include the inclusion of Iranian staff.

ITALY - Country Summary

In 1973 the Italian Bible Institute will launch an extension program.   The school sponsored by the Greater European Mission will have the cooperation of other mission groups.

Instituto Biblico Evangelico
00141 Roma - Via Cimone, 100
Italy

JAMAICA - Country Summary

| Year | Inst | Cent | Teachers | | | | | Students | | | | |
			Full	Part	Miss	Natl	Tot	Cert	Dipl	Bach	Lic	Tot
1971	1	2										20
1972	2											40
1973												
1974												
1975												

COUNTRY: Jamaica

Jamaica Theological Seminary
Box 121
Kingston 8, Jamaica

		Teachers					Students				
Year	Cent	Full	Part	Miss	Natl	Total	Cert	Dipl	Bach	Lic	Total
1972											40
1973											
1974											
1975											

(Erdel 1973)

SPONSORING GROUPS: The Missionary Church

COUNTRY: Jamaica

United Theological College of the West Indies

		Teachers					Students				
Year	Cent	Full	Part	Miss	Natl	Total	Cert	Dipl	Bach	Lic	Total
1971	2										20
1972											
1973											
1974											
1975											

(Extension Seminary 1971 No. 4:9).

JAPAN - Country Summary

Year	Inst	Cent	Teachers					Students				
			Full	Part	Miss	Natl	Tot	Cert	Dipl	Bach	Lic	Tot
1973	1	1	4	11	4	11	15	0	0	9	11	20
1974												
1975												

COUNTRY: Japan

Covenant Seminary
17-8 Nakameguro, 5 Chome
Meguro ku, Tokyo, Japan

| | | Teachers | | | | | Students | | | |
Year	Cent	Full	Part	Miss	Natl	Total	Cert	Dipl	Bach	Lic	Total
1973	1	4	11	4	11	15	0	0	9	11	20
1974											
1975											

SPONSORING GROUPS: Evangelical Covenant Church of America
Mission Covenant Church of Sweden
German Alliance Mission

OTHER PARTICIPANTS: None.

SUPPORTED BY: Mission subsidy and student fees.

STUDENT FEES: The student pays approximately $200 per
year plus books.

RECOGNITION OF
    STUDIES:

ORDINATION: This program may lead to ordination.

CANDIDATES FOR
FULL TIME SERVICE:

ACCREDITATION:

CLASS FREQUENCY: Three hours three mornings or three
evenings per week.

PREPARATION OF   No extension materials have been prepared
    MATERIALS: locally.

PLANS:

KENYA - Country Summary

Year	Inst	Cent	Teachers					Students				
			Full	Part	Miss	Natl	Tot	Cert	Dipl	Bach	Lic	Tot
1972	1	5	5	5	5	5	10	90	0	0	0	90
1973												
1974												
1975												

COUNTRY: Kenya

Kima Theological College
P. O. Box 75
Maseno, Kenya

Year	Cent	Teachers					Students				
		Full	Part	Miss	Natl	Total	Cert	Dipl	Bach	Lic	Total
1972	5	5	5	5	5	10	90	0	0	0	90
1973											
1974											
1975											

SPONSORING GROUPS: Church of God in East Africa
Missionary Board of the Church of God, Anderson, Indiana.

OTHER PARTICIPANTS: None.

SUPPORTED BY: The above named groups.

STUDENT FEES: The student pays $1.05 per course.

RECOGNITION OF
STUDIES: A certificate of achievement is given after
4, 18, and 27 courses are completed.   The
total program is 34 courses.

ORDINATION: This program is primarily geared to pastoral
training leading to ordination.

CANDIDATES FOR
FULL TIME SERVICE: 60%.

ACCREDITATION: The residence institution is accredited.

CLASS FREQUENCY: Weekly.

PREPARATION OF
MATERIALS: Two members of the institution have prepared extension materials.

PLANS: Possibilities for expansion are numerous.
The only limitations are materials and
staff.

MALAYSIA - Country Summary

			Teachers					Students				
Year	Inst	Cent	Full	Part	Miss	Natl	Tot	Cert	Dipl	Bach	Lic	Tot
1972	1	15	1	5	3	3	6	0	0	100	0	100
1973												
1974												
1975												

NATIONAL COORDINATOR: Rev. Duain Vierow
                         21 Jalan Abdul Samad
                         Kuala Lumpur, Malaysia

PUBLICATIONS: Newsletter of the Malaysia TEE Fellow-
                           ship
                         21 Jalan Abdul Samad
                         Kuala Lumpur, Malaysia

COUNTRY: Malaysia

Evangelical Lutheran Church in Malaysia and Singapore
Lay Training Program
21 Jalan Abdul Samad
Kuala Lumpur, Malaysia

		Teachers					Students			
Year	Cent	Full	Part	Miss	Natl	Total	Cert	Dipl	Bach	Lic	Total
1972	15	1	5	3	3	6	0	0	100	0	100
1973											
1974											
1975											

SPONSORING GROUPS: Evangelical Lutheran Church
Church of Sweden Mission

OTHER PARTICIPANTS: None.

SUPPORTED BY: The church budget, part of which comes from the Church of Sweden Mission.

STUDENT FEES: The student pays nothing but a contribution is requested for each course.

RECOGNITION OF STUDIES: Certificates are awarded upon completion of each course and a Diploma upon completion of the program.

ORDINATION: The program is considered to be lay training but can lead toward commissioning to carry on a local ministry.

CANDIDATES FOR FULL TIME SERVICE: None.

ACCREDITATION: None.

CLASS FREQUENCY: Weekly.

PREPARATION OF MATERIALS: Three members of the institution have prepared extension materials.

PLANS: Other churches have expressed an interest and plans are being discussed for a larger, more cooperative effort.

MEXICO - Country Summary

Year	Inst	Cent	Teachers					Students				
			Full	Part	Miss	Natl	Tot	Cert	Dipl	Bach	Lic	Tot
1967	2											
1968	2											
1969	2											
1970	3											
1971	4											
1972	5	45	7	67	29	45	74	253	327	18	0	598
1973												
1974												
1975												

NATIONAL COORDINATOR: David Legters
                        Seminario Teológico Presbiteriano de
                            Mexico
                        Av. Universidad No. 1943
                        Mérida, Yucatán, Mexico

AFFILIATION: ALISTE

COUNTRY: Mexico

Departamento de Extensión
La Buena Tierra
Apartado 407
Saltillo, Coah.,
Mexico

Year	Cent	Teachers					Students				
		Full	Part	Miss	Natl	Total	Cert	Dipl	Bach	Lic	Total
1972	5	3	0	3	0	3	55	15	0	0	70
1973											
1974											
1975											

SPONSORING GROUPS: Church of God, Anderson, Indiana.

OTHER PARTICIPANTS: None.

SUPPORTED BY: Board of Missions of the Church of God National churches.

STUDENT FEES: The student pays for his books and other materials and gives a voluntary offering.

RECOGNITION OF STUDIES: Certificates are given upon completion of each course to encourage the student.

ORDINATION: The majority of those who study are laymen. Some are pastors already ordained.

CANDIDATES FOR FULL TIME SERVICE: About 20%.

ACCREDITATION: None.

CLASS FREQUENCY: Once or twice per week.

PREPARATION OF MATERIALS: Two members of the institution have prepared extension materials.

PLANS: Plans are to arrange circuits to remote places to prepare pastors.

COUNTRY: Mexico

Departamento de Extensión
Seminario Luterano Augsburgo
Apartado Postal 20-416
Mexico 20, D.F., Mexico

		Teachers					Students			
Year	Cent	Full	Part	Miss	Natl	Total	Cert	Dipl	Bach	Lic	Total
1971	4	1	4	1	4	5	0	25	0	0	25
1972	5	1	5	0	6	6	0	44	0	0	44
1973											
1974											
1975											

SPONSORING GROUPS: Several Lutheran groups in Mexico.

OTHER PARTICIPANTS: None.

SUPPORTED BY: Mission subsidy and national churches.

STUDENT FEES: The student pays $10.00 per year.

RECOGNITION OF   A certificate is given upon completion of
    STUDIES: 10 courses which is the basic curriculum

ORDINATION: This is considered training for lay workers.

CANDIDATES FOR
FULL TIME SERVICE: 10%.

ACCREDITATION: None.

CLASS FREQUENCY: 3 ten-day institutes per school year.

PREPARATION OF   Two members of the institution have pre-
    MATERIALS: pared extension materials.

PLANS: Plans are to offer continuing education
                     courses beyond the basic curriculum.

COUNTRY: Mexico

Instituto Bíblico "Vida y Verdad"
Apartado /196
H. del Parral, Chihuahua
Mexico

Year	Cent	Teachers					Students				
		Full	Part	Miss	Natl	Total	Cert	Dipl	Bach	Lic	Total
1970	6						16	10	15	0	41
1971	7						10	12	13	0	35
1972	7	2	2	4	0	4	11	8	5	0	24
1973											
1974											
1975											

SPONSORING GROUPS: Mexican Evangelistic Mission

OTHER PARTICIPANTS: None.

SUPPORTED BY: Evangelical Methodist Church of the U.S.A.
Mexican Evangelistic Mission.

STUDENT FEES: The student pays for the text book and manuals plus $1.00 per course per trimester.

RECOGNITION OF STUDIES: No certificates are given.

ORDINATION: The majority of the students do not expect to be ordained, but they could do so upon completing the course and meeting other denominational requirements.

CANDIDATES FOR FULL TIME SERVICE: Not known.

ACCREDITATION: None.

CLASS FREQUENCY: Frequency varies in the centers. In some they are held weekly, in others every two weeks, and in still others every three weeks.

PREPARATION OF MATERIALS: One member of the institution has prepared extension materials.

PLANS: Plans are to open a nocturnal center in the cities, and to develop the idea of giving certificates for different levels of completion.

COUNTRY: Mexico

Seminario Teólogico Bautista Mexicano
Corregidora /1333 Ote.,
Torreón, Coahuila, Mexico

Year	Cent	Teachers					Students				
		Full	Part	Miss	Natl	Total	Cert	Dipl	Bach	Lic	Total
1967											
1968											
1969											
1970	8										278
1971	10										352
1972	20	1	40	15	26	41	75	245	10	0	335
1973											
1974											
1975											

SPONSORING GROUPS: Mission Board of the Southern Baptist Church
National Baptist Convention of Mexico

OTHER PARTICIPANTS: None.

SUPPORTED BY: Mission subsidy and student fees.

STUDENT FEES: The student pays for his materials, an
average of $2.00 per month.

RECOGNITION OF
STUDIES: A Christian Worker's Diploma is given upon
completion of the first half of the course.
A Ministerial Preparation Diploma is given
upon completion of the entire course of 64
units of study. After completion of the
first three units of study they receive a
credential as students of the *"Plan de
Dispersión."*

ORDINATION: The program prepares both laymen and minsiters.

CANDIDATES FOR
FULL TIME SERVICE: 15%.

ACCREDITATION: The program is in the process of being
approved for accreditation by AMIET.

CLASS FREQUENCY: In some centers - 4 days per week for one
or two months, in others weekly, in others
15 days each month.

PREPARATION OF
MATERIALS: Nine members of the faculty have prepared
extension materials.

PLANS: To open more zones for Intensive Capacitation.

COUNTRY: Mexico

Seminario Teológico por Extensión del Sureste
Calle 61, /529
Mérida, Yucatán,
Mexico

Year	Cent	Teachers					Students				
		Full	Part	Miss	Natl	Total	Cert	Dipl	Bach	Lic	Total
1969	20	0	20	13	7	20					200
1970	20										200
1971	5										78
1972	8	0	20	7	13	20	112	15	3	0	130
1973											
1974											
1975											

SPONSORING GROUPS: Two presbyteries of the Presbyterian Church
                      of Mexico.

OTHER PARTICIPANTS: The Explorer Agency

SUPPORTED BY: National churches and student fees.

STUDENT FEES: The student pays for his books (about $0.80
                      per course) and an additional $0.40 for
                      each weekly session.

RECOGNITION OF   Degrees awarded are a Certificate, a Dip-
  STUDIES: loma, a Bachelor of Theology and a Bachelor
                      of Christian Education degree. Other recog-
                      nition is given to those who are not pre-
                      pared for the certificate level.

ORDINATION: The majority of the students are laymen
                      with perhaps one third looking to ordina-
                      tion. There is a program that can lead to
                      ordination.

CANDIDATES FOR   30%.
FULL TIME SERVICE:

ACCREDITATION: None, but it is seeking accreditation from
                      the Seminario Teológico Presbiteriano of
                      Mexico.

CLASS FREQUENCY: Weekly.

PREPARATION OF   One member of the faculty has prepared
  MATERIALS: extension materials.

PLANS: Plans are for new centers to be opened in
                      other parts of the Yucateca Peninsula.

NIGERIA - Country Summary

Year	Inst	Cent	Teachers					Students				
			Full	Part	Miss	Natl	Tot	Cert	Dipl	Bach	Lic	Tot
1970	1											
1971	2											
1972	2	12	8	2	2	8	10	35	82	2	2	121
1973												
1974												
1975												

COUNTRY: Nigeria

Biliri Bible Training School
E.C.W.A. Biliri via Gombe
N.E. State, Nigeria

		Teachers					Students				
Year	Cent	Full	Part	Miss	Natl	Total	Cert	Dipl	Bach	Lic	Total
1970											
1971											
1972	11	8	1	1	8	9	35	82	0	0	117
1973											
1974											
1975											

SPONSORING GROUPS: Sudan Interior Mission
Evangelical Churches of West Africa

OTHER PARTICIPANTS: Sudan United Mission
Fellowship of Christian Churches, Sudan

SUPPORTED BY: National churches and a subsidy from the
Sudan Interior Mission.

STUDENT FEES: The student pays $10.00 for books.

RECOGNITION OF   Recognition is given upon completion of
   STUDIES: each course.

ORDINATION: This program is considered lay training.

CANDIDATES FOR   100%. All are church leaders who farm
FULL TIME SERVICE: for a living.

ACCREDITATION: The institution meets S.I.M./E.C.W.A
standards for B.Th. in Kwara State.

CLASS FREQUENCY: Weekly.

PREPARATION OF   No member of the institution has pre-
   MATERIALS: pared extension materials.

PLANS: The school plans to open new centers in the
districts.

COUNTRY: Nigeria

United Missionary Society Theological College
Box 171
Ilorin, Kwarastate, Nigeria

Year	Cent	Teachers					Students				
		Full	Part	Miss	Natl	Total	Cert	Dipl	Bach	Lic	Total
1971											
1972	1	0	1	1	0	1	0	0	2	2	4
1973											
1974											
1975											

SPONSORING GROUPS: United Missionary Church of Africa

OTHER PARTICIPANTS: Baptists
                     Methodists

SUPPORTED BY: Student fees and mission subsidy in the
                     U.S.A. and Canada.

STUDENT FEES: The student pays $3.05 per semester hour.

RECOGNITION OF   A certificate is given for each course com-
   STUDIES: pleted. The institution grants a Bachelor
                     of Theology degree.

ORDINATION: This program could lead to ordination but
                     is primarily lay training.

CANDIDATES FOR
FULL TIME SERVICE: None.

ACCREDITATION: The institution is recognized by the State
                     Education Board.
CLASS FREQUENCY: Bi-weekly.

PREPARATION OF   Three members of the institution have pre-
   MATERIALS: pared extension materials.

PLANS:

WEST PAKISTAN - Country Summary

Year	Inst	Cent	Teachers					Students				
			Full	Part	Miss	Natl	Tot	Cert	Dipl	Bach	Lic	Tot
1972	3	7	3	9	8	4	12	15	10	11+	29	65+
1973												
1974												
1975												

NATIONAL COORDINATOR: John Meadowcroft
P. O. Box 13
Gujranwala, West Pakistan

ORGANIZATIONS: PACTEE

COUNTRY: West Pakistan

The Extension Seminary of Theology
27-B Satellite Town
Rahim Yar Khan, Pakistan

		Teachers					Students				
Year	Cent	Full	Part	Miss	Natl	Total	Cert	Dipl	Bach	Lic	Total
1972	3	1	1	2	0	2	15	10	5	6	26
1973											
1974											
1975											

SPONSORING GROUPS: International Christian Fellowship
Pakistan Christian Fellowship Church

OTHER PARTICIPANTS: Associated Reformed Presbyterian Church

SUPPORTED BY: Donations within Pakistan from missionaries and the TEE project fund from the U.S.A. and Canada.

STUDENT FEES: The student pays about $0.20 per course plus about $0.65 per book.

RECOGNITION OF STUDIES: Certificates are given at the end of each term. Also, a simple certificate is given at the end of 6 credits, a certificate of theology after 12 credits, a diploma of theology after 18 credits and a B.D. after 30.

ORDINATION: The program is intended to be lay training, continued training for pastors, and a pastoral training program.

CANDIDATES FOR FULL TIME SERVICE: Not known.

ACCREDITATION: Accredited by PACTEE.

CLASS FREQUENCY: Weekly.

PREPARATION OF MATERIALS: Two members of the institution have prepared extension materials.

PLANS: Plans are to organize new centers in more distant villages of tribal Christians, in other towns, and in other areas as a service to other missions at their invitation.

COUNTRY: West Pakistan

Gujranwala Theological Seminary
P. O. Box 13
Gujranwala, Pakistan

		Teachers					Students			
Year	Cent	Full	Part	Miss	Natl	Total	Cert	Dipl	Bach	Lic	Total
1972	2	0	2	2	0	2	0	0	6	23	29
1973											
1974											
1975											

SPONSORING GROUPS: United Presbyterian Church of Pakistan
Church of Pakistan (Union of Anglican,
Methodist and Scotch Presbyterian)
Lahore Church Council
Associate Reformed Presbyterian Church

OTHER PARTICIPANTS: Finnish Missionary Society
World Mission Prayer League
Danish Pathan Mission
Full Gospel Church
Assembly of God
Brethren Church

SUPPORTED BY: Assessments on affiliated churches who obtain most of the money from foreign sources.

STUDENT FEES: The student pays $1.50 in fees and $1.50
for materials.

RECOGNITION OF   Certificates are given after 6 credits, a
STUDIES: Certificate of Theology after 12 credits,
a Diploma in Theology after 18 credits, and
a Bachelor of Theology after 30 credits.

ORDINATION: This program could lead to ordination, but
this is not its primary aim.

CANDIDATES FOR
FULL TIME SERVICE: 20%.

ACCREDITATION: None.

CLASS FREQUENCY: Weekly.

PREPARATION OF   Two members of the institution have pre-
MATERIALS: pared extension materials.

PLANS: The seminary hopes to expand to different
centers and to begin classes in the vernacular (Urdu).

COUNTRY: West Pakistan

Karachi Institute of Theology
Selwyn House, Trinity Close
Fatima Jinnah Rd.
Karachi 4, Pakistan

		Teachers					Students				
Year	Cent	Full	Part	Miss	Natl	Total	Cert	Dipl	Bach	Lic	Total
1972	2	2	6	4	4	8	0	0	All	0	
1973											
1974											
1975											

SPONSORING GROUPS: Church of Pakistan
Associate Reformed Presbyterian Church
Conservative Baptist Foreign Mission
International Fellowship of Evangelical
Students

OTHER PARTICIPANTS: None.

SUPPORTED BY: Gifts from churches and individuals in the
U.S.A. plus student fees.

STUDENT FEES: The student pays $1.00 per course.

RECOGNITION OF
STUDIES:

ORDINATION: The program is considered lay training but
a curriculum intended to lead to ordination
is being worked on by PACTEE which the institution hopes to follow.

CANDIDATES FOR
FULL TIME SERVICE: 1%.

ACCREDITATION: None.

CLASS FREQUENCY: Weekly.

PREPARATION OF   No member of the institution has prepared
MATERIALS: extension materials.

PLANS:

PANAMA – Country Summary

Year	Inst	Cent	Teachers					Students				
			Full	Part	Miss	Natl	Tot	Cert	Dipl	Bach	Lic	Tot
1972	1	6	1	3	3	1	4	0	36	0	0	36
1973												
1974												
1975												

NATIONAL COORDINATOR: Gilbert Reimer
Seminario Bethel
El Amanecer
La Chorrera, Panama

AFFILIATION: ALISTE

COUNTRY: Panama

Seminario Bethel
El Amanecer
La Chorrera, Panama

		Teachers				Students				
Year	Cent	Full	Part	Miss	Natl	Total	Cert	Dipl	Bach	Lic	Total
1972	6	1	3	3	1	4	0	36	0	0	36
1973											
1974											
1975											

SPONSORING GROUPS: Gospel Missionary Union
                      Free Will Baptist

OTHER PARTICIPANTS: None.

SUPPORTED BY: Professors are missionaries with salaries
                      from the exterior. Students pay for books
                      and a small matriculation fee.

STUDENT FEES: The student pays $1.00 per semester matri-
                      culation fee plus $1.00 to $3.00 for books.

RECOGNITION OF   Certificates are given each semester for the
   STUDIES: work completed. In addition the following
                      are awarded: A Certificate in Christian
                      Education (9 courses), A Christian Worker's
                      Certificate (9 courses or Christian Educa-
                      tion Certificate plus 4), and a Certificate
                      of the Proclamation of the Word (9 courses
                      or another certificate plus 4).

ORDINATION: The program is especially for laymen. How-
                      ever, if the student earns the three certi-
                      ficates and completes 8 more courses, he
                      receives a diploma indicating he is ready
                      for ordination.

CANDIDATES FOR
FULL TIME SERVICE: Not known.

ACCREDITATION: None.

CLASS FREQUENCY: Weekly.

PREPARATION OF   No faculty member has prepared extension
   MATERIALS: materials.

PLANS:

PERU - Country Summary

Year	Inst	Cent	Teachers					Students				
			Full	Part	Miss	Natl	Tot	Cert	Dipl	Bach	Lic	Tot
1970	2	8						25	11		0	36
1971	3	39								15	0	150
1972	1	17	2	13	7	8	15	90	105	6	0	201
1973												
1974												
1975												

NATIONAL COORDINATOR: Charles Porter
                                  Instituto Bíblico Bautista
                                  Casilla 448
                                  Iquitos, Peru

AFFILIATION: ALISTE

COUNTRY: Peru

Centro Teológico de San Martín
Misión Evangélica
Tarapoto, San Martín, Peru

		Teachers					Students			
Year	Cent	Full	Part	Miss	Natl	Total	Cert	Dipl	Bach	Lic	Total
1970	3						16	1			17
1971	10										50
1972											
1973											
1974											
1975											

(CLATT survey)

COUNTRY: Peru

Instituto Bíblico Bautista de Iquitos
Casilla 231
Iquitos, Peru

		Teachers					Students				
Year	Cent	Full	Part	Miss	Natl	Total	Cert	Dipl	Bach	Lic	Total
1970											
1971											
1972	17	2	13	7	8	15	90	105	6	0	201
1973											
1974											
1975											

SPONSORING GROUPS: Association of Baptists for World Evangelism

OTHER PARTICIPANTS: Baptist "Mid-Missions"

SUPPORTED BY: Missionary contributions, student fees, and help from local churches.

STUDENT FEES: The student pays $4.60 per semester.

RECOGNITION OF STUDIES: Upon completion of course, the student receives a certificate. The institution awards a Bachelor of Theology degree, a Diploma in Theology and a Certificate in Theology.

ORDINATION: The program is considered appropriate for laymen and for pastors. It is not necessary for ordination.

CANDIDATES FOR FULL TIME SERVICE: About 5%.

ACCREDITATION: None.

CLASS FREQUENCY: Generally, weekly.

PREPARATION OF MATERIALS: One member of the faculty has prepared materials for extension.

PLANS: Plans are to expand to all parts of the country.

COUNTRY: Peru

Seminario de Extensión Teológico
Iglesia del Nazareno
Apartado 85
Chiclayo, Peru

		Teachers					Students			
Year	Cent	Full	Part	Miss	Natl	Total	Cert	Dipl	Bach	Lic	Total
1971	4							15			15
1972											
1973											
1974											
1975											

(CLATT survey)

PHILIPPINES - Country Summary

			Teachers					Students				
Year	Inst	Cent	Full	Part	Miss	Natl	Tot	Cert	Dipl	Bach	Lic	Tot
1972	2	16	2	19	6	15	21	14	107	0	0	121
1973												
1974												
1975												

NATIONAL COORDINATOR: Vernon Carvey
                            Box 1416
                            Manila, Philippines

PUBLICATIONS: Philippines TEE Bulletin
                            Box 1416
                            Manila, Philippines

ORGANIZATIONS: PAFTEE

COUNTRY: Philippines

Conservative Baptist Bible College - Extension Department
P. O. Box 1882
Manila, Philippines

		Teachers					Students				
Year	Cent	Full	Part	Miss	Natl	Total	Cert	Dipl	Bach	Lic	Total
1969											
1970											
1971											
1972	13	0	12	4	8	12	0	107	0	0	107
1973											
1974											
1975											

SPONSORING GROUPS: Conservative Baptist Foreign Mission
                      Society.

OTHER PARTICIPANTS: None.

SUPPORTED BY: Mission subsidy and student fees.

STUDENT FEES: The student pays $1.50 per semester
                      course. The texts are subsidized so that
                      the student pays only $0.15 per text.

RECOGNITION OF   Certificates are given at the end of each
  STUDIES: year. Plans call for diplomas to be given
                      upon completion of 8, 16 and 32 courses.

ORDINATION: Most students do not plan for ordination.
                      Those completing the full course would be
                      candidates for ordination.

CANDIDATES FOR
FULL TIME SERVICE: None.

ACCREDITATION.   None.

CLASS FREQUENCY: Weekly.

PREPARATION OF   Two members of the faculty have prepared
  MATERIALS: extension materials.

PLANS: Plans are for expansion depending on
                      course material preparation.

COUNTRY: Philippines

The International Biblical Seminary
P. O. Box 66
Cagayan de Oro City L 305,
Philippines

		Teachers				Students				
Year	Cent	Full	Part	Miss	Natl	Total	Cert	Dipl	Bach	Lic	Total
1972	3	2	7	2	7	9	14	0	0	0	14
1973										
1974										
1975										

SPONSORING GROUPS: International Missions, Inc.
Bumila Fellowship of Baptist Churches, Inc.

OTHER PARTICIPANTS: None

SUPPORTED BY: Subsidy from the U.S.A., Canada and New Zealand for texts. The rest is self-supporting.

STUDENT FEES: The student pays $0.80 for texts, $0.32 registration fee and $5.00 tuition per year.

RECOGNITION OF STUDIES: Certificates are given upon completion of the school year. If students complete the full course they will be granted the degree Bachelor of Biblical Arts.

ORDINATION: This program may lead to ordination.

ACCREDITATION: None.

CLASS FREQUENCY: Bi-weekly.

PREPARATION OF MATERIALS: Two members of the faculty have prepared extension materials.

PLANS: The seminary hopes to open new centers as they have students in other areas.

COUNTRY: Philippines

Mindanao Baptist Bible College
P. O. Box 99
Davao City, Philippines

		Teachers					Students			
Year	Cent	Full	Part	Miss	Natl	Total	Cert	Dipl	Bach	Lic	Total
1973	1	3	3	2	4	6	0	18	22	0	40
1974										
1975										

SPONSORING GROUPS: Philippine Baptist Mission (Southern Baptist)
                     Luzon Baptist Convention
                     Mindanao Baptist Convention
                     Chinese Baptist Convention

OTHER PARTICIPANTS: None.

SUPPORTED BY: Foreign Mission Board of the Southern Baptist
                     Convention.

STUDENT FEES: Students pay approximately $1.00 per course.

RECOGNITION OF   Certificates will be given in three stages
   STUDIES: or levels.

ORDINATION: The denomination does not require theo-
                     logical training for ordination. The school
                     is primarily for pastors, however.

CANDIDATES FOR
FULL TIME SERVICE: 80-90%.

ACCREDITATION: None. Although the related seminary is
                     accredited.

CLASS FREQUENCY: Weekly.

PREPARATION OF   Four members of the faculty have prepared
   MATERIALS: extension materials, two programmed.

PLANS: Centers are to be opened in eight regional
                     areas.

COUNTRY: Philippines

Oro School of the Bible
30 Victoria Street
Cagayan de Oro City, Philippines

Year	Cent	Teachers					Students				
		Full	Part	Miss	Natl	Total	Cert	Dipl	Bach	Lic	Total
1971											
1972											
1973	1	1	2	1	2	3	5	5	0	0	10
1974											
1975											

SPONSORING GROUPS: Christian Advent Churches in the Philippines

OTHER PARTICIPANTS: Assemblies of God
Pentecostal Church of God
Bethany Home (Baptist)
Philippine Gospel Church
Southern Baptist Church

SUPPORTED BY: Mission subsidy and tuition.

STUDENT FEES: The student pays approximately $3.00

RECOGNITION OF   The school grants a diploma and a certi-
   STUDIES: ficate.

ORDINATION: The program is appropriate as lay training
                     but can lead to ordination.

CANDIDATES FOR
FULL TIME SERVICE: About 25%.

ACCREDITATION: None.

CLASS FREQUENCY: Monthly.

PREPARATION OF   No member of the institution has prepared
   MATERIALS: extension materials.

PLANS: Plans are to have full time workers.

PUERTO RICO - Country Summary

Year	Inst	Cent	Teachers					Students				
			Full	Part	Miss	Natl	Tot	Cert	Dipl	Bach	Lic	Tot
1970	1	5						130			19	149
1971	1	6						120			8	128
1972												
1973												
1974												
1975												

AFFILIATION: ALISTE

COUNTRY: Puerto Rico

Instituto Bíblico Menonita
Apartado 146
Aibonito, Puerto Rico 00609

		Teachers					Students			
Year	Cent	Full	Part	Miss	Natl	Total	Cert	Dipl	Bach	Lic	Total
1970	5						130			19	149
1971	6						120			8	128
1972											
1973											
1974											
1975											

(CLATT Surveys)

RHODESIA - Country Survey

Year	Inst	Cent	Teachers					Students				
			Full	Part	Miss	Natl	Tot	Cert	Dipl	Bach	Lic	Tot
1972	1	4										51
1973												
1974												
1975												

COUNTRY: Rhodesia

Brethren in Christ Church

Year	Cent	Teachers					Students				
		Full	Part	Miss	Natl	Total	Cert	Dipl	Bach	Lic	Total
1972	4										51
1973											
1974											
1975											
(Holland 1973)											

SIERRA LEONE - Country Summary

Year	Inst	Cent	Teachers					Students				
			Full	Part	Miss	Natl	Tot	Cert	Dipl	Bach	Lic	Tot
1972	1	5	0	2	2	0	2	45	18	0	0	63
1973												
1974												
1975												

COUNTRY: Sierra Leone

Sierra Leone Bible College
Box 890
Freetown, Sierra Leone

Year	Cent	Teachers					Students				
		Full	Part	Miss	Natl	Total	Cert	Dipl	Bach	Lic	Total
1972	5	0	2	2	0	2	45	18	0	0	63
1973											
1974											
1975											

SPONSORING GROUPS: Missionary Church
Wesleyan Church
United Brethren in Christ
European Baptist Mission

OTHER PARTICIPANTS: Methodist Church
E.L.W.A. - Monrovia, Liberia
Christians in Action
West African Methodist

SUPPORTED BY: Mission subsidy and national church gifts.

STUDENT FEES: The student pays 1.50 (Leone) per course.

RECOGNITION OF   Courses are equivalent to those in the resi-
  STUDIES: dence program as to recognition.

ORDINATION: Ordination is for the individual church to
decide but the program usually helps the
candidate.

CANDIDATES FOR
FULL TIME SERVICE: Most of them.

ACCREDITATION: Affiliated with the London Bible College a
and ETTA. No official accreditation.

CLASS FREQUENCY: Weekly.

PLANS: A full time teacher for extension is coming
to start an extensive program upcountry
late in 1973.

SOUTH AFRICA - Country Summary

Year	Inst	Cent	Teachers					Students				
			Full	Part	Miss	Natl	Tot	Cert	Dipl	Bach	Lic	Tot
1972	3	18	7	5	9	3	12	90	54	27	0	171
1973												
1974												
1975												

COUNTRY: South Africa

Durban Bible College
Postal: P. O. Box 7, Jacobs, Natal, South Africa
Location: 39 Samphalpur Rd., Merebank, Durban N.H.

		Teachers					Students				
Year	Cent	Full	Part	Miss	Natl	Total	Cert	Dipl	Bach	Lic	Total
1972	3	7	3	8	2	10	0	40	22	0	62
1973											
1974											
1975											

SPONSORING GROUPS: Evangelical Alliance Mission

OTHER PARTICIPANTS: Baptist Union of South Africa
Bethesda Church (Full Gospel Pentecostal)
Independent churches and Bible churches
associated with TEAM and AEF.

SUPPORTED BY: Mission subsidy.

STUDENT FEES: The student pays $20.00 per school year
plus a $1.00 matriculation and buys his own
books.

RECOGNITION OF
STUDIES: Recognition is given after completion of
the full course (6 years).

ORDINATION: This is training for a pastoral ministry.

CANDIDATES FOR
FULL TIME SERVICE: 80%.

ACCREDITATION: Associated with the Association of Evangelical Bible Schools and Colleges of Africa
and Madascar (AEBICAM).

CLASS FREQUENCY: Twice weekly.

PREPARATION OF
MATERIALS: Two members of the faculty are now working
on extension materials.

PLANS: Plans are to open more extension centers
within a 60 mile radius.

COUNTRY: South Africa

Evangelical Bible Institute
P. O. Box 629
Rustenburg, Transvaal
South Africa

		Teachers				Students				
Year	Cent	Full	Part	Miss	Natl	Total	Cert	Dipl	Bach	Lic	Total
1972	3	0	2	1	1	2	14	0	0	0	14
1973	4	0	2	1	1	2	21	0	5	0	26
1974											
1975											

SPONSORING GROUPS: The Evangelical Alliance Mission
                     Evangelical Church (African)

OTHER PARTICIPANTS: None.

SUPPORTED BY: Mission subsidy.

STUDENT FEES: The student pays less than $1.00 per
                     semester course.

RECOGNITION OF   Plans are to give certificates for each
   STUDIES: course completed at the end of the year.
                     Graduation will be after 16 subjects are
                     completed.

ORDINATION: The program is labeled "Lay Training" but
                     could lead to ordination.

CANDIDATES FOR
FULL TIME SERVICE: Less than 1%.

ACCREDITATION: No. They would like to work out accredi-
                     tation with AEBICAM in the future.

CLASS FREQUENCY: Bi-weekly.

PREPARATION OF   Local translation of AEBICAM materials
   MATERIALS: into regional dialects.

PLANS: Four new centers are in the process of
                     being formed.

COUNTRY: South Africa

The Free Methodist Extension Bible School
P. O. Box 1263, Witbank
Republic of South Africa

| | | Teachers | | | | Students | | | | |
Year	Cent	Full	Part	Miss	Natl	Total	Cert	Dipl	Bach	Lic	Total
1972	12	1	2	3	0	3	69	14	0	0	83
1973											
1974											
1975											

SPONSORING GROUPS: Free Methodist Mission

OTHER PARTICIPANTS: Students from various groups.

SUPPORTED BY: Mission subsidy.

STUDENT FEES: The student pays $2.30 for fees and books
                     per course.

RECOGNITION OF   Certificates are given upon completion of
STUDIES: each course. A Christian Worker's Diploma
                     is to be given upon completion of a parti-
                     cular level.

ORDINATION: The program is both lay and ministerial
                     training. Completion of the pastors course
                     and the deacons course meets academic re-
                     quirements.

CANDIDATES FOR
FULL TIME SERVICE: About 10%.

ACCREDITATION: None. The institution has applied to
                     AEBICAM.

CLASS FREQUENCY: Every two weeks.

PREPARATION OF   Two members of the faculty have prepared a
MATERIALS: programmed course on pastoral care which is
                     available in Zulu.

PLANS: Plans are to open new centers in strategic
                     areas and to train more perceptive students
                     as student monitors and eventually teachers.

SPAIN - Country Summary

Twenty-six delegates attended a workshop with Peter Savage
in Madrid in March of 1971.   Three, that is half, of the Bible
schools in Spain were represented.   At that time the Federation
of Independent Churches in Spain was operating an extension program, but it appears that this has been discontinued.   Thirty-
seven students in seven centers were reported to CLATT for last
year.

TAIWAN - Country Summary

			Teachers					Students				
Year	Inst	Cent	Full	Part	Miss	Natl	Tot	Cert	Dipl	Bach	Lic	Tot
1971	1											
1972	1	2	0	3	1	2	3	4	2	2	0	8
1973												
1974												
1975												

NATIONAL COORDINATOR: Rev. Hugh Sprunger
P. O. Box 165
Taichung, Taiwan 400
ROC

COUNTRY: Taiwan

China Evangelical Seminary
P. O. Box 28-4, Shihlin
Taipei, Taiwan 111
Republic of China

		Teachers					Students				
Year	Cent	Full	Part	Miss	Natl	Total	Cert	Dipl	Bach	Lic	Total
1971											
1972	2	0	3	1	2	3	4	2	2	0	8
1973											
1974											
1975											

SPONSORING GROUPS: Overseas Crusades
                     Conservative Baptists
                     Free Methodists
                     Oriental Missionary Society

OTHER PARTICIPANTS: General Conference Mennonite Mission
                     Southern Baptist Church
                     Finnish Missionary Society (Lutheran)

SUPPORTED BY: Contributions from various groups.

STUDENT FEES: The student pays for books plus a matri-
                     culation fee of approximately $1.25.

RECOGNITION OF   A certificate is given showing completion
STUDIES: of each course and another upon graduation
                     (100 hours).

ORDINATION: Most of the groups consider the program to
                     be theological training for laymen rather
                     than ministerial training.

CANDIDATES FOR
FULL TIME SERVICE: Not known.

ACCREDITATION: None.

CLASS FREQUENCY: Generally, weekly.

PREPARATION OF   A senior student is working on a translation/
MATERIALS: adaptation of Mark from the English Intertext.
                     Jeremiah and Principles of Church Growth
                     were done in the Free Methodist and Conser-
                     vative Baptist theological institutions.

PLANS: Plans are to open a third center in Taichung
                     in February 1973 and to expand the number
                     of courses available for study.

TANZANIA – Country Summary

			Teachers					Students				
Year	Inst	Cent	Full	Part	Miss	Natl	Tot	Cert	Dipl	Bach	Lic	Tot
1969												
1970												
1971												
1972												
1973												
1974												
1975												

COUNTRY: Tanzania

Diocese of Victoria Nyanza
P. O. Box 278
Mwanza, Tanzania

		Teachers					Students				
		---	---	---	---	---	---	---	---	---	---
Year	Cent	Full	Part	Miss	Natl	Total	Cert	Dipl	Bach	Lic	Total
1969											
1970											
1971											
1972											
1973											
1974											
1975											

SPONSORING GROUPS: Anglican Church

OTHER PARTICIPANTS: Lutheran Church
                     Moravian Church

SUPPORTED BY: Subsidy by Australian based mission
                     Local church
                     A small endowment

STUDENT FEES: Varies according to diocese.

RECOGNITION OF   Diploma in Theology granted upon com-
    STUDIES: pletion.

ORDINATION: Students may be ordained.

CANDIDATES FOR
FULL TIME SERVICE: About 90%.

ACCREDITATION: None. This program is an extension of St.
                     Philips Theological College, Box 20, Kongwa,
                     Tanzania.

CLASS FREQUENCY: No regular classes have been held. A
                     seminar in 1972 had to be cancelled.

PREPARATION OF   The staff of the Theological College prepares
    MATERIALS: notes and bibliographies for those students
                     who are 500 miles from the college. The
                     diocese hopes to use AEBICAM materials when
                     available.

PLANS: Plans are to appoint a traveling tutor.

THAILAND - Country Summary

			Teachers					Students				
Year	Inst	Cent	Full	Part	Miss	Natl	Tot	Cert	Dipl	Bach	Lic	Tot
1971												
1972	1	3	0	10	5	5	10	0	30	15	0	45
1973												
1974												
1975												

NATIONAL COORDINATOR: James W. Gustafson
48 Soi Yenakas 2
Tungmahamek, Bangkok, Thailand

PUBLICATIONS: Thai TEE Bulletin
433/3 Suan Plu
Bangkok, Thailand

ORGANIZATIONS: Thai CoCoTEE

COUNTRY: Thailand

Thailand Baptist Theological Seminary
433 Suan Plu
Bangkok, Thailand

		Teachers					Students			
Year	Cent	Full	Part	Miss	Natl	Total	Cert	Dipl	Bach	Lic	Total
1973	1	2	1	1	2	3	0	1	2	0	3
1974											
1975											

SPONSORING GROUPS: Thailand Baptist Mission (Southern)

OTHER PARTICIPANTS: Church of Christ in Thailand
                    American Baptist Mission

SUPPORTED BY: Mission subsidy.

STUDENT FEES: The student pays $1.00 per course plus
                     $0.50 matriculation fee. He does not pay
                     for texts.

RECOGNITION OF   Certificates are given for completion of
   STUDIES: each course.

ORDINATION: This is considered both lay and pastoral
                     training.

CANDIDATES FOR
FULL TIME SERVICE: 33%.

ACCREDITATION: None.

CLASS FREQUENCY: Weekly.

PREPARATION OF   One member of the faculty has prepared
   MATERIALS: extension materials.

PLANS: Plans are to organize new centers.

COUNTRY: Thailand

Thailand Theological Seminary
Box 37
Chiang Mai, Thailand

		Teachers				Students				
Year	Cent	Full	Part	Miss	Natl	Total	Cert	Dipl	Bach	Lic	Total

1968 (experimental)

Year	Cent	Full	Part	Miss	Natl	Total	Cert	Dipl	Bach	Lic	Total
1971	1	0	6	5	1	6	0	0	15	0	15
1972	3	0	10	5	5	10	0	30	15	0	45
1973											
1974											
1975											

SPONSORING GROUPS: Church of Christ in Thailand
United Presbyterian Church in the U.S.A.
Disciples of Christ
American Baptist Mission
Kyodan (United Church of Japan)
Marburger Mission (Germany)
Church of South India

OTHER PARTICIPANTS: Korea Evangelistic Inter-mission Alliance
Evangelical Covenant Church of America
Roman Catholic Church (Jesuits)

SUPPORTED BY   Gifts and subsidies from missions and churches
in Thailand and the U.S.A.
Foundation for Theological Education
Theological Education Fund
C.E.L.T.

STUDENT FEES: The student pays for his own books plus
$2.50 per credit unit in the cities. In the
villages he pays only a $2.50 registration
fee per term.

RECOGNITION OF   A certificate is given at the end of the
    STUDIES: school year for all work completed.

ORDINATION: The program is basically lay training but
can lead to ordination or commissioning as
a church worker or pastor-elder.

CANDIDATES FOR
FULL TIME SERVICE: Not known.

ACCREDITATION: Accredited by the Association of Theological
Schools of Southeast Asia.

COUNTRY: Thailand

Thailand Theological Seminary (continued)

CLASS FREQUENCY: Generally, weekly.

PREPARATION OF   Five members of the seminary are presently
MATERIALS: at work preparing extension materials.

PLANS: Plans are to open two new centers in 1973.

TRINIDAD - Country Summary

Year	Inst	Cent	Teachers					Students				
			Full	Part	Miss	Natl	Tot	Cert	Dipl	Bach	Lic	Tot
1972	2	5	2	7	6	3	9	5	40	5	0	50
1973												
1974												
1975												

COUNTRY: Trinidad

Nazarene Training College
P. O. Box 1245
Port of Spain, Trinidad

		Teachers					Students				
Year	Cent	Full	Part	Miss	Natl	Total	Cert	Dipl	Bach	Lic	Total
1972	3	0	3	2	1	3	4	22	5	0	31
1973											
1974											
1975											

SPONSORING GROUPS: Church of the Nazarene

OTHER PARTICIPANTS: None at present.

SUPPORTED BY: Mission subsidy and student fees.

STUDENT FEES: The student pays $5.00 per credit hour
                     (cost of books included).

RECOGNITION OF   As yet nothing has been decided concerning
STUDIES: certificates to be awarded.

ORDINATION: This is considered to be both lay and
                     ministerial training.

CANDIDATES FOR
FULL TIME SERVICE: Not known.

ACCREDITATION: None.

CLASS FREQUENCY: Weekly.

PREPARATION OF   As yet no member of the faculty has prepared
MATERIALS: extension materials.

PLANS: The program is in the beginning stages, but
                     plans are to open centers in Guyana, Trini-
                     dad and the Virgin Islands.

COUNTRY: Trinidad

Open Bible Institute
P. O. Box 82
San Fernando, Trinidad

Year	Cent	Teachers					Students				
		Full	Part	Miss	Natl	Total	Cert	Dipl	Bach	Lic	Total
1972	2	2	4	4	2	6	1	18	0	0	19
1973											
1974											
1975											

SPONSORING GROUPS: Open Bible Standard Missions
                     Open Bible Standard Churches of Trinidad

OTHER PARTICIPANTS: Several students from the Assembly of God

SUPPORTED BY: Tuition of students and support of missionary
                     teachers by the mission.

STUDENT FEES: The student pays $5.00 matriculation fee per
                     13 week term.

RECOGNITION OF   The student receives a certificate for each
    STUDIES: course completed.

ORDINATION: This is considered lay training, but some
                     may go on to the non-resident night school
                     which grants a diploma.

CANDIDATES FOR   10%.
FULL TIME SERVICE:

ACCREDITATION: None.

CLASS FREQUENCY: Twice per week.

PREPARATION OF   They are writing and adapting their own
    MATERIALS: materials to fill needs.

PLANS: Plans are to open other centers for short
                     package courses.

UNITED STATES - Country Summary

Extension programs in the United States are quite varied.
They differ from those in other areas in that, although there
is a great deal of emphasis on home study, in some institutions
very little is said of workbooks and no mention is made of programmed instructional materials. These programs do fit into
the extension category, however, since their goal is to produce
full or part-time Christian leadership through training other
than traditional residence studies. Most of these programs are
quite new and some have yet to begin, but plans and programs
are at least being elaborated for participation in the extension
seminary movement.

New York Theological Seminary tried an experimental one
year program in 1970-71 which would give an equivalent to one
year of studies in a B.D. program. Students were to partici-
page in a Core Group of twelve students with a faculty advisor.
Each student was to seek employment in either a church, social
agency or action group. The Core Group would meet for biblical
studies and the students could take classes at New York Theoloci-
cal Seminary or other local seminaries.

In the fall quarter of 1972 the School of World Mission of
Fuller Theological Seminary offered one course by extension in
a local church. The pastors and laymen attended one class a
week in the early morning hours. A more comprehensive program
is planned for the 1973-74 school year. Fuller Theological Seminary will open extension centers in San Diego, Los Angeles and
Fresno, California and Seattle, Washington. Some centers will
be geared for lay training; others will offer in two years the
equivalent to one year residence work toward the M.Div. degree.
At present this program is designed only to feed the residence
school since it is impossible to receive a full theological education under the program. For more information write to:

> Director of Extension
> Fuller Theological Seminary
> 135 North Oakland Avenue
> Pasadena, California 91101

Other extension programs with or without credits are offered
by the following seminaries:

> Director of Extension
> American Baptist Theological Seminary
> Nashville, Tennessee 37207

> Pittsburgh Theological Seminary
> Pittsburgh, Pennsylvania 15206

UNITED STATES - Country Summary (continued)

San Francisco Theological Seminary
San Anselmo, California 94960

The Birmingham Extension Seminary for Theological Education,
Birmingham, Alabama was formed in January of 1973. It was able
to attract fifty-three students with only two weeks of advertising. Many of the students have had years of practical experience but no opportunity to attend a residence seminary program. In February of 1973 twenty-one students studied toward
the Master of Divinity degree, fourteen toward the Master of Religious Education and eighteen enrolled as auditors.

The Lutheran Church in America is developing an expanded
diaconate program. To provide in-service training for the communities formed, some kind of theological education by extension
will be appropriate.

Melodyland Schools opened their School of Theology in
January of 1973. Classes meet from Monday through Friday in the
evenings and on Saturday morning. Enrollment for the first period was 115 and the school is served by a faculty of thirteen.

Melodyland Schools
P. O. Box 6000
Anaheim, California 92806

The Los Angeles Christian Training Center is sponsored by
the Los Angeles Southern Baptist Association and accreditation
is given through the Golden Gate Baptist Seminary and California
Baptist College. Four levels of studies are given and two
courses each quarter are offered in Spanish.

Los Angeles Christian Training Center
8219 Florence Avenue
Downey, California 90240

Also located in the Los Angeles area is the Bible Seminary
of the Americas. At this institution also some of the courses
are taught in Spanish. Classes are available for those who have
completed eight years of school, for those who have completed
high school and for those with two or more years of college.
The requirements for a three credit course offered during the
twelve week quarters are as follows:

5 hours of study per week X 12   60
6 hours of class attendance (every other week)   6
    Practical application   24
                                    Total 90 hours

UNITED STATES - Country Summary (continued)

Students may take as many or as few courses as they like and
are able to handle and there is no time limit for completing the
requirements for a diploma. Each summer there will be two two-
week sessions taught five days a week for one hour credit.

The most extensive system of extension education for pastors and laymen is set out in a booklet entitled *Training for
Non-Stipendiary Ministry Today*. The booklet, edited by H.
Boone Porter, Jr., is subtitled A Directory of Training Programs
and Schools Within the Episcopal Church. The forms of preparation for those studying for lay or ordained service vary greatly
from one program to another. Some methods mentioned are home
study, evening classes, weekend sessions, directed study, seminars and study under local clergy. The booklet lists over
forty programs in the United States (including one primarily for
Sioux Indians), Latin America and the Philippines. Copies of
the booklet for fifty cents each may be obtained from:

> The Rev. Marshall T. Rice
> Secretary Treasurer of Non-STOP
> Box 764
> Ridgewood, New Jersey 07451

The American Baptist Seminary listed above has the largest
student body of any program in the United States. For the period ending January 31, 1973, it reports an enrollment of 693
students in more than thirty-seven centers. Other centers had
not reported data for students. Classes meet weekly. This is
a lower academic level program than some others in the United
States and its curriculum includes two years of study of English which might be considered remedial in other institutions.
A four year course leading to a Certificate in Christian Training and a five year course granting the Diploma in Theology are
offered. New centers are established wherever permission is
given to a local ministerial association or other denominational group by the Seminary. Qualified teachers are recruited
locally and at least fifteen students must be enrolled to open
a new center. A ten dollar registration fee is paid the Seminary and other finances are worked out locally. There are now
centers in at least sixteen states.

URUGUAY – Country Summary

			Teachers					Students				
Year	Inst	Cent	Full	Part	Miss	Natl	Tot	Cert	Dipl	Bach	Lic	Tot
1970	1											
1971	1											
1972	1	2	8	2	6	4	10	0	10	41	0	51
1973												
1974												
1975												

NATIONAL COORDINATOR: Terry Barratt
                        Seminario por Extensión Anglicano
                        Santiago 1862
                        S.M. Tucuman, Argentina

AFFILIATION: ALISTE

COUNTRY: Uruguay

Seminario Evangélico Menonita de Teología
Avenida Millan 4392
Montevideo, Uruguay

		Teachers						Students			
Year	Cent	Full	Part	Miss	Natl	Total	Cert	Dipl	Bach	Lic	Total
1970											
1971											
1972	1	8	2	6	4	10	0	10	41	0	51
1973											
1974											
1975											

SPONSORING GROUPS: Mennonite Church

OTHER PARTICIPANTS: None.

SUPPORTED BY: Mission subsidy and national churches.

STUDENT FEES: The student pays approximately $25.00 per
                      month.

RECOGNITION OF
    STUDIES: The institution awards a Bachelor of Theolog
                      degree.

ORDINATION: The program is considered to be both lay
                      training and ministerial preparation. Or-
                      dination does not depend upon completed
                      studies.

CANDIDATES FOR
FULL TIME SERVICE: Does not apply.

ACCREDITATION:

CLASS FREQUENCY: Weekly.

PREPARATION OF   No member of the faculty has prepared ex-
    MATERIALS: tension materials.

PLANS:

VENEZUELA - Country Summary

			Teachers					Students				
Year	Inst	Cent	Full	Part	Miss	Natl	Tot	Cert	Dipl	Bach	Lic	Tot
1970	2											
1971	3											
1972	3	19	2	19	11	10	21	100	95	2	0	197
1973												
1974												
1975												

NATIONAL COORDINATOR: Rodolfo Blank
Instituto "Juan de Frias"
Apartado Postal 216
Puerto Ordaz, Estado Bolivar
Venezuela

AFFILIATION: ALISTE

COUNTRY: Venezuela

Instituto Teológico Juan de Frías
Apartado Postal 216
Puerto Ordaz, Estado Bolívar
Venezuela

		Teachers					Students				
Year	Cent	Full	Part	Miss	Natl	Total	Cert	Dipl	Bach	Lic	Total
1970											
1971											
1972	4	0	2	2	0	2	0	20	2	0	22
1973											
1974											
1975											

SPONSORING GROUPS: Conference of Lutheran Churches of Venezuela.

OTHER PARTICIPANTS: None.

SUPPORTED BY: Mission subsidy and national churches.

STUDENT FEES: The student buys his texts and manuals.

RECOGNITION OF   Certificates are given for each course com-
STUDIES: pleted and a diploma is given for deacons,
                        teachers and catequists after completing
                        10 courses.

ORDINATION: The program is to prepare laymen and pastors.
Ordination does not depend on a theological
education.

CANDIDATES FOR
FULL TIME SERVICE: 50%.

ACCREDITATION: The institution is affiliated with the
Seminario Luterano Augsburgo de Mexico.

CLASS FREQUENCY: Weekly.

PREPARATION OF   One member of the faculty has prepared ex-
MATERIALS.   tension materials.

PLANS: Plans are to open new centers and expand
the bachalaureate program.

COUNTRY: Venezuela

Seminario Local
Cruzada Mundial Evangélica
Apartado 501
Barquisimeto, Venezuela

		Teachers				Students				
Year	Cent	Full	Part	Miss	Natl	Total	Cert	Dipl	Bach	Lic	Total
1970											
1971	4						0	15	0	0	15
1972	6	2	2	2	2	4	0	25	0	0	25
1973	1	0	1	0	1	1	0	6	0	0	6
1974											
1975											

SPONSORING GROUPS: World Evangelization Crusade
Convention of Churches associated with W.E.C

OTHER PARTICIPANTS: None.

SUPPORTED BY: National churches.

STUDENT FEES: The student pays only the price of the texts used.

RECOGNITION OF STUDIES: Certificates are given upon completion of a series.

ORDINATION: This is presently considered lay training.

CANDIDATES FOR FULL TIME SERVICE: 2%.

ACCREDITATION: None. The institution hopes to affiliate with another seminary for higher level studies.

CLASS FREQUENCY: Every two weeks or more frequently.

PREPARATION OF MATERIALS: No extension materials have been prepared locally.

PLANS: Due to a lack of personnel, the future of the school is very uncertain.

COUNTRY: Venezuela

Seminario Teológico Bautista de Venezuela
Apartado 27
Los Teques, Venezuela

		Teachers					Students				
Year	Cent	Full	Part	Miss	Natl	Total	Cert	Dipl	Bach	Lic	Total
1971											
1972	9	0	15	7	8	15	10u	50	0	0	150
1973											
1974											
1975											

SPONSORING GROUPS: Baptist Convention of Venezuela

OTHER PARTICIPANTS: None.

SUPPORTED BY: Baptist Convention of Venezuela

STUDENT FEES: The student pays $10.00 per semester.

RECOGNITION OF
STUDIES: Degrees given are: Certificate in
Theology or Religious Education, Bachelor
in Theology or Religious Education and
Licentiate in Theology or Religious Edu-
cation.

ORDINATION: Ordination does not depend upon completion
of any course of studies.

CANDIDATES FOR
FULL TIME SERVICE: 15%.

ACCREDITATION: Accredited by the accrediting agency of
Latin American Baptist Seminaries.

CLASS FREQUENCY: Weekly.

PREPARATION OF
MATERIALS: Two members of the faculty have prepared
extension materials.

PLANS: Plans are to open new centers and prepare
better materials.

ZAMBIA - Country Survey

Year	Inst	Cent	Teachers					Students				
			Full	Part	Miss	Natl	Tot	Cert	Dipl	Bach	Lic	Tot
1972	1	8										110
1973												
1974												
1975												

COUNTRY: Zambia

Choma Bible Institute
Box 131
Choma Zambia

		Teachers					Students			
Year	Cent	Full	Part	Miss	Natl	Total	Cert	Dipl	Bach	Lic	Total
1970	5	1	0	1	0	1	50				50
1971	5	2	0	2	0	2	80				80
1972	8	2	2	4	0	4	100				100
1973											
1974											
1975											

SPONSORING GROUPS: Brethren in Christ Church

OTHER PARTICIPANTS: None.

SUPPORTED BY: US mission funds and student fees.

STUDENT FEES: $1.00 per ten weeks.

RECOGNITION OF   Certificates given at the end of each term.
  STUDIES:

ORDINATION: Could lead to ordination.

CANDIDATES FOR   Probably none.
FULL TIME SERVICE:

ACCREDITATION: None.

CLASS FREQUENCY: Weekly.

PREPARATION OF   Two members of the faculty have prepared
  MATERIALS: extension materials.

PLANS: New centers to be opened in 1974.

COUNTRY: Spain

Escuela Evangélica de Teología de Barcelona
c. Travesía de San Antonio 6, 4°, 1ª
Barcelona 12, Spain

Year	Cent	Teachers					Students				
		Full	Part	Miss	Natl	Total	Cert	Dipl	Bach	Lic	Total
1969											
1970											
1971											
1972	8	2	3	2	3	5	21	7	9	0	37
1973											
1974											
1975											

SPONSORING GROUPS: The Federation of Independent Evangelical Churches of Spain (FIEIDE).

OTHER PARTICIPANTS: None, but the school is open to any evangelical denomination.

SUPPORTED BY: Funds from the FIEIDE.

STUDENT FEES: The student pays only for his books.

RECOGNITION OF STUDIES: A certificate is awarded upon the completion of each course. After completion of each section of the curriculum a corresponding diploma is given. Degrees granted are Lic. in Theol., Dip. in Theol., Dip. Min., Cert. of Christian service.

ORDINATION: May lead to ordination.

CANDIDATES FOR FULL TIME SERVICE: 2%.

ACCREDITATION: None.

CLASS FREQUENCY: In Barcelona, weekly. In other places every two weeks or monthly.

PREPARATION OF MATERIALS: Three members of the institution have prepared extension materials.

PLANS: Uncertain at the moment. The lack of personnel makes reorganization necessary.

COUNTRY: Rhodesia

Rusitu Bible Institute - Extension Department
P. O. Box 576
Umtali, Rhodesia

		Teachers					Students				
Year	Cent	Full	Part	Miss	Natl	Total	Cert	Dipl	Bach	Lic.	Total
1972	4	3	5	4	4	8	0	26	3	0	29
1973											
1974											
1975											

SPONSORING GROUPS: Africa Evangelical Fellowship (Inderdenomi-
                     national)

OTHER PARTICIPANTS: African Reformed Church
                     Salvation Army
                     Central Africa Presbyterian Church
                     Baptist Church

SUPPORTED BY: Free will support from England, Canada and
                     the U.S.A.

STUDENT FEES: The student pays $75.00 per year.

RECOGNITION OF   Certificates are given after every 10
   STUDIES: units of study. One unit = 12 hours.

ORDINATION: The program can lead to ordination but is
                     mainly lay training.

CANDIDATES FOR
FULL TIME SERVICE: About 5%.

ACCREDITATION: None. It is being pursued.

CLASS FREQUENCY: Weekly.

PREPARATION OF   Two members of the institution have pre-
   MATERIALS: pared extension materials.

PLANS: New centers are being opened next term in
                     three other areas.

COUNTRY: Taiwan

Taiwan Theological College - The Night Class
20, Lane 2, Sec. 2. Yang Teh Ta Road
Shihlin, Taipei
Republic of China

		Teachers					Students				
Year	Cent	Full	Part	Miss	Natl	Total	Cert	Dipl	Bach	Lic	Total
1972											
1973											
1974											
1975											

SPONSORING GROUPS:

OTHER PARTICIPANTS: Some students from other denominations.

SUPPORTED BY: Subsidy from the College.

STUDENT FEES: The student pays $5.00 per semester course.

RECOGNITION OF   A Diploma in Theology is granted with no
   STUDIES: intermediate goals.

ORDINATION: This is lay training only.

CANDIDATES FOR
FULL TIME SERVICE: None.

ACCREDITATION: The college is accredited by the Associa-
                    tion of Theological Schools of South East
                    Asia.

CLASS FREQUENCY: Two nights per week.

PREPARATION OF   Twelve members of the institution have pre-
   MATERIALS.   pared materials.

PLANS:

COUNTRY: Rhodesia

Lund Bible School
P/BAG 9030
Fort Victoria, Rhodesia

		Teachers					Students			
Year	Cent	Full	Part	Miss	Natl	Total	Cert	Dipl	Bach	Lic	Total
1973	2	3	2	3	2	5	5	9	0	0	14
1974											
1975											

SPONSORING GROUPS: Free Methodists

OTHER PARTICIPANTS: Dutch Reformed

SUPPORTED BY: Subsidy from U.S. based mission.

STUDENT FEES: The student pays only for books.

RECOGNITION OF   Certificates are given on completion of
STUDIES: each course. A Certificate in Theology is
                     awarded. Plans call for certificates in
                     Teacher Training for Sunday School, Lay
                     Workers, Lay Ministers, etc.

ORDINATION: It can lead to ordination.

CANDIDATES FOR
FULL TIME SERVICE: 30%.

ACCREDITATION: None.

CLASS FREQUENCY: Weekly.

PREPARATION OF   Four members of the institution have pre-
MATERIALS: pared extension materials.

PLANS: New centers will be opened by demand.

COUNTRY: Brazil

Instituto Batista de Educacão Teológica por Extensão (IBETE)
Rua Jaão Ramalho, 466
São Paulo, SP, Brazil

		Teachers				Students				
Year	Cent	Full	Part	Miss	Natl Total	Cert	Dipl	Bach	Lic	Total
1969										
1970										
1971										
1972	30	3	0	3	0	3	10%	55%	28%	12%
1973										
1974										
1975										

SPONSORING GROUPS: União Batista Evangelica
                      Baptist General Conference of North America

OTHER PARTICIPANTS: None.

SUPPORTED BY: 60% national, 40% North American.

STUDENT FEES: $2.50 per month and additional variable
                        fees.

RECOGNITION OF   Certificates are given at the institute
  STUDIES: level.

ORDINATION: The program is for lay training as well
                        as for ordination.

CANDIDATES FOR
FULL TIME SERVICE:

ACCREDITATION:

CLASS FREQUENCY:

PLANS: They expect to have within a year 50 centers
                        with 1200 students and within three years
                        160 centers with 3000 students in 4 states.

COUNTRY:　Ecuador

Instituto Bíblico del Pacífico
Casilla 187
Esmeraldas, Ecuador

		Teachers					Students				
Year	Cent	Full	Part	Miss	Natl	Total	Cert	Dipl	Bach	Lic	Total
1969											
1970											
1971											
1972	11	0	4	3	1	4	62	5			67
1973											
1974											
1975											

SPONSORING GROUPS:　Missionary Church

OTHER PARTICIPANTS:　Christian and Missionary Alliance.

SUPPORTED BY:　　　Mission subsidy and student fees.

STUDENT FEES:　　　$1.00

RECOGNITION OF　　Certificates are given at the end of each
　STUDIES:　　　　course and Diplomas at the end of ten.

ORDINATION:　　　This may lead to ordination.

CANDIDATES FOR　　None.
FULL TIME SERVICE:

ACCREDITATION:　　None.

CLASS FREQUENCY:　Bi-weekly.

PREPARATION OF　　None.
　MATERIALS:

PLANS:　　　　　　Two new centers in other towns next year.

COUNTRY: Ethiopia

Milate Heywar Bible School
Box 2323
Ambo Ethiopia

| | | Teachers | | | | Students | | | | |
Year	Cent	Full	Part	Miss	Natl	Total	Cert	Dipl	Bach	Lic	Total
1971	1	0	2	1	1	2					
1972	3	0	6	3	3	6	10	17			27
1973											
1974											
1975											

SPONSORING GROUPS: Baptist General Conference
                      BEA Churches

OTHER PARTICIPANTS: Christian Missionary Fellowship

SUPPORTED BY: Subsidy through BGCM and BEA churches.

STUDENT FEES: They pay for books only.

RECOGNITION OF   Credit cards are given on completion of
   STUDIES: courses. Students will receive a certifi-
                      cate on completing 48 hours - equivalent
                      to one year of residence study.

ORDINATION: Students who are accepted for third year
                      in residence school could be considered
                      for ordination.

CANDIDATES FOR   Unknown.
FULL TIME SERVICE:

ACCREDITATION: None.

CLASS FREQUENCY: Weekly or bi-weekly

PREPARATION OF   Three members of the faculty have prepared
   MATERIALS: programmed materials.

PLANS: Expansion of the program to teach non-liter-
                      ates with a tape and picture curriculum.

COUNTRY: Niger

L'Ecole Biblique D'Aguie
B. P. 121
Maradi, Republic of Niger

Year	Cent	Teachers					Students				
		Full	Part	Miss	Natl	Total	Cert	Dipl	Bach	Lic	Total
1972	6	1	3	4	0	4	50				50
1973											
1974											
1975											

SPONSORING GROUPS: Sudan Interior Mission

OTHER PARTICIPANTS: None.

SUPPORTED BY: Subsidy from churches in the US, Canada, Europe and Niger.

STUDENT FEES: They pay for texts and workbooks.

RECOGNITION OF STUDIES: Certificates are given for each course.

ORDINATION: The program is not yet sufficient for ordination.

CANDIDATES FOR FULL TIME SERVICE:

ACCREDITATION: None.

CLASS FREQUENCY: Weekly. Monthly visit by director.

PREPARATION OF MATERIALS: One member of the faculty has prepared extension materials.

PLANS: Two courses will be added and there will be an attempt to establish a curriculum by 1974.

Appendices

135 North Oakland Avenue
Pasadena, California 91101
December 1, 1972

Dear co worker in extension:

Ten years have passed since theological education by extension was
launched in Guatemala. It is time to survey the extent of the movement
and to evaluate its performance and possibilities. Attached is a questionnaire requesting information useful in this evaluation. The data will be
compiled and will help various individuals and agencies in their study of
TEE.

In order to give some guidelines in answering the questions, the
right side of the questionnaire contains sample answers from the United
Biblical Seminary of Colombia. Perhaps a comparison of your extension
program with one that has been in operation for some six years will be of
help to you. Therefore we ask that you return to us by air mail a carbon
copy of the data relating to your own institution. Your answers may be
returned on half sheets of paper, thereby reducing postal costs.

The few minutes you take from your busy schedule will help to provide a global picture of extension which should provide insights for all
involved in this type of program. We welcome also any reports or promotional materials regarding your insitution. These will be helpful even
though it is necessary for them to be translated here. Thank you for
your cooperation in this project.

Wayne C Weld
Wayne C. Weld

SURVEY OF THEOLOGICAL EXTENSION PROGRAMS

YOUR DATA   (SAMPLE ANSWERS)

1. Name of the Institution.   1. (United Biblical Seminary
   [   ]   of Colombia)

2. Address.   2. (Apartado Aéreo 1141
   [   ]   Medellín, Colombia)

3. Year in which the extension program began.   3. (1966)
   [   ]

4. Indicate any previous type of theological edu- 4. (Residence - day)
   cation program which your institution sponsored.

   ___Residence - day

   ___Residence - night

   ___Residence - short term

   ___Correspondence

   ___Other (please specify)

   [   ]

5. What year was the previous type of theological 5. (1944)
   training initiated?
   [   ]

6. If your institution is related to another   6. (not applicable)
   institution of theological education give the
   name and address.
   [   ]

7. What missions or Churches officially cooperate 7. (Interamerican Missionary
   in your institution?   Society
   [   ]   Evangelical Covenant Church
                                                      Latin America Mission
                                                      General Conference Men-
                                                         nonite Church
                                                      Mennonite Brethren Church
                                                      Cumberland Presbyterian
                                                         Church)

8. Other evangelical groups that participate in your institution through students or some other way.

8. (Wesleyan Mission World Evangelization Crusade Gospel Missionary Union Christian and Missionary Alliance Lutheran Church in America Overseas Crusades Presbyterian Church of Colombia Panamerican Mission Foursquare Gospel Church)

9. How is your institution financed?

9. (Subsidy from missions based in the U.S. and Canada and from national Churches.)

10. How much does the student pay for tuition or books? (in US $ equivalents)

10. (Students pay about US $3.00 for a semester course. They pay for all texts and workbooks. Matriculation fee is $1.00 per semester.)

11. Number of full time faculty or administrative personnel.

11. (Three)

12. Number of part time faculty or administrative personnel.

12. (Twenty-five)

13. How many of these are missionaries?

13. (Twelve)

14. What are the academic levels of your students? How many are enrolled at each level?

14. (Certificate - literate, 2 or 3 years of primary 250 students

Diploma - completed primary school 90 students

Bachelor - 4 to 6 years of high school 20 students)

15. Number of centers operated.   15. (Twenty-five)

16. Degrees granted.   16. (Bachelor of Theology
                                                       Diploma in Theology)

17. Are there intermediate goals or is recognition 17. (Certificates are given
given before completing the whole course of studies?   at the end of each semester.
                                                        Plans call for diplomas as
                                                        Sunday School teachers,
                                                        Evangelists, Christian
                                                        Workers, etc. after ten or
                                                        twelve subjects have been
                                                        studied and another diplo-
                                                        ma after the second third
                                                        of the whole course.)

18. What calendar does your school year follow?   18. (Two semesters of sixteen
                                                       weeks each.)

19. Is your program considered "lay training" or   19. (Most students do not hope
could it lead to ordination?   for ordination, but it
                                                       would be granted on termina-
                                                       ting the whole course or ever
                                                       before completion according
                                                       to denominational requiremen

20. Have you elaborated a full curriculum intended 20. (The CATA curriculum used
to lead to ordination?   throughout Latin America is
                                                       used at the diploma level.
                                                       Other levels are not defined
                                                       yet.)

21. What percentage of your students are preparing 21. (About 10 %)
for a full time ministry?

22. Are there alternate courses of specialized   22. (Plans are being considered for
studies?   studies in preparation for
                                                        work as evangelist, pastor,
                                                        teacher, deacon with some
                                                        core courses and electives
                                                        according to interest.)

23. How many years of study would be required to terminate the whole course as for ordination?

23. (At the diploma level there are 36 subjects. Four per year would require nine years for a degree leading to ordination in some Churches. The curriculum for the other levels has not been defined yet.)

24. What are the levels of residence theological institutions in your country or region?

24. (Two seminaries for high school graduates. Several Bible institutes for those who have completed primary or for functional literates.)

25. Is your institution accredited by any regional or other accrediting agency?

25. (No. However, only one seminary in the area has been considered for accreditation by the regional association of theological schools.)

26. Would course work done through extension be accepted as equivalent to the same courses offered in a residence program?

26. (All credits are transferable to the residence program of the same seminary.)

27. How many have completed your course of study?

27. (Two who began in residence.)

28. What percentage of those enrolled for one term continue to study another?

28. (About 50% continue, although sometimes with interruptions.)

29. How often are classes held?

29. (Weekly except bi-weekly classes in some isolated areas.)

30. Are periodic meetings held to unite students at various centers for fellowship, encouragement and special courses?

30. (In some areas monthly meetings have been held at centrally located points.)

31. What plans do you have for expanding your present program?

31. (New centers will be organized in other cities and perhaps within several congregations in one city.)

5

32. How many subjects are presently offered?

32. (Two or three subjects
    offered at each center e
    semester. Previously of;
    Bachelor - 8 subjects
    Diploma - 18 subjects
    Certificate - 12 subject

33. For how many subjects do you have programmed
materials?

33. (About five subjects at
    each level.)

34. Where are your instructional materials prepared?

34. (Locally, Guatemala,
    Bolivia, Ecuador)

35. How many persons in your institution have prepared materials for extension?

35. (Six, but only two for
    programmed materials)

36. Have you conducted workshops for writers?

36. (Three workshops for wri†
    over a three year period.

37. Have you conducted workshops for teachers?

38. (In some areas a workshop
    for teachers is held befc
    each school year.)

38. Will sufficient materials be made available to
continue your program of studies without delay?

38. (Provisional materials ar
    being used until somethin
    better is prepared.)

Please attach any other comments or materials which will be helpful in defining
and describing your extension program. Thank you for your assistance.

135 N. Oakland Avenue
Pasadena, California 91101
1 diciembre de 1.972

Estimado colaborador en extensión:

Diez años han pasado ya desde que la educación teológica por extensión
tuvo su conienzo en Guatemala. Es tiempo de notar la amplitud del movimiento
y de evaluarlo según su rendimiento y sus posibilidades. Adjunto un cuestionario que pide información útil en esta evaluación. Los datos serán recopila-
dos y ayudarán a muchos en su estudio en cuanto a este programa.

Para dar algunas pautas en contestar las preguntas, el lado derecho del
cuestionario presenta respuestas modelo tomadas del Seminario Bíblico Unido
de Colombia. Tal vez una comparación del programa de su institución con otro
que ha funcionado ya por seis años sea útil. Por lo tanto, pedimos quenos
devuelvan por correo aéreo una copia de los datos relacionados a su institución. Las respuestas pueden ser enviadas en medias hojas para ahorrar portes.

Los pocos minutos que saca de sus muchas actividades y responsabilidades
nos ayudarán a proveer un cuadro completo de extension. Tal cuadro proveerá
conceptos importantes para todos los que están involucrados en extensión.
Solcitamos, por lo tanto, que nos envíen también cualquier informe o material promocional de su institución.

Le agradecemos anticipadamente por su colaboración en este proyecto. No
deje que no se tome en cuenta su institución.

Su servidor en Cristo,

Wayne C. Weld

CENSO DE PROGRAMAS DE EDUCACION TEOLOGICA POR EXTENSION

DATOS SUYOS   (RESPUESTA MODELO)

1. Nombre de la Institución.   1. (Seminario Bíblico Unido
                                                        de Colombia)

2. Dirección.   2. (Apartado Aéreo 1141
                                                        Medellín, Colombia)

3. Año en que se inició el programa de extensión. 3. (1966)

4. Indique cualquier tipo de educación teológica   4. (Residencia - diurna)
que su institución auspiciaba.

___Residencia - diurna

___Residencia - nocturna

___Residencia - corto plazo

___Correspondencia

___Otro (Indique tipo)

5. ¿En qué año se inició el tipo previo de pre-   5. (1944)
paración teológica?

6. Si su institución tiene afiliación con otra   6. (no aplica)
institución de educación teológica dé el nombre
y dirección.

7. ¿Qué misiones oiglesias cooperan oficial-   7. (Sociedad Misionera Inter-
mente en su institución?   americana
                                                      Misión del Pacto Evangé-
                                                      lico
                                                      Misión Latinoamericana
                                                      Iglesia Menonita de Col.
                                                      Hermanos Menonitas
                                                      Iglesia Presbieriana
                                                      Cumberland)

8. Otros grupos evangélicos que participan en su institución de alguna manera.

8. (Misión Wesleyana
Crusada Mundial
Unión Misionera Evan.
Alianza Cristiana y
Misionera
Iglesia Luterana
SEPAL
Iglesia Presbiteriana
Misión Panamericana
Iglesia Cuadrangular)

9. ¿Cómo se sostiene económicamente su institución?

9. (Subvención de misiones norteamericanas y de iglesias nacionales.)

10. ¿Cuánto pagan los alumnos por pensión y libros? (en equivalencia de $ US)

10. (Alumnos pagan unos $3.00 por materia semestral. Compran textos y manuales. Matrícula es de $1.00 por semestre.)

11. Número de profesores o administradores de tiempo completo.

11. (3)

12. Número de profesores o administradores de tiempo parcial.

12. (25)

13. ¿Cuántos de ellos son extranjeros?

13. (12)

14. Indique los niveles académicos de los alumnos. ¿Cuántos están matriculados en cada nivel?

14. (Certificado - 2 o 3 años de primaria 250 alumnos

Diploma - primaria completa 90 alumnos

Bachillerato - 4 años o completo 20 alumnos

15. Número de centros

15. (25)

16. Grados otorgados

16. (Bachiller de Teología
    Diploma en Teología)

17. ¿Hay metas intermedias o se da reconoci-
    miento antes de terminar el curso completo de
    estudios?

17. (Certificados se dan al
    terminar cada semestre. S
    espera ofrecer diplomas
    para maestros de Esc. Dom
    evangelistas, obreros, et
    después de 10 o 12 materi
    y otro diploma al termina
    el segundo tercio del cur
    completo.)

18. ¿Qué calendario sigue la institución?

18. (Dos semestres de 16 sema
    nas cada uno.)

19. ¿El programa se considera apto para laicos o
    puede conducir a la ordenación?

19. (La mayoría de los alumno
    no esperan ordenarse, per
    podría serlo al terminar
    el curso completo y llena
    otros requisitos denomina-
    cionales.)

20. ¿Se ha elaborado un pénsum completo que
    pueda conducir a la ordenación?

20. (El pénsum de CATA se usa
    en el nivel diploma. Los
    otros niveles no están de-
    finidos todavía.)

21. ¿Qué porcentaje de los alumnos se preparan
    para un ministerio de tiempo completo?

21. (Unos 10%)

22. ¿Hay cursos alternativos de estudios espe-
    ciales?

22. (Se preparan cursos para
    evangelistas, pastores,
    maestros, diáconos con al-
    gunas materias básicas par
    todos y materias optativas
    según el interés del alumn

23. ¿Cuántos años de estudio se requieren para terminar el curso como para ordenación?

23. (En el nivel diploma hay 36 materias. 4 por año requerería 9 años para un grado que satisface los requisitos de ordenación en algunas denominaciones. Otros niveles no definidos.

24. ¿En qué nivel académico operan las instituciones de residencia en su país o región?

24. (2 seminarios para bachilleres. Unos institutos bíblicos para los que han terminado primaria o que son alfabetos.)

25. ¿Está acreditada su institución ante alguna agencia acreditadora?

25. (No. Pero sólo un seminario en la región se ha considerado para acreditación por ALET.)

26. ¿Se reconocen los estudios por extensión como equivalentes de estudios realizados en algún programa de residencia?

26. (Créditos aceptados en el programa de residencia del mismo seminario.)

27. ¿Cuántos han terminado el curso completo?

27. (2 que empezaron en residencia.)

28. ¿Qué porcentaje de los matriculados en un semestre siguen estudiando otro semestre?

28. (Unos 50%, aunque a veces estudios interrumpidos.)

29. ¿Con qué frecuencia se ofrecen clases?

29. (Semanalmente pero cada 15 días en algunos sectores remotos.)

30. ¿Se convocan reuniones periódicamente para compañerismo, estímulo y materias especiales?

30. (En algunos sectores reuniones mensuales se han realizado en locales centrales.)

31. ¿Qué planes tienen para extender el programa actual?

31. (Centros nuevos se organizarán en otras ciudades y tal vez dentro de congregaciones en unas ciudades.)

32. ¿Cuántas materias se ofrecen actualmente?

32. (2 o 3 materias en cada centro. Total ofrecidas anteriormente:
Bachiller - 8
Diploma - 18
Certificado - 12

33. ¿Para cuántas materias hay materiales programados?

33. (Unas 5 materias en cada nivel.)

34. ¿Dónde se preparan los materiales para instrucción?

34. (Colombia, Guatemala, Bolivia, Ecuador)

35. ¿Cuántas personas en su institución han preparado materiales para extensión?

35. (6 pero sólo 2 materiales programados.)

36. ¿Se han realizado talleres para escritores?

36. (3 talleres para escritores en 3 años.)

37. ¿Se han realizado talleres para profesores?

37. (En unos sectores un taller se organiza antes de cada año escolar.)

38. ¿Tendrá suficientes materiales disponibles para seguir el curso de estudios sin demora?

38. (Se usan materiales provisionales hasta que haya algo mejor.)

Favor de ajuntar observaciones o materiales que puedan ayudar a definir o describir el programa de extensión. Muchas gracias por su colaboración.

EXTENSION

THE MONTHLY AIR MAIL

NEWSLETTER

135 NORTH OAKLAND AVENUE   PASADENA, CALIFORNIA 91101

BER 1972   VOL. I NO.1

WHY ANOTHER NEWSLETTER?

ie need has arisen for a monthly air mail
etter on theological education by extension.
newsletter will be sent to those whose re-
ibilities require them to be right up to
on what is happening in this worldwide move-
and who are able to share insights that are
ed up in their own activities. Although sev-
bulletins related to extension programs now
t, almost all are restricted to one region
ie world and are sent by surface mail to
r subscribers. Not only is worldwide coordi-
on and sharing necessary, but this must be
zed as rapidly as possible by means of
ly reports which arrive within a few days
rinting.

veral of us presently at the School of World
on of Fuller Theological Seminary have re-
d to produce the kind of newsletter that
keep abreast of new developments. Our news
es will be key men in extension programs
ghout the world and the various organiza-
s which presently are active in some phase
tension work. As lists of available mate-
s, notices of workshops and other meetings,
les or observations which contain valuable
hts, and reports of the expansion of the
sion movement reach us, they will be sent
o those concerned.

is is not an attempt to control the exten-
movement from the United States. Local and
nal organizations must make decisions about
ams and production of materials. However,
akthrough in one area of the world might
de the insight needed in some other area.
ght be possible to adapt materials prepared
other country or to see how adaptation has
done by others rather than to start from
ch in preparing course materials. We in-
all those who have items which would be of
est and importance to others to submit
to us. The utility of this newsletter will
d in part on the voluntary submission of
ial from persons such as yourself.

is first copy is being sent free to persons
nstitutions which we feel have a vital in-
t in the extension movement. Next month's
etter will go only to those who subscribe
ans of the coupon which you will find at
nd of this issue.

     Wayne C. Weld, Editor

**Future issues of EXTENSION will contain two
sheets.** This first issue was reduced to its
present size because many copies are being sent
out as an enclosure with other materials.

     **An Asia-wide TEE Consultation for coordina-
tors** and others involved in TEE will be held
the last week in November or first week in December in Bangkok, Thailand. For more details
write to: TAP-Asia, 33A Chancery Lane, Singapore 11.

     **An evaluation and reorganization of CATA and
CLATT** (Advisory Committee for Autodidactic Texts
and Latin American Committee for Theological
Texts) after five years of operation is planned
for Medellín, Colombia on January 8-13. Plans
to accelerate and improve the writing, production and distribution of extension materials
will be discussed. The meetings, to be held in
Spanish, will gather delegates from institutions
throughout Latin America.

     **A TEE organizational meeting for the Near
East and North Africa** has been set for this
month. This is a result of a workshop held at
Beirut July 3-14. One of those involved in the
projected meeting is Samuel F. Schlorff, 33 bis
Cours Gambetta, 13100 AIX-EN-PROVENCE, France.

     **More than 2,000 students in nearly thirty
institutions** now study by extension in Brazil
according to Richard Sturz of AETTE. These students are included in the 4,879 extension students for all of Latin America that CLATT reports for 1971. CLATT is presently conducting
another official census which should indicate
the phenomenal growth of this movement throughout Central and South America.

     The Malaysian workshop on TEE was held Sep-
tember 18-29 in Kuala Lumpur. The prohibition
of evangelistic work among the Moslems and the
probable expulsion of missionaries within a
few years lend urgency to the preparation of
leaders. Twenty-one participants representing
nine evangelical groups came to discuss the
possibilities of TEE with Peter Savage. An ad-
hoc committee will meet again in December. Its
coordinator is Rev. Duain Vierow, 21 Jalan
Abdul Samad, Kuala Lumpur, Malaysia.

     Twelve centers with 200 students in India
are reported by TAFTEE (The Association for
Theological Extension Education).

CLATT Catalog No. 3 of available materials
was distributed in September. This four page
list of programmed and provisional materials in
Spanish can be ordered from:
CLATT
Peter Wagner, Secretary
135 N. Oakland Avenue
Pasadena, California 91101

All programmed instruction materials in any
language produced anywhere in the world will be
listed in the CAMEO Release presently being prepared. This Release is free to all IFMA and
EFMA Boards and others who ask for it. Write to:
CAMEO
8210 West 16th Place
Lakewood, Colorado 80215

Programmed instruction materials in Portuguese are coordinated by Richard Sturz. For a
current list of materials write to:
AETTE
Richard Sturz, Secretary
Caixa Postal 30.259
01000 Sao Paulo, Brazil

Preparation of programmed instructional materials is the subject of many of the articles
in Programming News. The first issue (July
1971) contained articles entitled "What are
Programmed Materials?" and "The History of Programming."
Programming News
Merevale, Forest Guernsey
Channel Islands, United Kingdom

The AEBICAM BULLETIN (Association of Evangelical Bible Institutes and Colleges of Africa
and Madigascar) reports on progress in TEE in
that area. In addition to reports from the
cooperating institutions it carries notices such
as that of the meeting of the AEBICAM executive
committee in Limuru, Kenya on January 31.
AEBICAM BULLETIN
Rev. Fred Holland, Editor
Box 131
Choma, Zambia

TAP-Asia has compiled reports on TEE from the
following countries: India, Pakistan, Sumatra,
Philippines, Indonesia and Thailand. Also included in the mimeographed booklet are lists of
textbooks and assettes availabe for TEE. Many
of the materials are in English as well as the
language of the country in which prepared. This
report may be requested from:
Dr. Bong Ro, S.E. Asia Coordinator
TAP-Asia
33A Chancery Lane
Singapore 11

This first issue of EXTENSION is being sent
to 502 theological schools around the world.
Sets of address labels for these schools may be
purchased for $25.00 including air postage from
William Carey Library
305 Pasadena Avenue
South Pasadena, California 91030

The Evangelical Churches of West Africa
Nigeria launched an experimental program i
early in 1971. The results were so impress
that the number taking part has doubled.
missionaries working part time coordinate
instruct ten pastors who in turn hold TEE s
nars for 130 evangelists. Programmed inst
tion materials in the Hausa language for O
Testament and Evangelism have just become a
able in mimeographed form. Sunday School m
uals are being adapted for a third course.

Courses on TEE and Programming will be o
fered during the winter quarter at the Scho
of World Mission, Fuller Theological Semina
by James Emery, one of the pioneers of the
extension program in Guatemala.

A workshop on TEE including writing programmed instructional materials will be con
ducted at Missionary Internship headquarter
by Dr. Ted Ward and Mr. Samuel Rowen on Feb
ruary 19-23. For more details write to:
Missionary Internship
Box 457
Farmington, Michigan 48024

TEE and Programmed Instructional Materia
in Indonesia brought twenty-four delegates
a workshop in Sukabuni during the first thr
weeks of September. Three extension progra
are presently in operation or in preparatio
that country: The National Council of Churc
is expanding its outreach to 3,000 leaders.
Southern Baptists will open four centers in
1973. The Christian and Missionary Alliance
enrolled 150 students last January on the is
lands of Temor, Alor and Rot. Plans now include a program for 75 students in West Bor

A writers' workshop for Pakistan will be
sponsored by the Committee for Theological
Education by Extension (CTEE) in Gujranwala
December 15-17.

Revision workshops for programmed materi
for TEE in Africa meet as follows:
January 10-25 in Salisbury, Rhodesia. Writ
Rev. F. L. Holland, Box 131, Choma, Zambia.
February 19-March 3 in Jos, Nigeria. Writ
Rev. Peter Dominy, Box 643, Jos, Nigeria.
A workshop for new writers will be held in
Nigeria from March 1 to 23 or 30.

To receive the next and subsequent issues
EXTENSION send your check for U.S. $7.25 wi
your name and address to
EXTENSION
Wayne C. Weld, Editor
135 North Oakland Avenue
Pasadena, California 91101

NAME _____

ADDRESS_____

_____

THE MONTHLY AIR MAIL

NEWSLETTER

EXTENSION

135 North Oakland Avenue   Pasadena, California 91101

DECEMBER 1972   VOL. I NO. 2

A Programming Techniques Workshop
will be held in Wheaton, Illinois on
March 19-24, 1973. Cost is $50.00
plus food, plus travel. Applications,
accompanied by the $10.00 registra-
tion fee (included in the $50.00),
must be sent before January 31 to:
    R. B. Buker, CAMEO Coordinator
    2210 Park Place
    Boca Raton, Florida 33432

WEF Programming News of October
1972 features an article by Peter
Savage entitled Preparing to Write.
Among other useful suggestions it pro-
poses the following steps that the potential writer will take:
1) Defining the TOPIC AREA
2) Defining the TARGET POPULATION
3) Stating the EDUCATIONAL GOALS
4) Analysis of TARGET POPULATION
5) Build a Pyramid of Objectives and
   Sub-Objectives
6) Establish Strategy

TAP-Asia is producing the report
of nine Programmed Instruction workshops held in Asia last summer. Those
who want these reports as well as other
detailed TEE information from that area
should send $10.00 for TAP-Asia member-
ship to:
    Dr. Bong Ro, S.E. Asia Coordinator
    TAP-Asia
    33A Chancery Lane
    Singapore 11

Theological Education by Extension edited by Ralph Winter, which
relates the history of the movement
in Latin America, will be updated for
a second edition soon.

Extension in Haiti was stimulated
by a workshop in June conducted by
Harold Alexander and James Sauder.
TEE students in June numbered 250. A
second workshop in August was attended
by 30 professors from 5 organizations.
Student enrollment has risen to 650.
Coordination of TEE in Haiti is by
    Centre d'Information et de Sta-
        tistique Evangelique (CISE)
    B.P. 458
    Port-au-Prince, Haiti

Inquiries concerning TEE in the
Near East and North Africa should be
directed to:
    Bob Meloy
    P.O. Box 126
    Tripoli, Lebanon

Evangel Publishing House of
Kisumu, Kenya has agreed with AEBICAM
to publish all of the TEE materials
to be used in Africa. The first text,
Talking with God, is also available
in Swahili under the title Kuzungumza
na Mungu. Prices are $1.50 and $1.00
respectively, with discounts for
quantity orders. Bringing People to
Christ, an evangelism text, will be in
print in January. This book written
by Jonah Moyo and Grace Holland in
Zambia will also be translated into
Swahili. Eight more texts are being
validated for production at present
and plans call for printing of these
materials in French as well as in
English and Swahili. For more information write:
    Evangel Publishing House
    P.O. Box 969
    Kisumu, Kenya

The Consultation of Theological Institutions that have extension programs to be held in Medellín, Colombia on January 8-13 contemplates an evaluation of what has been done in Latin America and a reorganization of agencies to expedite the movement. The meetings will be held in Spanish, but the titles of the papers to be presented are translated into English below to indicate the concerns of the meeting.

1. The Intertext Project in Spanish.
2. Orientation for Workshops.
3. The Problem of the Semi-literate in the Development of a Plan of Studies.
4. Finances and Budgets.
5. Reports of CATA (Advisory Committee for Autodidactic Texts).
6. The 16 Steps for the Production and Distribution of Intertexts.
7. The Constitution of the Evangelical Association of Theological Texts for Extension (AETTE).
8. Group Dynamics and Suggestions for the Future.
9. Seminary Curricula.
10. Development of Professors and Materials for Theological Education in Latin America.
11. Theological Education by Extension-A Critique of Its Development and Method by a TEF committee.
12. The Evaluation of Extension Studies.
13. The Professor-teaching vs. the Student-learning.

Discussions on Theological Training in Africa will be held in Limuru on February 8, 1973. The discussions, sponsored by AEBICAM, will include TEE and Programmed Instruction. The cost us US $5.00 (Kenya SH35/-). Those who desire to attend must send reservations before January 1 to:

Mr. Eric Maillefer, AEAM
Box 49332
Nairobi, Kenya

TEE workshops on the role of the professor in TEE will be conducted next year by Harold Alexander. The nine three-day workshops will probably be held in such places as Abijan, Jos, Bujumbura, Addis Abba, Limuru, and Salisbury. Other centers of TEE will be considered for workshops during the visit of Mr. Alexander in July and August. These workshops will be coordinated by AEBICAM, Box 131, Choma, Zambia.

CAMEO has published a Bibliography of Programmed Texts. The list of over 100 texts does not include many which are being validated, but it does contain some titles which will not be in production for as long as two years from now. For all the books the language and distributor are named. For some, the level, when available, and the price are also indicated. Listings are from 23 institutions or agencies in English, French, Indonesian, Portuguese, Spanish, Thai and Vietnamese.

This bibliography points up the need for a clearer definition of levels of study which would permit a more useful interchange of materials across language or regional barriers. Perhaps in listing materials it would be helpful to indicate the text book which would be used if the course were offered in residence or which is used in conjunction with the programmed instruction.

TEE in Indonesia has plans to reach 3,000 potential leaders as reported in the last issue. However, the first program to be in operation outside of that sponsored by the Christian and Missionary Alliance is beginning with 124 students. This is the work of the West Indonesia Protestant Church, a member of the Indonesian National Council of Churches. Most of the first students are church elders.

The Church Growth Book Club offers
the following books on extension.
Many are available at a considerable
discount to those who become members
through a $1.00 yearly subscription
to the Church Growth Bulletin.
AN EXTENSION SEMINARY PRIMER -
  Covell and Wagner
DECIDE FOR YOURSELF: A THEOLOGICAL
  WORKBOOK - Lewis, Intervarsity
DEVELOPING PROGRAMMED INSTRUCTION-
  AL MATERIALS - Espich & Williams
EL SEMINARIO DE EXTENSION: UN MA-
  NUAL - Emery
INDUCTIVE STUDY OF THE BOOK OF
  JEREMIAH - Kinsler
INDUCTIVE STUDY OF THE BOOK OF
  MARK - Kinsler
PREPARING INSTRUCTIONAL OBJECTIVES-
  Mager
PRINCIPIOS DEL CRECIMIENTO DE LA
  IGLESIA - Weld & McGavran
PRINCIPLES OF CHURCH GROWTH -
  Weld and McGavran
PROGRAMMED INSTRUCTION FOR THEOLO-
  GICAL EDUCATION BY EXTENSION -
  Ward and Ward
THEOLOGICAL EDUCATION BY EXTENSION
  Winter
Order from:
  The Church Growth Book Club
  305 Pasadena Avenue
  South Pasadena, California 91030

An extension class in Principles
and Procedures of Church Growth is
being taught in Pasadena, California
by Donald McGavran and Peter Wagner.
The class offered for credit by
Fuller Theological Seminary is attended by local pastors and meets
in one of the central churches of
the city.

In Zambia the Brethren in Christ
Church has 110 people enrolled in
eight centers. Nearly half of
those enrolled attended at least 7
of 10 lessons. In Rhodesia the
same denomination has 51 people
enrolled in 4 centers.

THEOLOGICAL NEWS, the quarterly
news-letter of the Theological Assistance Program (TAP) of the World Evangelical Fellowship, features a guest
editorial by Dr. Bong Rin Ro in its
October 1972 issue. He concludes
with the following suggestions:
  First, we must develop B.D. level
    seminaries.
  Second, we must encourage the
    establishing of centres for
    advanced theological studies
    (CATS) to train graduate theo-
    logians.
  Third, pedagogical seminaries
    should be planned to improve
    seminary training.
  Fourth, TEE methods must be de-
    veloped to train pastors and
    key lay leaders on-the-job.

You may order THEOLOGICAL NEWS from
Bruce J. Nicholls
Union Biblical Seminary
Yeotmal, Maharashtra, India
Subscription rates: $2.00 per annum
air-mail and $1.00 surface mail.

In Transvaal, South Africa the
Free Methodist Extension Bible School
launched an extension program last
August. 83 students are enrolled in
12 centers. Most centers are in the
urban areas of Johannesburg and
Pretoria. Interest indicates an increase in enrollment for 1973. The
principal, Donald Crider, reports
that programmed course on pastoral
care has been developed in Zulu.

A World Directory of Mission Related Educational Institutions will
be available in January 1973. The
retail price of this 900 page book
is $19.95. For members of EFMA or
IFMA the price is $10.00 plus $1.25
for handling. The check for $11.25
must accompany order.
  William Carey Library
  305 Pasadena Avenue
  South Pasadena, California 91030

TAP-Asia is producing the report
of nine Programmed Instruction workshops held in Asia last summer.
Those who want these reports as well
as other detailed TEE information
from that area should send $10.00 for
TAP-Asia membership to:
    Dr. Bong Ro, S.E. Asia Coordinator
    TAP-Asia
    33A Chancery Lane
    Singapore 11

WEF Theological News for October 1972 contains the following
summary of these nine workshops:
Between July and October this year
Programmed Instruction Workshops
have been held throughout Asia. Each
workshop was under local sponsorship but the coordination of dates
and resource personnel was under-
taken by the TEE ministry of TAP-
Asia. Mr. Ian McCleary, the TEE
General Coordinator, led workshops
in the Philippines, New Guinea and
South Vietnam. Six participated in
the Vietnam workshop and a further
workshop is being planned for 1973.
Mr. Martin Dainton, the Associate
Coordinator, led two workshops:
(1) Lebanon, 17 participants from
Jordan, Egypt, North Africa and
Lebanon itself; and (2) Thailand,
23 participants including 3 from
Bangladesh. Rev. Peter Savage of
Bolivia led a further 4 workshops:
Indonesia, 24 representing 7 major
church denominations, India, 16
representatives from Theological
Colleges and TAFTEE centres, Malaysia, 21 participants (3 from Indonesia), 11 of whom formed an ad hoc
fellowship to further TEE in W. Malaysia, and Taiwan, 11 participants.
mostly from Theological Colleges.

EXTENSION readers are reminded
that we welcome your news items for
our next or subsequent issues. One
of our goals is to call attention
to other TEE news sources.

Three workshops for new writers of
programmed texts will be conducted
next year by AEBICAM. The dates and
places are as follows:
    Jos 12 Feb. to 9 Mar.
    Kenya 15 May to 8 June
    Salisbury 18 Sept. to 12 Oct.
For further information write AEBICAM,
P.O. Box 131, Choma Zambia. For the
Jos workshop contact J. Flueddemann,
SIM, Jos, Nigeria.

The TEE workshop held November
8-10 in Torreon, Coah, Mexico was
attended by 20 persons from 6 evangelical groups. The workshop pointed
up the need for more materials in
Spanish and for more visual materials
prepared to explain extension education
and programmed instruction to those who
have no experience in this area.

The CLATT survey of TEE in Latin
America is still incomplete. The total student enrollment reported in
Central and South America and the
Caribbean stands at 4894 with at least
twenty institutions still not re-
porting.

If you have not yet subscribed to
EXTENSION or know someone else who
should receive the twelve issues of
our trial year, send your check for
U.S. $7.25 with your name and address
to:
    EXTENSION
    Wayne C. Weld, Editor
    135 North Oakland Avenue
    Pasadena, California 91101

NAME _____

ADDRESS_____

       _____

THE MONTHLY AIR MAIL
NEWSLETTER
EXTENSION

135 North Oakland Avenue   Pasadena, California 91101

JANUARY 1973   VOL. I NO. 3

In Indonesia where the church has doubled its numbers in five years hundreds of churches do not have pastors. TEE workshops were attended by participants which represented more than 2,500 congregations. The Southern Baptists with 200 churches are phasing out their residential program and will begin an "in service" seminary training by extension this year.

Of the thirty participants in the workshop in Manila, over 50% were Filipinos. The academic level of the group was very high. Many came from groups which have set them aside specifically for TEE work.

Leaders of the workshops sponsored by TAP-Asia felt that a Workshop Leaders' Training Course should be set up for late 1973 or early 1974. This would bring together key writers from several countries who are potential workshop instructors for their own countries.

A preliminary analysis of the student body of the United Biblical Seminary of Colombia indicates that of the 224 students included in the study 162 were male and 105 were married. Ages ranged from 13 to 71. The average age was 32. Christian experience ranged from two months to 45 years with an average of 7 years. Of these students 195 hold some office or activity in the church

and many hold more than one. 15 of the students were full time pastors, but 30 more served as self supporting pastors or lay preachers. Approximately one third of all students taught in Sunday School and 20 were Sunday School Superintendents.

The Guyana Baptist Theological Institute has a program of "Ministerial Training by Guided-Study" which operates at three academic levels. The curriculum provides for scholarly attainment and prepares the pastor for speaking to the modern Caribbean men on various educational levels. It is hoped that it will become a Caribbean cooperative effort in ministerial education. Each country may adapt the program to meet her existing needs and opportunities. Qualified persons are encouraged to contribute to the program by helping to prepare guides in the suggested areas of study.

The Latin American Committee on Theological Texts (CLATT) has ceded its functions to other organizations to arise in the International Consultation on Programmed Texts to be held in Medellin, Colombia, January 8 to 13. Adding estimates to reports from institutions the last CLATT bulletin gives a total of 9,030 extension students in 742 centers throughout Latin America.

(continued on page 2 column 1)

The yearly statistics since the found-
ing of the movement are as follows:

1962	5 students
1963	50
1964	88
1965	90
1966	143
1967	200
1968	300
1969	1,000
1970	2,500
1971	4,879
1972	9,030

The largest program reported is
that of the Presbyterian Seminary
of Brazil with 3,000 students.

At a meeting of a special committee of the American Association
of Theological Schools on January
10-11 Dr. Ralph Winter will present
a paper entitled "The Extension
Model in Theological Education:
What it Is and How it may be Used."

Dr. John Sinclair, Latin American Secretary for COEMAR, makes the
following remarks which reflect on
the benefits of theological education by extension in Guatemala:
"During the past year I have been
involved on three separate occasions
in Guatemala in consultations with
both lay and ordained leadership of
the Presbyterian Church of Guatemala. We have dealt with a variety
of issues on church life, inter-
church relations and analysis of
national problems."
"I have been impressed by the new
confidence with which problems are
approached and the ability of the
Guatemalan brethren to handle ideas
and sort them out from 'feelings'.
There still remain deep convictions
and sharp cultural differences but
the change is in the way in which
the leaders respond to problems.
There is still the freedom to differ and yet to disagree but knowing
wherein the disagreements lie."

"Whether this change is due only
to the change in our relationships
as two sister churches and a process
of 'growing up', I am not sure. But
I am convinced that the intensive
commitment of that church to theological education by extension has provided a broad cross-section of the
leadership with secular and theological training without which this marked
growth toward maturity would not have
occured."

A vast mushrooming of "tent making
ministry" programs of theological education has occurred in the Episcopal
Church in the United States. Currently
there are twenty-five programs in
ninety-two dioceses. The Episcopal Boar
of Theological Education wants to improve, coordinate and standardize these
programs which are considered inferior
by those who received a traditional
preparation for ordination. Presumably
high quality TEE will help this situation.

The Study Center of the Evangelical
Church of Iran operates an extension
program under the auspices of the Near
East School of Theology in Beirut. The
Study Center which has functioned since
1965 offers courses in Persian in group
which meet with a professor for four
hours each month after doing the required reading. The English language
program leads to a Bachelor of Theology
degree differs little from traditional
residence programs. For information
write to:

> Kenneth Thomas
> Study Center
> P. O. Box 1505
> Tehran, Iran

Inaugurated in January 1971 TAFTEE
began to function in five centers throu
out India by August of that same year.
In November 1972 the number of centers
had risen to 12 and the number of stude
increased from 120 to 250.

(continued on bottom of page 3)

The urgent need for TEE in Malaysia is seen in the following chart provided
by Prof. Peter Savage which indicates that only one Church is confident of enough
trained leaders to carry on its program if missionaries left.

Name	Began Work	Churches	Groups	If all missionary forces left, how many trained leaders could carry on?
Evangelical Mission of Borneo	1928	260	20	about 20 - 25
Anglican Diocese of West Malaysia	1850	30	-	10
O.M.F. in Malaysia	1951	6-12	15?	"few", "none", "some"
Ev.Lutheran Church in Malaysia & Singapore	1907	5-6	10-13	8 to 13
Lutheran Church in Malaysia & Singapore	1963	25	-	20 to 25
Presbyterian Church in Singapore & Malaysia	1880	40	30?	20% in English work 80% in Chinese work
Malaysia Evening Bible College	1969	-	3	
Assemblies of God in Indonesia	1954	170	-	51
Huria Kristen Batak Protestants(Indonesia)	1860	1,500	-	about 2,000

(continued from last paragraph page 2)

Nine of fourteen members of the
executive committee are Indians and
further indigenization is planned.

Ten courses have been developed,
but five have been withdrawn for
revision or replacement. There is a
desparate need for writers.

Four courses should be available
at the lower diploma level by mid
1973. These will be produced in
several regional languages.

Meanwhile, at the other end of
the scale, a very large number of
college graduates, including nearly
a dozen with doctorates are studying
by extension.

Theological News reports that the response to a questionnaire regarding upgrading of standards for theological schools and extension centers has been favorable. Replies urge that entrance standards should be flexible in the case of older and mature students, that special attention be given to the accreditation of TEE programs that in the 8-10 comprehensive examinations in both core and optional subjects emphasis be given to the evaluation and interpretation of areas of knowledge rather than on detailed subject content.

Dr. Bong Rin Ro reports in Theological News the following rapid progress of TEE in the Philippines: The Bethel Bible Institute (Assemblies of God) has recently opened a TEE center in Manila with 16 students, most of whom are working at the college level. The Halls of Life Bible College (Foursquare Gospel Church) in Kadingilan, Mindanao also expects to have 16 students. The Baptist Bible Training School (Southern Baptists) in Davao City has already produced two text books for TEE. The Rev. Robert Samms, the national TEE coordinator in the Philippines is giving able leadership to the program.

The following courses are being prepared by various groups in cooperation with AEBICAM (Africa):

1. Christian Experience
2. I Corinthians
3. New Testament Survey, Part 1
4. New Testament Survey, Part 2
5. Pastoral Theology
6. Evangelism
7. Homiletics
8. Church Growth, Part 1
9. Mark's Gospel
10. New Testament Survey, Part 3
11. O. T. Survey, Part 1
12. O.T. Survey, Part 2
13. O.T. Survey, Part 3
14. Bible Times & Geography
15. Pastoral Epistles

In a letter dated December 27 and under the signature of Dr. Bong Rin R TAP-ASIA, reports that some funds are available for the production of PI materials for Theological Education. The letter says, "We would be gratefu if you would inform those in your cou try who are interested in TEE, of the availability of money for use in producing these materials, and if you wo forward these requests to our Singapo office, if possible by February 15, 1 at the latest." Further information available concerning those who qualif for financial assistance by writing t

Dr. Bong Rin Ro
TAP-Asia
33 Chancery Lane
Singapore 11

The Sumatra School of Theology op ated by the Assemblies of God opened extension centers in April 1972 - 197 in established churches, two in priva homes, two in rented buildings, and o in a school-owned building. There we 112 students.

EXTENSION

THE MONTHLY AIR MAIL
NEWSLETTER

135 NORTH OAKLAND AVENUE   PASADENA, CALIFORNIA 91101

FEBRUARY 1973   VOL. I NO. 4

PAFTEE Philippines Association for Theological Education by
Extension was to be launched January 25-26 in Cebu City. Membership
is open to theological institutions
and church bodies or missions engaged
in a program of TEE and which are in
accord with the doctrinal statement
of PAFTEE. The association will establish policies and guidelines for
the TEE program, including the following:

a. Establish the levels on which
TEE texts will be developed.

b. Develop the curriculum for each
of these levels.

c. Determine the length of courses
(in weeks); number of study periods
weekly and other format matters.

d. Develop guidelines for the development, testing and production of
TEE texts.

e. Develop procedures for the
adaptation of texts into the languages of the Philippines.

In its third mandate the Theological Education Fund has included in
its budget $245,000 for projects in
theological education by extension.
This is equal to the amount budgeted
for all other types of experiments
in theological education.

TAP - ASIA reports that in Thailand
cassettes are being used to instruct
tribal Christians at their Bible
school at Phayao. Programmed Instruction Material is being prepared to meet
the needs of the Blue Meo Christians.
It has been used with good effect
among the Yao Christians.

Many institutions still consider
extension studies to be lay training
and seek to continue traditional
residence education for men expect-
ing to be ordained into the ministry.
The Lutheran Theological Seminary in
La Paz, Bolivia may have a more real-
istic plan. Its residence program
is for laymen, mostly young men who
have not really settled down yet, but
who want to know more of God's Word.
But all who register for extension
studies are expected to be mature
Christians who are already serving as
pastors or at least as responsible
officials in a local church.

Mr. Martin Dainton, editor of
Programming News, reports that the
Protestant Church of West Indonesia
hopes to start in June 1973 a course
for pastors and church elders. The
writing of programmed materials and
supervision of students will be done
by a team appointed by church au-
thorities. The only missionary assistance in this project is the loan to
the church of a specialist in educational technology as advisor.

The T.E.F. Committee meeting to
be held in London from July 11 to
16 will treat the theme "Innovative
Patterns in Theological Education."
The proposed outline agenda includes
a presentation by Dr. Ross Kinsler
entitled "Extension Theological Education as One New Pattern" (Re-
flections on its goals, development, structure.)

PIM workshops, sponsored by the TEE National Office in the Philippines, were conducted by Miss Patricia Harrison in Baguio City, Jan. 15-20; Cebu City, Jan. 22-27 and Davao City, Jan. 29-Feb. 3.

The "Juan de Frias" Theological Institute by Extension operates under the belief that God has given various gifts to different people within the church. Therefore a corporate ministry can be trained by offering alternate courses through extension studies. The Institute has designed courses for catechists and Sunday School teachers who receive a certificate in Christian Education. Another series of studies for deacons and administrators leads to a certificate in Christian Service and a third course for evangelists and lay preachers grants a certificate in the Proclamation of the Word. Those who aspire to the ministry select courses from the above three areas.
(in Puerto Ordaz, Venezuela).

In Education Newsletter No. 4 of 1972 two new emphases of the Theological Education Fund in its third mandate are stated: "(1) the wider concept of ministry, and, therefore, the wider range of forms and styles of theological training; (2) the greater concern for financial viability of theological education in the Third World." The TEF Committee will consider programs which demonstrate contextualization, the "capacity in theological education to respond to the context." This contextualization should be reflected in the following aspects: missiological, structural, theological and pedagogical.

In the paper which he presented to a meeting of the Special Committee of the American Association of Theological Schools in January, Dr. Winter defined extension in this general way:

"An extension student, then, is someone who, no matter how he studies, is still carrying a responsible productive load in the world beyond the school. In this light a program can be "extension" for one student and not for another, and a method deserving the label extension is therefore one which is designed to allow the learner to participate in society productively while continuing his studies."

The AATS representatives responded very favorably to the presentation and plan to devote an entire issue of Theological Education to extension later in the year.

Covenant Seminary in Tokyo, Japan has adopted a new system so that students can get complete seminary training while continuing full time employment. Classes will be given every other day. Some students will take only morning classes and others will take only evening classes. The student may take as many or as few classes as his work schedule allows.

On August 30 representatives of the various programs of extension in Ecuador gathered in Guayaquil. The seven denominations represented reported a total of some 395 students in 52 centers. The most ambitious program is that of the Gospel Missionary Union which operates 35 centers for 219 students. Most of the students are Quechuas as well as are twenty of the professors. The extension studies are supplemented by radio broadcasts of four classes a week.

TEE information in Asia:
1. TEE Report in Asia, August, 1972.
Includes TEE materials, cassettes
catalog, TEE directory.
2. Report of PI Workshops in Asia
for TEE, January, 1973. Reports of
workshops in 9 countries.
3. TEE Filmstrip: "TEE Could Be the
Answer" (20 minutes). For the explanation and promotion of TEE in Asia.
For further information write to:
TAP - Asia
33A Chancery Lane
Singapore 11

The Evangelical Theological Association for Training by Extension
(AETTE) will hold its Sixth Assembly in Sao Paulo on February 8 and 9.
The 25 member institutions represent
a student body of several thousand.
Topics to be considered include:
approval of Inter-Texts, authors'
rights, analysis of the objectives
of AETTE, restructuration, plans for
1973-74 and a consideration of the
Third Mandate of the Theological Education Fund.

Fuller Theological Seminary has
proposed the establishment of four
extension centers for the fall of
1973. These centers, to be operated
in San Diego, Los Angeles, Fresno and
Seattle, will be geared to train for
both the non-ordained and ordained
according to the various models of
programs set up. Credits will be
transferrable to the residence program.

In Singapore there is a new development of TEE in the Anglican
Church under the leadership of Bishop
Chiu Ban It and Rev. James Wong. 23
professional Christian leaders are
being enrolled according to TAP -
ASIA.

The Advisory Committee for
Autodidactic Texts (CATA) and the
Latin American Committee for Theological texts (CLATT) ceased to
exist last month. In their place a
new organization was born in a meeting convened by CATA in Medellin,
Colombia. Because these two organizations, which functioned for five
years, have had such an importance for
extension programs in other parts of
the world as well, the rest of this
issue will be devoted to that meeting
and its consequences.

The meetings were attended by 53
delegates from some twenty countries
and forty institutions which operate
or anticipate extension programs.
The new organization formed to take
over the functions of CATA and CLATT
is the Latin American Association of
Institutions and Theological Semina-
ries by Extension (ALISTE). The
International Coordinator is
Prof. Jose Carrera G.
Seminario Presbiteriano
Apartado 3
San Felipe, Reu., Guatemala

Whereas CATA was composed of four
technical experts and CLATT was an ad
hoc committee providing coordination
between writers and publishers, ALISTE
is an association of institutions with
extension programs. Members will so-
licit entrance, subscribe to the statement of faith and pay annual dues. A
five member Directive Committee will
serve until the next international
assembly of the association in 1976.

ALISTE will promote workshops for
writers and professors and help to
coordinate the production of materials and their distribution. The
publication of catalogs of extension
materials, information about existing
programs and articles of interest
will help to accomplish these goals.

ALISTE publications will supplement the Extension Seminary, a quarterly bulletin published in English
and Spanish at the Presbyterian Seminary in Guatemala.

The Intertext project has been
suspended. Due to lack of communication between institutions and de-
lays in the production and distribution of materials, as many as
four manuals for the same course
have been produced. The writers
assigned by CATA have been unable to
take time from other responsibilities
to prepare texts. Meanwhile, other
writers are being prepared through
work shops and other studies and are
now producing better provisional
materials. It is expected that
through a process of natural selection the best materials will gain
wide use and subsequently will be
recommended for revision with a view
toward printing in larger quantities.

The Intertext project was limited
to diploma level materials. ALISTE
will attempt to maintain information
also on higher and lower level TEE
materials although courses prepared
for semi-literates are likely to be
more regional in vocabulary and content.

National and regional coordinators of ALISTE are as follows:

David Legters
Sem. Teol. Pres. de Mexico
Av. Universidad No. 1943
Merida, Yucatan, Mexico

Vernon Reimer
Seminario Biblico Unido
Apartado Aereo 5945
Cali, Colombia

Enrique Guang T.
Seminario Biblico Alianza
Apartado 2006
Guayaquil, Ecuador

Terry Barratt
Seminario por Extension Anglicano
Santiago 1862
S.M. Tucuman, Argentina
(for Uruguay & Paraguay also)

Sergio Correa
Seminario Biblico por Extension
Moneda 1898
Santiago, Chile

Robert Andrews
Seminario Teologico Luterano
Casilla 266
La Paz, Bolivia

Charles Porter
Institute Biblico Bautista
Casilla 448
Iquitos, Peru

Rodolfo Blank
Instituto "Juan de Frias"
Apartado Postal 216
Puerto Ordaz, Estado Bolivar
Venequela

James Sauder
Institutos Biblicos Interamericanos
Apartado 77
La Ceiba, Honduras

Gilbert Reimer
Seminario Bethel
El Amanecer
La Chorrera, Panama

If you have not yet subscribed to
EXTENSION or know someone else who
should receive the twelve issues of
our trial year, send your check for
U.S. $7.25 with your name and address
to:
    EXTENSION
    Wayne C. Weld, Editor
    135 North Oakland Avenue
    Pasadena, California 91101

NAME _____

ADDRESS _____

_____

THE MONTHLY AIR MAIL
NEWSLETTER
EXTENSION

135 North Oakland Avenue   Pasadena, California 91101

MARCH 1973   VOL. I NO. 5

○ ALISTE (Latin American Association of Institutions and Theological Seminaries by Extension) an-
nounces that the address of its
International Coordinator is:
Lic. Jose G. Carrera
6 Avenida A 4-68, Zona 1
Guatemala, Guatemala

The quota for institutions that
want to become active members is
$24.00 (US) per year. Those that
prefer to become cooperating or
fraternal members (without vote)
pay half that amount. Individuals
who wish to receive bimonthly bulletins with notices and catalogs
of materials may do so by paying
$6.00 per year to the treasurer:
Wayne C. Weld
847 Santa Barbara Street
Pasadena, California 91101
USA

○ The Conservative Baptist (CBFMS)
Evangelism Committee for the Philippines reported for 1972 that,
"A factor not yet adequately mea-
sured is the impact of Theological
Education by Extension (TEE) on our
work. More than 130 students are
studying in various centers and
while not yet scientifically mea-
sured, TEE is making a definite impact on our work."

○ A teacher training workshop was
held at the Central Taiwan Theological College on January 29-30 with
21 persons from 8 different groups.

○ In addition to Theological Education by Extension by Winter and An
Extension Seminary Primer by Covell
and Wagner, with which most of our
readers will be familiar, two fairly
comprehensive although not readily
available studies have been made on
the extension seminary movement.
Kenneth Mulholland wrote a thesis at
Lancaster Theological Seminary in
1971 entitled Theological Education
by Extension with Special Reference
to Honduras. Vance Field wrote a
thesis at Western Evangelical Seminary in 1972 with the title Theological Education by Extension. This
study has special reference to the
work of Christian and Missionary
Alliance programs in extension.

○ The South East Asia Graduate
School of Theology has a program for
Burmese graduate students who are
unable to leave their country which
has some similarity to extension studies. The professors who live outside the country must depend on correspondence and tapes and very infrequent visits. This seems to be a
case where programmed materials might
be an aid.

○ The committee on TEE for the Near
East plans workshops for Lebanon and
Egypt during 1973. The large Protestant community in Egypt seems the
most promising area. However there
is some opposition from the traditional clergy. The Near East School of
Theology already has an extension
program in Iran.

◯ In an article translated from the UNICO (Colombia, South America) bulletin Peter Savage suggests the following criteria for evaluating extension studies.

1) Is the movement of extension studies really reaching the "Functional ministers" of each denomination that for many factors are not able to enter the residence system? Who are the students in extension centers?

2) Have the studies, the plan of studies, the curriculum that is currently being offerred to extension students, helped the student to better and to develop his ministry? As ministers of God has the student (a congregational leader) been developed? In the life of the community, liturgy, evangelism and mission has the leader shown himself to be more capable and consequently is the church more dynamic in its ministry as the people of God and in its mission to a lost world?

3) Is the method that is being used efficient? Do the programmed materials contribute to the learning of the student? What role does the professor play? Does the lack of an adequate professor or of regular attendance at weekly classes impede the student's learning? Is there danger of brain washing?

4) There is no doubt that the students who attend extension centers bring their context with them--the reality in which they live. Nevertheless, we should ask if the professor and the programmed materials are related to "the known" of the student--his context. Are the materials presented nothing more than packages of knowledge that the student by decision of the professor has to digest?

◯ In January of this year the TEE committee in Malaysia began the publication of a TEE newsletter. One of its first functions was to announce a meeting with the Vicar General of The Anglican Church West Malaysia on January 30 at Luther House, Jalan Utara, Petaling Jaya. TEE in Malaysia began with a workshop in Singapore in 1971, was enlarged by another in Kuala Lumpur in September 1972 and continued by an ad hoc committee of three.

The TEE Fellowship is seeking to collect a "bank" of extension materials and asks for the cooperation of others, particularly in Asia in the exchange of materials. In writing of materials please state: target population, objectives, teacher's guides, tests, other information such as cost, availability etc. Information on materials or a request for the Malaysia TEE newsletter should be addressed to:
Rev. Duain Vierow
21 Jalan Abdul Samad
Kuala Lumpur, Malaysia

◯ The new executive secretary of AEBICAM (Association of Evangelical Bible Institutes and Colleges of Africa and Madagascar) is Byang Kato. In a major reorganization Fred Holland who has been TEE coordinator for the area continues as secretary of the English speaking areas for theological training.

As a result of workshops and coordination of various denominations in Jos, Nigeria 14 teams of missionaries and nationals are producing programmed materials.

AEBICAM will sponsor a writers' workshop in Kenya from May 14 to June 9, 1973.

◯ The China Evangelical Seminary Committee on Theological Education by Extension in Taiwan reports that revision/adaptation of Principles of Church Growth is complete and that revision/adaptation of Jeremiah and translation/adaptation of Mark are progressing.

The Committee will sponsor three workshops with the assistance of Peter Savage during the summer months. Two-day meetings will be scheduled in Kaohsiung, Taichung and Taipei. The first day will be the consultations with church leaders on the background and program of TEE and the second day will be a training seminar for prospective teachers. The last two weeks of the summer program will be for training writers in programmed instruction techniques.

The Committee will study the transfer of extension credits to recognized resident theological institutions. Presently the graduation certificate carries no degree.

◯ Inaugurated in January 1971 TAFTEE - India began to function in five centers by August of that year. Now sixteen months have passed and the five centers with their 120 students have become thirteen centers with close to 250 students.

◯ Ministry in Context: The Third Mandate Programme of the Theological Education Fund (1970-77) recently published has ten pages on Theological Education by Extension. It offers a critique of its development and method and states some tentative guidlines for TEF support of the further development of this program.

◯ The Rev. Homer Goddard, Ph.D. has been appointed Director of Extension Ministries of Fuller Theological Seminary and began his responsibilities February 1, 1973. A two-year curriculum equivalent to a maximum of one year at the resident program will be designed by the Seminary.

◯ PAFTEE (Philippines Association for TEE) was organized January 25 with the participation of twelve groups. One of the reasons given for the rapid advance of TEE in the Philippines according to Robert Samms, PAFTEE Director, is the number of workshops that have been held. During the six months before PAFTEE's birth 124 persons had attended four workshops on programmed instruction. If only 10 per cent of those who attended actually write materials a good start toward preparing quality materials for all the courses to be offered will have been made.

◯ The recently formed Birmingham Extension Seminary for Theological Education, Birmingham, Alabama was able to attract 53 students with only two weeks of advertising. Many of the students have had years of practical experience but no opportunity to attend a residence seminary program. The initial enrollment, according to The Presbyterian Layman of February 1973, shows 21 students pursuing the Master of Divinity degree, 14 working under a Master of Religious Education program and 18 enrolled as auditors.

◯ Student enrollment in Haiti has reached nearly 600 in the four extension programs operated by various missions and churches. In the nearly 40 centers more than half of the teachers are Haitians. In March there will be two regional seminars to prepare center teachers.

◯ The results of a survey by UNICO (Union of Bible Institutions of Colombia) indicate that there are already four times as many extension as resident students in the country. The following table appeared in the latest UNICO bulletin.

INSTITUTION	RESIDENCE	EXTENSION				
		Centers	Certif.	Dipl.	Bach.	Lic.	Total
Christian & Miss. All.	81	18	150	42	18		210
World Evang. Crusade	47						
Colom. Mennonite Ch.		2		5	8		13
SELITE (Luth. Ch. in A.)		6		33	4		37
United Biblical Sem.							
Bogota Division		3		28	4		32
Cali Division		12	41	37	7		85
Caribbean Division		34	314				314
Medellin Division	16	1		7			7
Baptist Theol. Sem.	60	3	20	70		18	108
	204	79	525	222	41	18	806

◯ The second AEBICAM text is now ready. It is Bringing People to Jesus, a 224 page text on evangelism written by Grace Holland and Jonah Moyo. The first text, Talking with God has been revised. The books may be ordered from the
Evangel Publishing House
P. O. Box 969
Kisumu, Kenya

Bringing People..US$1.80 Ksh10/-
Talking... $1.00
5-39 copies 33% discount
40 or more copies - 40% discount

◯ The pilot project on TEE is now in its second semester in North Sumatra. Six national teachers served 9 extension centers the first semester. Starting enrollment was 94 and 71 completed. Drop-outs were from language difficulty, local church opposition and other factors. All 71 students have enrolled for the second semester for a total of 117 students. Three more centers have been opened. Three of the five tribes in the North Sumatra area are now being served.

◯ Perhaps the largest extension program operated by a single institution is that of the Presbyterian Edward Lane Bible Institute of Patrocinio, Brazil. The Institute had 60 to 80 residence students in the past. With the initiation of the extension' program the number of residence students dropped to 35 to 40. However, the number of extension students rose from 300 in 1970 to 500 in 1971 and 700 in 1972.

◯ If you have not yet subscribed to EXTENSION or know someone else who should receive the twelve issues of our trial year, you may receive back issues and the next seven current issues now for $5.00. Send your check (in US $) with your name and address to:
EXTENSION
Wayne C. Weld, Editor
135 North Oakland Avenue
Pasadena, California 91101

NAME _____

ADDRESS _____

_____

THE MONTHLY AIR MAIL

NEWSLETTER

EXTENSION

135 NORTH OAKLAND AVENUE   PASADENA, CALIFORNIA 91101

APRIL 1973   VOL. I NO. 6

The Thai TEE Bulletin issued its first number in February, 1973. This is the informative organ of the Consultative Committee for Theological Education by Extension in Thailand (CoCoTEE). The bulletin will be published in both English and Thai. The first number included the story of the formation of CoCoTEE, the curriculum agreed on by that committee, information on programmed instruction and news from abroad. It also announced the Thai TEE Seminar to be held in Bangkok on 29 May – 1 June, 1973. For information on the seminar or a copy of the bulletin write to:
Jack Carter
433/3 Suan Plu (Nanta)
Bangkok, Thailand

At the three workshops held in the Philippines by Miss Pat Harrison during the month of January, good use was made of three mimeographed manuals which she and Ian McClery compiled for that purpose. Total attendance for the three workshops was 120. Considerable use was made of groups working with tutors, and this approach seemed to make possible much more individual assistance, Miss Harrison reports.

The new executive director of PAFTEE (Philippines Association for TEE) is::
Vernon Carvey
Box 1416
Manila, Philippines

The first Intertext in Spanish Principles of Church Growth is being reprinted by William Carey Library. The first 2000 copies were sold out a short time ago. A limited printing will be done with the expectation that the book will be revised by the end of this year. Any comments or criticisms of the book in Spanish or English by the readers of EXTENSION will be welcomed by the editor of this newsletter. These would be helpful for any later revision of the English version as well.

Fred Holland of Africa's AEBICAM has announced the following tentative schedule of workshops for Africa. Further details will be given when available.
Workshops for Francophone Africa with Dr. Paul White:

July	9-11	Senegal
	13-17	Upper Volta
	19-21	Niger
	24-28	Chad
	31-Aug 3	Bangui
Aug.	6-9	Dahomey
	10-14	Gagon
	17-21	Kinshasa

Workshops with Harold Alexander are to be as follows:

July	4-6	Ivory Coast
	9-11	Jos, Nigeria
	12-14	Ethiopia
	17-20	Zaire East
	23-26	Kenya
	30-Aug 1	Salisbury
Aug.	2-4	Pretoria

APRIL 1973   PAGE 2

◯On March 25 a committee appointed
by the Episcopal Board of Theological
Education met for a three day consideration of the need for some uniformity and quality control in the
burgeoning programs of ministerial
training that are developing within
a number of the diocese of the Episcopal Church in the United States.
In 25 different diocese there are
programs for ministerial training
which could be called extension programs whereby men are being trained
for lay responsibilities, non-stipendiary ministries and fully ordained ministries. A booklet was
used as a resource for this discussion entitled Training for Non-
Stipendiary Ministry Today: A Directory of Training Programs and
Schools Within the Episcopal Church.
This may be secured for $0.50 by
writing to:
Rev. Marshall T. Rice
Box 764
Ridgewood, New Jersey 07451

◯On April 13-14 Peter Savage is
conducting a workshop on TEE at the
Seminario Biblico Latinoamericano in
San Jose, Costa Rica.

◯Martin Dainton of TAP-Asia led a
workshop on PI in Bangkok September
25 to October 8, 1972. Participants
included 3 missionaries from Bangladesh, 4 Thai, 2 Karen and 14 missionaries from Thailand.

The first TEE programmed text in
Thai, a translation from English of
a study of the Book of Acts will be
published in June, 1973. Copies of
this preliminary edition will sell
for about 10 baht (US $.50). Thai
CoCoTEE has also agreed to publish
a Thai translation of Mark later.

At its January 1973 meeting Thai
CoCoTEE adopted a curriculum of 30
courses at the 4th grade level. All
introductory material will be taught
as an integral part of the study of
the books of the Bible themselves.
(Thai TEE Bulletin, February 1973).

◯ PRELIMINARY SUMMARY OF EXTENSION PROGRAMS IN THE CARIBBEAN
Data as of December, 1972

Country	Inst.	Cent.	Teachers	Cert	Dipl	Students Bach	Lic	Total
Guadeloupe	1	4	2					57
Guyana	1	6						145
Haiti	4	32	33	450	235	1	0	685
Jamaica	2							40
Trinidad	1	3	3	4	22	5	0	31
TOTALS								
5	9	45	38	454	257	6	0	959

LATIN AMERICA
REGIONAL SUMMARY

Country	Inst.	Cent.	Teachers	Cert	Dipl	Students Bach	Lic	Total
Argentina	7	49	75	160	338	1	0	499
Bolivia	4	29	35	193	53	19	0	265
Brazil	6	58	74	1149	207	57	0	1413
Chile	1	9	7	0	60	10	0	70
Colombia	7	106	98	658	249	41	22	1061
Dominican Republic	2	13	8	45	62	18	0	125
Ecuador	5	66	92	489	125	59	3	676
Guatemala	4	59	35	280	308	54	0	642
Honduras	2	22	17	83	0	0	0	83
Mexico	5	45	74	253	327	18	0	598
Panama	1	6	4	0	36	0	0	36
Peru	1	17	15	90	105	6	0	201
Puerto Rico estimate	1			120			10	130
Uruguay	1	1	10	0	10	41	0	51
Venezuela	3	19	21	100	95	2	0	197

TOTALS

15	50	499	565	3620	1975	326	35	6047

Note: Many figures, particularly those of brazil are incomplete. It is estimated that there are at least 30 institutions and 5,000 students not
included above.

Certificate - less than full primary
Diploma - full primary school
Bachelor - nine or more years of formal education
Licentiate - two or more years of college

APRIL 1973

The first TEE and PIM workshops in Australia were held in October 1972 and January 1973 respectively. These were in connection with the TEE program being developed by the Armidale Diocese of the Church of England. Ray Morris, of the Andes Evangelical Mission, Bolivia conducted the one-day workshop in Tamworth on the concept of TEE. The meeting was attended by a group of Anglican clergy and lay people.

From February 12-16 Miss Pat Harrison conducted an intensive PIM workshop at the University of New England, Armidale. Seven potential course writers attended.

The Armidale Diocese of the Church of England is pioneering a series of extension courses at several academic levels. Last year courses in Christian Education of Children attracted some 90 students of several denominations in two main centers. This year courses in Homiletics and Local Church Principles are being offered. An economic recession in the area has forced the churches to turn to unpaid lay leadership which can be trained through TEE.

The Christian and Missionary Alliance College of Theology is training all its pastors at degree level by TEE. It has 25 students in Sydney, Melbourne and Canberra. The Alliance is also conducting TEE courses among Aborigines in Western Australia.

Plans for a second PIM workshop in Papua, New Guinea during August are underway. An association of Bible Schools has been formed for the country and there is considerable interest in TEE there.

Our thanks to Miss Pat Harrison for the above news. Why don't you send us all the printable news from your area?

The Presbyterian Seminary in Guatemala where TEE began just ten years ago is proposing the establishment of a two year course for the training of teachers and for writers of programmed materials. There would be opportunity for practical work as well as investigation. It is believed that this would be better than a series of workshops of short duration. Classes would be offered by Ross Kinsler, James Emery and other experts to be sought for this training. Your opinion regarding such a program would be welcomed by the ALISTE coordinator and rector of the Seminary

Lic. Jose G. Carrera
6 Avenida A 4-68, Zona 1
Guatemala, Guatemala

The Eleventh Annual Convention of the National Society for Programmed Instruction will be at the Fairmont Hotel in San Francisco, California on April 18 to 21, 1973. Dr. Robert Mager is one of the featured speakers. For the fifteen hours of workshops and sessions it is possible to receive one semester unit of credit from the California State University, San Francisco. For more details contact:

Miriam Sierra-Franco
Chairman, Registration
23 Starview Way
San Francisco, California 94131

If you have not yet subscribed to EXTENSION or know someone else who should receive the twelve issues of our trial year, you may receive back issues and the next six current issues now for $5.00. Send your check (in US $) with your name and address to:

EXTENSION
Wayne C. Weld, Editor
135 North Oakland Avenue
Pasadena, California 91101

NAME _____

ADDRESS _____

_____

THE MONTHLY AIR MAIL

NEWSLETTER

EXTENSION

135 NORTH OAKLAND AVENUE   PASADENA, CALIFORNIA 91101

MAY 1973

VOL. I NO. 7

○ At a recent AEAM (Association of Evangelicals of Africa and Madagascar) Dr. Paul White was named Secretary for Theological Education in Francophone Africa. For information regarding TEE in this area you may write him at:
B. P. 1010
97481 St. Denis
Reunion, Indian Ocean

○ Dr. White reports a new extension program on the island of Reunion. Seventeen students are enrolled in two centers at three academic levels. Eleven study at diploma level, two at high school level and four at university level. This represents a good percentage of the leadership of the church since it was only begun two years ago and there are forty baptized members.

○ The following workshops will be held by Dr. White this summer under the auspices of the newly formed Theological Commission of the AEAM:
Dakar, Senegal   July 4-6
Bobo-Dionlasso, Haute Volta
                        July 11-13
NiAmey, Niger   July 16-18
Fort Lamy, Tchad   July 23-25
Bangui, Central Africa Republic
                        July 30-August 1
Cotenon, Dahomey   Aug. 6-8
Muila, Gabon   Aug. 13-14
Boma, Zaire   Aug. 20-22
The seminars will stress the basic principles involved in setting up TEE programs.

○ The American Baptist Theological Seminary, Nashville, Tennessee 37207 reports 693 students in thirty-seven centers for the period ending January 31, 1973. Enrollment in several other centers was not included in the report. Classes meet weekly. A four year course leading to a Certificate in Christian Training and a five year course granting the Diploma in Theology are offered.

New centers are established where permission is given by the Seminary, the application is sponsored by a local ministerial association or other agency of the denomination, qualified teachers are recruited and at least fifteen students apply. A $10 enrollment fee is paid the Seminary and other finances are worked out locally. There are now centers in at least sixteen states.

○ Seventeen texts for TEE in Africa are now in various stages of preparation. They are part of a forty text series for the certificate level. The texts on Prayer and Evangelism have been completed. At the five week workshop in Jos, Nigeria earlier this year, writing was completed on Acts and other materials are nearing completion. Sixteen teams of national-missionary writers attended the workshop. Eleven teams are scheduled to meet in May in Kenya for a similar five week workshop. Both workshops are under the direction of Fred Holland, the TEE coordinator for Anglophone Africa.

MAY 1973

○ In Singapore there is a new development of TEE in the Anglican Church under the leadership of Bishop Chiu Ban It and Rev. James Wong. Forty Christian lay-leaders from various professions are enfolled. The Baptist, Lutheran and Presbyterian churches are also applying TEE.

○ AETTE (Evangelical Theological Association for Training by Extension) had its sixth Assembly in Sao Paulo, Brazil on February 8 and 9. This is the oldest association of extension institutions and now has twenty-eight institutions and two individuals as members. At the meetings in February the re-elected president, Lowell Bailey, explained the five levels of learning. The out-going Executive Secretary, Richard Sturz, spoke on the psychology of learning and the new Secretary, Harmon Johnson, affirmed that in Brazil, of those that enter seminaries or institutes, the majority do not finish; of those that finish, many do not enter the ministry; of those that enter the ministry, many are not suitable. A grand part of the problem resides in an inadequate curriculum, frequently imported by missionaries without modification.

○ AETTE made plans to sponsor workshops for PI writers. The first of six two-day sessions at two week intervals was to be held April 9 and 10. Those interested in more details may write to the professor:
Dr. Julieta Breternitz
Caixa Postal 30.259
Sao Paulo, SP., Brazil

○ The new Executive Secretary of AETTE is
John Klassen
Caixa Postal 5938
01000 Sao Paulo, SP., Brazil

○ In the AEBICAM sponsored workshops for writers, those who attend agree to permit their materials to be produced for other programs and countries. Before printing, however, field testing for validation is done with forty to sixty students and then necessary revisions are made. For materials produced in local vernaculars less strict control is exercised. Guidelines in the preparation of these texts require that they be evangelical, culturally relevant, follow linear programming techniques and use a basic vocabulary. Fred Holland states that the materials are so thoroughly African that usage in other areas would be impossible.

○ A newsletter on TEE is edited in French and distributed in Burundi, Rwanda and eastern Zaire. It may be obtained from:
John F. Robinson
B. P. 304
Bunia, Republic of Zaire

○ A twenty minute filmstrip and cassette presentation has been prepared by TAP-Asia. It is entitled "TEE Could Be the Answer." It is available now from:
Dr. Clyde Taylor
World Evangelical Fellowship
100 Western Union Building
Washington, D.C. 20005
The sale price of the filmstrip is $10.00 or it may be rented for $3.00.

○ The new address of the TEE coordinator in Thailand is
Rev. James W. Gustafson
167/1 Naresuan Road
Udorn Thani, Thailand

○ The translation of Ross Kinsler's programmed text on Mark will be completed in Taiwan in May 1973. Centers now operate in the cities of Kaohsiung, Hsi-Lo, Taichung and Taipei.

AFRICA - REGIONAL SUMMARY

Country	Institutions	Centers	Teachers	Cert	Students Dipl	Bach	Lic	Total
Ethiopia	1	5	11	95	25	0	0	120
Iran	1	4	4	0	0	16	10	26
Kenya	1	5	10	90	0	0	0	90
Nigeria	2	12	19	35	82	2	2	121
Rhodesia	1							51
Sierra Leone	1	5	2	45	18	0	0	63
South Africa	3	18	12	90	54	27	0	171
Zambia	1							110
TOTAL	11	59	48	355	179	45	12	752

ASIA - REGIONAL SUMMARY

Country	Institutions	Centers	Teachers	Cert	Dipl	Bach	Lic	Total
Hong Kong	1	12	20	0	0	0	52	52
India	1	13	19	0	0	10	210	220
Indonesia	3	14	32	53	34	145	1	458
Malaysia	1	15	16	0	0	100	0	100
W. Pakistan	3	7	12	15	10	11	29	55
Philippines	2	16	21	13	107	0	0	121
Taiwan	1	2	3	4	2	2	0	8
Thailand	1	3	10	0	30	15	0	45
TOTAL	14	83	138	76	183	292	303	1029

NOTE: The figures above reflect student enrollment as of December, 1972. In Africa it is estimated that there were at least 50 per cent more institutions and students

Certificate - less than full primary
Diploma - full primary school
Bachelor - nine or more years of formal education
Licentiate - two or more years of college

May 1973

◯ Programming News has been renamed
Programming in recognition of its
function, not to carry news but to
share developments in programming.
It will be issued in February, April,
August and November yearly. The
February, 1973 issue contains an
article on "Cognitive Psychology:
An Introduction" by Neale Grinkley,
Instructor in Religious Educa-
tion, Birmingham, United Kingdom.
This issue also lists the types of
learning as set forth in the text:
The Conditions of Learning by
R. M. Gagne. New York, Holt, Rine-
hart and Winston, 2nd Edition,
1972.

From a chapter by B. S. Bloom
in the book (Vols. 1 and 2) Tax-
onomy of Educational Objectives:
The Classification of Educational
Goals, a guideline as to the kind
of learning we want to produce is
given.

◯ The January, 1973 issue of
Theological News lists several
sources of cassettes on theological topics. Some offerings are
largely devotional, but some offer
Bible studies or other courses
which might supplement other means
of TEE. One of the most extensive
collections is listed by TAP-ASIA,
33A, Chancery Lane, Singapore 11.

◯ Cassette lessons are being used
by the Voice of Peace in Chiang
Mai, Thailand, to train lay leaders
in their Cassette Bible School.

◯ In the extension program to be
initiated in the fall by Fuller
Theological Seminary, use of video
tapes and a direct telephone connection between the students in
the various cities and the professors is anticipated. TEE offers
opportunities for experimentation
in effective ways of teaching that
should benefit traditional programs
as well.

◯ The National Baptist Convention
(Southern) in Chile has elected a
missionary, James Bitner, to plan
and direct seminary extension work.
This is a case in which the national
Church has felt the need for TEE and
has taken the initiative in designa-
ting personnel for the program. The
Church hopes to launch its program
in March, 1974.

◯ "Teeing Off With TEE," an article
by Samuel F. Rowen, one of the early
promotors of TEE in the Caribbean,
appeared in the April 27 issue of
Christianity Today. The article indicates the growth and importance
of the movement and some of the more
prominent programs and structures.
Rowen cites evidence that this is
not just a fad in theological education, but a manifestation of concern for a more theologically prepared laity and also for continuing
education for those now serving as
titular or functional pastors.
    The article concludes with a warn-
ing lest this innovation in theological education distract from basic
issues which must be faced in ministerial training and lest TEE become
another imported form which lacks
cultural relevance for the people
whom it is to serve.

◯ If you have not yet subscribed to
EXTENSION or know someone else who
should receive the twelve issues of
our trial year, you may receive back
issues and the next five current issues now for $5.00. Send your check
(in US $) with your name and address
to: EXTENSION
       135 North Oakland Avenue
       Pasadena, California 91101

NAME _____

ADDRESS _____

       _____

Bibliography

AEBICAM BULLETIN, April 1972 to present, (Box 131, Choma, Zambia).

AETTE
n.d.   La Constitución de la Asociación Evangélica de Textos Teológicos de Extensión AETTE.

ALEXANDER, J. E.
1965-66 "New Formulas for Theological Education," *Religion in Life,* 35:30-44.

ALISTE, February 1973 to present (Lic. José G. Carrera, 6 Avenida A 4-68, Zona 1, Guatemala, Guatemala).

AMERICAN BAPTIST THEOLOGICAL SEMINARY
1972   *Catalog for 1972-73, Department of Seminary Extension.* Nashville, Tennessee.

1973   Semi-Annual Report of the Department of Seminary Extension, July 1, 1972-January 11, 1973.

ASHBY, G. W.
1967   "Theological Training: Any Criticisms?   #1," *Ministry,* 3:115-116.

BARRY, F. R.
1962   "Selection and Training of Candidates for the Ministry: A New Deal in Training," *Expository Times,* 74:43-46.

BENTON, William
1961   "The Voice of Latin American and Its Significance in Today's World," New York, *Encyclopedia Britannica, Britannica Book of the Year 1961.*

BIDDULPH, George Burton
  1956 "A Philosophy of Curriculum for a Seminary in Colom-
        bia, S.A.." An unpublished M.R.E. thesis, Fuller
        Theological Seminary.

BOARD OF CHRISTIAN EDUCATION OF THE UNITED PRESBYTERIAN CHURCH
        IN THE U.S.A.
  1965 Report of the Consultation on Continuing Education to
        the General Council, Philadelphia, Pennsylvania.

BOLETIM DA AETTE, 1968 to present, (Caixa Postal 5938,
        01000 Sao Paulo, Brazil).

BRIDSTON, Keith R.
  1967 "Form and Function in the Education of Ministers,"
        Theological Education, 4:543-555.

BROUGHAM, David R.
  1970 "The Training of the Chinese in Indonesia for the
        Ministry." An unpublished M.A. thesis, Fuller Theo-
        logical Seminary.

BURKE, F. H.
  1967 "Church Growth, With or Without Trained Leaders:
        Africa," *Church Growth Bulletin*, 6:7-9.

CARR, Lucille L.
  1966 "A Seminary and Church Growth." An unpublished M.A.
        thesis, Fuller Theological Seminary.

CAMEO RELEASES, Spring 1968 to present, (5010 Sixth Avenue,
        Denver, Colorado 80204).

CAMEO
  1971 *1970 TEE Workshop Reports.* (Mimeographed)

  1972 *1971 TEE Workshop Reports.* (Mimeographed)

CATA
  1968 *Acta No. 1* December 12.

  1969 *Acta No. 2* November 25-December 2.

CENTRO DE ESTUDIOS TEOLOGICOS
        Un Estudio para Educación Teológico en el Ecuador.
        (Mimeographed)

CHAO, Jonathan
  1972 "Foreign Missions and Theological Education: Taiwan,
        a Case Study," *Evangelical Missions Quarterly*, 9:1-16.

CLATT BOLETIN, September 1968 to January 1973.

COCKBURN, Alexander and BLACKBURN, Robin, eds.
1969 *Student Power.* Baltimore, Penguin Books.

COMITE CONTINUADOR DE SEMINARIOS LUTERANOS DE EXTENSION EN LA
AMERICA LATINA
1972 *Acta No. 1* June 11.

1973 *Acta No. 2* January 6-12.

COMMITTEE ON EXTENSION RESIDENTIAL PILOT SCHEME IN THE COCHA-
BAMBA VALLEY
"A Memorandum of the Extension Seminary Program," Cocha-
bamba, Bolivia, Andes Evangelical Mission.

COMMITTEE ON THEOLOGICAL EDUCATION
1967 *The Seminary as a Christian Community.* New York, DOM,
National Council of Churches.

CONSERVATIVE BAPTIST FOREIGN MISSIONARY SOCIETY
1967a Mimeographed letter with documents, July 27.

1967b *Decentralized Seminary Bulletin,* Vol. 1 No. 1 October.

1968 *Bulletin of Extension Seminary Training,* Vol. 2 No. 1
March; Vol. 2 No. 2 July.

CONSULTATION ON THEOLOGICAL EDUCATION
1970 *Changing Demands on Theological Education in the Light*
of Developing Patterns of Ministry. New York, COEMAR
and the Commission on Ecumenical Scholarships and Theological Education, DOM, NCC.

CONSULTATION ON THEOLOGY OF THE INDONESIAN COUNCIL OF CHURCHES
1971 "Our Hope for Theological Education in the Future,"
South East Asia Journal of Theology, 13:25-29.

COOLEY, Frank L.
1970 "Theology and Theological Education in Southeast Asia
Today," *South East Asia Journal of Theology,* 12:16-28.

COVELL, Ralph
1970a *Report on Taiwan Workshops.*(Typed)

1970b *Report on Theological Extension Consultation, Singapore*
September 12, 1970. (Mimeographed)

COVELL, Ralph R. and WAGNER, C. Peter
1971 *An Extension Seminary Primer.* South Pasadena, California, William Carey Library.

COX, Harvey
1970 *"Seminários en Transición,"* *Simposio Año III*, No. 5:
      30-36.

CRANE, W. H.
1965 "Lay Training in the S.C.M. in Africa," *Ministry*,
      5:174-178.

CRIDER, Donald
1972 Letter to author, November 21.

EMERY, James
1963 "Preparation of Leaders in a Ladino-Indian Church,"
      Practical Anthropology, 10:127-34.

1972 *"Cursos de Estudios del Seminario,"* Document No. 9 for
      the Medellín Consultation of CATA.

1973 Lectures at Fuller Theological Seminary School of
      World Mission.

ERDEL, Paul
1973 Leter to author, March 26.

ESPICH, James E. and WILLIAMS, Bill
1967 *Developing Programmed Instructional Material.* Belmont,
      California, Fearon Publishers.

EVANS, Stanley
1962 "Selection and Training of Candidates for the Ministry:
      The Church of England," *Expository Times*, Vol. 73, No.
      7:209-211.

1963 "Selection and Training of Candidates for the Ministry:
      New Essays in Ordination Training," *Expository Times*,
      74:181-2.

EXTENSION, November 1972 to present, (135 No. Oakland Avenue,
      Pasadena, California 91101).

EXTENSION SEMINARY, 1966 to present, (Apartado 1881, Guatemala,
      Guatemala).

FIELD, Vance R.
1972 "Theological Education by Extension." An unpublished
      M.Div. thesis, Western Evangelical Seminary, Portland,
      Oregon.

FINKBEINER, Lester
1972 Letter to author, November 20.

FLEMING, John R.
  1965 "'Then and Now' in Theological Education in South East
        Asia," *South East Asia Journal of Theology,* 4:58-66.

FRANKLIN, Christine B.
  1973 Letter to author, February 19.

GEYER, Georgie Anne
  1970 *The New Latins.* Garden City, New York, Doubleday and
        Company.

GONZALES, Justo, ed.
  1965 *Por La Renovación del Entendimiento.* Librería La Refor-
        ma, Río Piedras, Puerto Rico.

GUZMAN CAMPOS, German
  1969 *Camilo Torres.* New York, Sheed and Ward. (Translated
        from the original Spanish by John D. Ring)

HAMMERS, Glorya
  1973 Letter to author, February 13.

HARRISON, Patricia J., ed.
  1972a *Programmed Instruction Workshop, Book 1, Instructional
        Foundations - A Study Guide.* Theological Education by
        Extension Philippine National Office, Manila. (Mimeo-
        graphed for private circulation)

  1972b *Programmed Instruction Workshop, Book 2, Source Book -
        A Selection of Readings in Programming.* Theological
        Education by Extension Philippine National Office,
        Manila. (Mimeographed for private circulation)

  1972c *Programmed Instruction Workshop, Book 3, Program Manual -
        Selected Samples of Programmed Lessons.* Theological
        Education by Extension Philippine National Office.
        (Mimeographed for private circulation)

  1973 Letter to author, March 22.

HILL, James E.
  1969 "Theological Education for the Church in Mission: A
        Case History of the Baptist, Methodist and Free Brethren
        Churches in the Argentine Republic." An unpublished
        M.A. thesis, Fuller Theological Seminary School of
        World Mission.

HOLLAND, Fred
  1973 Interview with author, April 16.

HOPEWELL, James
 1965a *The Crisis in the Christian Ministry in Africa, I.* A
       paper prepared for the Christian Council Secretaries
       Meeting, January 9-12 at Enugu, East Nigeria. London,
       Theological Education Fund.

 1965b *Preparing the Candidate for Mission.* A paper prepared
       for the National Council of Churches Consultation on
       Theological Education in Warwick, New York. London,
       Theological Education Fund.

 1966 "Training a Tent-making Ministry," *International Review
       of Missions,* 219:333-39.

 1967a "Missionary and Seminary Structure," *International Re-
       view of Missions,* 22:158-163.

 1967b "Guest Editorial," *International Review of Missions,*
       56:141-4.

HWANG, C. H.
 1962 "A Rethinking of Theological Training for the Ministry
       in the Younger Churches Today," *South East Asia Journal
       of Theology,* 2:7-34.

ILLICH, Ivan
 1970 *Deschooling Society.* New York, Harrow Books, Harper
       and Row.

INTERNATIONAL MISSIONARY COUNCIL
 1939 *The World Mission of the Church.* Published for the
       American Board of Commissioners for Foreign Missions
       by International Missionary Council, New York.

ISIDRO, Gadiel T.
 1967 "We Need Seminaries," *Evangelical Missions Quarterly,*
       1:26-31.

JENCKS, Christopher and RIESMAN, David
 1968 *The Academic Revolution.* Garden City, New York,
       Doubleday and Company, Inc.

KINSLER, F. Ross
 1967 "An Extension Seminary in Guatemala," *Church Growth
       Bulletin,* 6:10-12.

 1969 *Confidential Report - CATA Workshops, August 8-23, 1969.*

 1972a *"El Proyecto de Intertextos en Español,"* Document No.
       1 for the Medellín Consultation of CATA.

KINSLER, F. Ross
1972b *Informes de CATA*," Document No. 5 for the Medellín
Consultation of CATA.

1972c "Development of Professors and Materials for Theological Education in Latin America," Document No. 10
for the Medellín Consultation of CATA.

1973 *"La Consulta de Medellín,"* *ALISTE*, 1:2-3.

CATA *Memos, Actas, Anuncios* 1968-1973 (Apartado 1881,
Guatemala, Guatemala.

KLASSEN, John
1973 Letter to author, April 4.

KRETZMANN, Martin Luther
1970a "Theological Education: A Critique," *Africa Theological Journal*, 3:17-29.

1970b "Notes Toward a Functional Theological Education Program in Africa and Asia," *Lutheran World*, 3:270-4.

KRUSCHE, Werner
1967 "Some Questions about Theological Education," *International Review of Missions*, 222:164-6.

LALIVE d'EPINAY, Christian
1967 "The Training of Pastors and Theological Education,
the Case of Chile," *International Review of Missions*,
222:185-192.

LAWSON, J. S.
1966 "The Role of Christian Laymen in Africa Today,"
Ministry, 1:2.

LORES, Rubén
1971 "A New Day," *World Vision Magazine*, 15:8-10.

MC CLEARY, Ian
1972 *Report on the TEE Consultations in Thailand, Malaysia,
Singapore and Indonesia, February 12-18, 1972*. (Mimeographed)

MACKIE, Steven G.
1966a "Patterns of Ministry and the Purpose of a Theological
School," *Theological Education*, 2:82-8.

1966b "Ministry in the Melting," *Study Encounter*, World
Council of Churches, Geneva, 2:64-70.

MACKIE, Steven G., ed.
1967 "Theological Education Tomorrow," *Study Encounter 3*,
      4:116-200.

MAGER, Robert F.
1962 *Preparing Educational Objectives*. Belmont, California,
      Fearon Publishers.

MARASCHIN, J. C.
1970 *"Novas Estructuras para a Educacão Teológica,"* *Simposio*,
      5:309.

1973 Letter to author, March 26.

MARKLE MEYER, Susan
1969 *Good Frames and Bad*. New York, John Wiley and Sons,
      Inc.

MIAO, Chester
1939 "Training of the Ministry in the Younger Churches,"
      International Review of Missions, 28:377-82.

MIGUEZ BONINO, José
1960 "Theological Education for a Church in Transition,"
      International Review of Missions, 28:377-82.

1973 Letter to author, February 23.

MIGUEZ BONINO, José, ed.
n.d. *Out of the Hurt and Hope*. New York, Friendship Press.

MILLER, Paul M.
1969 *Equipping for Ministry in East Africa*. Scottsdale,
      Pennsylvania, Herald Press.

MOORE, E. Maynard
1968 "Theological Education for a Revolutional Church,"
      Theological Education, 2:603-10.

MULHOLLAND, Dewey M.
1961 "A Curriculum for a Seminary in the Brazilian Hinter-
      land." Unpublished M.R.E. thesis, Fuller Theological
      Seminary.

MULHOLLAND, Kenneth B.
1971 "Theological Education by Extension with Special Re-
      ference to Honduras." Unpublished M.S.T. thesis,
      Lancaster Theological Seminary, Lancaster, Pennsylvania.

NANFELT, Peter N.
1970 *Extension Theological Education Seminar report:
      Djakarta, Indonesia, September 7-11, 1970*. (Mimeographed).

NEWBIGEN, Leslie
1963 *"Nuestros Métodos Misioneros bajo el Juicio de la Palabra de Dios,"* Comité de Cooperación Presbiteriana en América Latina (CCPAL), Bogotá, Colombia.

NEWSLETTER OF THE MALAYSIA THEOLOGICAL EDUCATION FELLOWSHIP, January 1973 to present, (Rev. Duain Vierow, 21 Jalan Abdul Samad, Kuala Lumpur, Malaysia).

NIDA, Eugene
1963 "Selection, Preparation and Function of Leaders in Indian Fields," *Practical Anthropology,* 10:6-16.

NIEBUHR, H. Richard and WILLIAMS, Daniel D.
1956 *The Ministry in Historical Perspective.* New York, Harper and Row.

NIEBUHR, H. Richard, WILLIAMS, Daniel D. and GUSTAFSON, James M.
1957 *The Advancement of Theological Education.* New York, Harper and Brothers.

NTWASA, S.
1972 "Training of Black Ministers Today," *International Review of Missions,* 61:177-82.

NYBLADE, Orville W.
1970 "An Idea of Theological Education in Tanzania," *Africa Theological Journal,* 3:69-79.

OLSEN, Walther
1973 Letter to author, January 8.

PAFTEE
1973 *Constitution and By-laws. Minutes of the Organizational Meeting, January 25.* Philippine Association for Theological Education by Extension.

PATON, David M., ed.
1965 *New Forms of Ministry,* World Council of Churches, Comission on World Mission and Evangelism, London, Edinburgh House Press.

PATTERSON, George
1972 "Modifications of the Extension Method for Areas of Limited Education Opportunity," *Extension Seminary,* 4:1-5.

PETERS, Harry
1940 "Training Pastors in Guatemala," *International Review of Missions,* 29:370-73.

PORTER, H. Boone, Jr.
1972 *Training for Non-Stipendiary Ministry Today: A Directory of Training Programs and Schools Within the Episcopal Church.* Kansas City, Missouri, Roanridge.

PROGRAMMING NEWS, since July 1971, (Merevale, Forest, Guernsey, Channel Islands, United Kingdom).

RAMBO, David
1968 "Training Competent Leaders for the Christian and Missionary Alliance Church of the Philippines." An unpublished M.A. thesis, Fuller Theological Seminary.

RANSON, C. W. *et al.*
1957 *Survey of the Training of the Ministry in Madagascar.*
London, International Missionary Council.

RECOMMENDATIONS OF THE CONSULTATION ON LUTHERAN THEOLOGICAL
EDUCATION BY EXTENSION MEETING IN MEXICO, June 8-10,
1972.

REIMER, Vernon
1972 *"Finanzas y Presupuesto,"* Document No. 4 for the
Medellín Consultation of CATA.

REYNHOUT, Hubert, Jr.
1947 *A Comparative Study of Bible Institute Curriculums,*
Providence, Providence Bible Institute.

1959 *The Bible School on the Mission Field.* Barrington,
Rhode Island, Barrington College.

ROWEN, Samuel F.
1967 *The Resident-Extension Seminary; A Seminary Program
for the Dominican Republic.* Miami, West Indies Mission.

n.d. *Theological Training by Extension.* (Mimeographed)

SAMMS, Robert L.
1972 *Report on TEE Philippines, TEE Report.* Singapore:
TAP-Asia.

SAPSEZIAN, A.
1971 "In Search of a Grass-roots Ministry," *International
Review of Missions,* 60:259-71.

SAVAGE, Peter
1969 *Informe del Secretario Regional - CATA, Zona Sur de
Sud América - Perú, Chile, Argentina, Bolivia, December 1, 1969.*

SAVAGE, Peter
   1971 *Memorandum: Workshop England and Spain, January -
       March, 1971.* (Mimeographed)

   1972a *Memorandum: Indonesian Workshop for TEE and PIM,
       September 27, 1972.* (Mimeographed)

   1972b *"Orientación para los Talleres de Trabajo,"* Document
       No. 2 for the Medellín Consultation of CATA.

   1972c *"El Problema del Semi-Analfabeto en el Diseño de un
       Plan de Estudios,"* Document No. 3 for the Medellín
       Consultation of CATA.

   1972d *"La Evaluación de los Estudios por Extensión,"*
       Document No. 12 for the Medellín Consultation of CATA.

   1973 Interview with author, April 6.

SAVAGE, Peter and KINSLER, F. Ross
   1972 *El Profesor-enseñando versus el Alumno-aprendiendo,"*
       Document No. 13 for the Medellín Consultation of CATA.

SCANLON, Clark
   1962 *Church Growth Through Theological Education.* Eugene,
       Oregon, Institute of Church Growth.

SCOPES, Wilfred
   1963 *Five Years - A Report from the Theological Education
       Fund, 1958-63.* New York, World Council of Churches.

SCOPES, Wilfred, ed.
   1962 *The Christian Ministry in Latin America and the Carib-
       bean.* New York, Commission on World Mission and Evan-
       gelism, World Council of Churches.

SEPULVEDA NIÑO, Saturnino
   1971 *Pecados de la Iglesia. Fundación: Investigaciones
       para el Cambio,* Bogotá, Colombia

SPECIAL COMMITTEE ON THEOLOGICAL EDUCATION
   1966 "New Challenges to Seminary Teachers in a Rapidly
       Changing World," DOM, NCC, New York.

SPRUNGER, Hugh D.
   1972 *Report of the Executive Director of the TEE Program,
       CES Board, Semi-Annual Meeting, December 18, 1972.*

STURZ, Richard J.
   1972 *Instrucão Programada no Brasil.* Mimeographed paper,
       January 1972.

SUTHERLAND, S. T.
1972 *Report on TEE in Vietnam.*

TAFTEE
      The Report of Extension Theological Education Work-
      shop, September 14-18, 1970

      A Progress Report, November 1972.

      Constitution.

      Minutes Executive Committee November 30, 1970.
      Minutes Executive Committee October 13, 1971.
      Minutes Executive Committee October 28-29, 1971.
      Minutes Executive Committee January 28-29, 1972.
      Minutes Executive Committee October 11, 1972.
      Minutes Second Annual Meeting October 12-13, 1972.

TAKIMA, Toshihiro
1969 "Concepts of Leadership and their Meaning for the Growth
      of Christian Churches: With Particular Reference to
      the Churches in India." An unpublished M.A. thesis,
      Fuller Theological Seminary.

TAKENAKA, Masao
1962 "Towards a New Structure of the Church in Asia,"
      South East Asia Journal of Theology, 3:27-39.

TAP-ASIA
1972a Theological Education by Extension Report, Singapore,
      August 1972.

1972b Replies to the Questionnaire on Needs of Theological
      Schools in Asia.

1972c Eight Workshops Throughout Asia Train Theological
      Leaders in Programmed Instruction Techniques. (Typed)

1973 Report of the Programmed Instruction Workshops for
      Theological Education by Extension.

TAYLOR, John V.
1967 "Preparing the Ordinand for Mission," *International
      Review of Missions,* 222:145-57.

TEE BULLETIN - PHILIPPINES, 1972 to present, (Box 1416, Manila,
      Philippines)

THEOLOGICAL EDUCATION FUND
1961 *Theological Education in the Pacific,* London, TEF.

THEOLOGICAL EDUCATION FUND
1964 *Theological Schools in Africa, Asia, The Caribbean,
      Latin America and the South Pacific.* New York, TEF.

1965 *Issues in Theological Education 1964-65.* New York,
      TEF.

THEOLOGICAL EDUCATION FUND COMMITTEE
1972 "Theological Education by Extension - A Critique of
      its Development and Method," Document No. 11 for the
      Medellín Consultation of CATA.

THEOLOGICAL EDUCATION FUND STAFF
1972 *Ministry in Context: The Third Mandate Programme of
      the Theological Education Fund (1970-1977).* Bromley,
      Kent, England, TEF.

THAI TEE BULLETIN, February 1973 to present, (433/3 Suan Plu,
      Bangkok, Thailand).

THEOLOGICAL NEWS - TAP OF WEF, May 1969 to present (John E.
      Langlois, Merevale Forest, Guernsey, Channel Islands,
      United Kingdom).

THOMAS, Owen C.
1967 "Professional Education and Theological Education,"
      Theological Education, 1:556-565.

TIPPETT, A. R.
1967 "A Historical Survey of the Character and Training of
      the Fijian Ministry," from *The Growth of an Indigenous
      Church,* mimeographed manuscript, Fuller Theological
      Seminary, Pasadena, California (19-41, 47-57).

TUGGY, A. Leonard
1972 *Conservative Baptist Bible College Extension Department
      Report, October 16, 1972.*

UNICO BULLETIN, July 1972 to present, (Vernon Reimer, Apartado
      Aereo 5945, Cali, Colombia).

UNICO
      Minutes April 21-24, 1968.
      Minutes December 15-16, 1968.
      Minutes April 17, 1969.

VANDERBILT, Maas
1972 "Breakthrough at the Fourth JEA Annual Meeting,"
      Japan Harvest, Summer 1972:4-78.

VOELKEL, Javier
  1969   "The Eternal Revolutionary."   An unpublished M.A. the-
         sis, Fuller Theological Seminary, Pasadena, California.

WAGNER, C. Peter
  1968-1973 *CLATT Boletín Informativo* 1-13.

  1970a *Report of CAMEO Workshop in Viet Nam.*   (Typed)

  1970b *Report of CAMEO Workshop in India.*

  1972   "*Los 16 Pasos para la Producción y Distribución de
         Intertextos,*" Document No. 6 for the Medellín Consulta-
         tion of CATA.
WARD, E.
  n.d.   *Manual Sobre las Técnicas de la Programación.*   Cocha-
         bamba, Bolivia, CATA.

WARD, Ted and WARD, Margaret
  1970   *Programmed Instruction for Theological Education by
         Extension.*   CAMEO.

WARD, Ted
  1972   Letter to Ed Hayes and other participants in the May
         18-20 conference in Denver.

WARD, Ted and MC KINNEY, Lois
  n.d.   *Non-Formal Education and the Church.*   Institute for
         International Studies in Education, Michigan State
         University, Lansing, Michigan. (Mimeographed)

WARD, Ted and ROWEN, Samuel F.
  1972   "The Significance of the Extension Seminary," *Evan-
         gelical Missions Quarterly,* 9:17-27.

WEBSTER, Douglas
  1963   *A Tent-Making Ministry - Toward a More Flexible Form
         of Ministry.*   New York, World Council of Churches.

  1964   *Patterns of Part-time Ministry in Some Churches in
         Latin America.*   London, World Dominion Press.

WEBSTER, Douglas and NASIR, K. L.
  1962   *Survey of the Training of the Ministry in the Middle
         East.*   Geneva, Commission of World Mission and Evan-
         gelism, World Council of Churches.

WEF - TAP
         Replies to the Questionnaire on Needs of Theological
         Schools in Asia.

WELCH, F. G.
  1963 *Training for the Ministry in East Africa.* Association for East African Theological Colleges, Limuru, Mercury Press, Nairobi, Kenya.

WELD, Wayne C. and MC GAVRAN, Donald A.
  1971 *Principles of Church Growth.* South Pasadena, California, William Carey Library.

WINTER, Ralph D.
  1963 "The Extension Seminary Plan in Guatemala." (Mimeographed)

  1964 "The Parity of the Ministry and 'Levels' of Training." (Mimeographed)

  1966a "Reading in the Guatemalan Environment," *New Frontiers in College-Adult Reading.* National Reading Conference, Inc., Marquette University, Milwaukee, Wisconsin 1-12.

  1966b *The Evangelical Seminary.* July, San Felipe, Reu, Guatemala.

  1966c "This Seminary Goes to the Student," *World Vision Magazine,* July-August:10-12.

  1967a "The Training Union of Greater Colombia." (Mimeographed)

  1967b "Designing the Right Kind of Ministerial Training," *Church Growth Bulletin,* 6:1-3.

  1967c "New Winds Blowing," *Church Growth Bulletin,* 6:12-13.

  1967d "Cultural Overhang and the Training of Pastors," *Church Growth Bulletin,* 2:5-6.

  1967e "Agonizing Reappraisal at the Quiche Bible Institute," *Church Growth Bulletin,* 4:8-10.

  1970a *"Educão Teológica por Extensão,"* *Simpósio,* 5:21-29.

  1970b "The Acorn that Exploded," *World Vision Magazine,* XIV:18.

  1973 "The Extension Model in Theological Education: What it is and What it Can Do." (Paper presented to the American Association of Theological Schools, January 11.

WINTER, Ralph D., ed.
  1967 *The Extension Seminary and the Programmed Textbook,*
        A Report of a Workshop in Armenia, Colombia, September
        4-9, 1967.   Fuller Theological Seminary, Pasadena,
        California.

  1969 *Theological Education by Extension.*   South Pasadena,
        California, William Carey Library.

ABOUT THE AUTHOR

Wayne Curtis Weld was born in Yakima, Washington on November 28, 1934. He attended primary and high school in Seattle and in 1956 graduated from the University of Washington with a degree in Sociology in the College of Education.

Following a three year tour of duty as a Marine Corps officer he enrolled at Fuller Theological Seminary, graduating with a B.D. degree in 1962. An additional year of studies at North Park Theological Seminary in Chicago prepared him for ordination and commissioning as a missionary by the Evangelical Covenant Church of America and he has served in that capacity since then.

The first assignment was eight months of study in the Spanish Language Institute in San Jose, Costa Rica. After this preparation the next three years were spent in educational and evangelistic work in Ibarra, Ecuador.

During the furlough year 1967-68 he earned an M.A. degree in Missions at the School of World Mission, Fuller Theological Seminary. His thesis was published under the title *An Ecuadorian Impasse*.

For their second term of service the Welds were assigned as teachers to the United Biblical Seminary in Medellin, Colombia. There, in addition to participation in the residence program, they worked in theological education by extension and in direct evangelistic work of visitation and home Bible studies. In 1970 Wayne authored with Donald McGavran of Fuller Seminary the first Intertext for extension, *Principios del Crecimiento de la Iglesia*. Wayne later translated this into English and it was published as *Principles of Church Growth*.

Wayne was married to Mary Anne Bergman on August 19, 1960. They have two boys. They expect to return to Medellin, Colombia in July, 1973, for four years of teaching, writing and evangelism with the Covenant Mission there.

BV
4164
W44

Weld, Wayne. 14651

The world directory
of theological
education by
extension

DATE			
SEP 4 '87			
NOV 2 '87			
OCT 26 '89			
MY 2'91			

© THE BAKER & TAYLOR CO.